Biology

for the IB Diploma

Exam Preparation Guide

First edition

Brenda Walpole

Cambridge University Press's mission is to advance learning, knowledge and research worldwide.

Our IB Diploma resources aim to:

- encourage learners to explore concepts, ideas and topics that have local and global significance

- help students develop a positive attitude to learning in preparation for higher education

- assist students in approaching complex questions, applying critical-thinking skills and forming reasoned answers.

CAMBRIDGE
UNIVERSITY PRESS

CAMBRIDGE
UNIVERSITY PRESS

University Printing House, Cambridge CB2 8BS, United Kingdom

One Liberty Plaza, 20th Floor, New York, NY 10006, USA

477 Williamstown Road, Port Melbourne, VIC 3207, Australia

4843/24, 2nd Floor, Ansari Road, Daryaganj, Delhi – 110002, India

79 Anson Road, #06–04/06, Singapore 079906

Cambridge University Press is part of the University of Cambridge.

It furthers the University's mission by disseminating knowledge in the pursuit of education, learning and research at the highest international levels of excellence.

Information on this title: education.cambridge.org

First published 2015

20 19 18 17 16 15 14 13 12 11 10 9 8 7 6 5 4

Printed in Malaysia by Vivar Printing

A catalogue record for this publication is available from the British Library

ISBN 978-1-107-49568-5 Paperback

All questions, answers and annotations have been written by the author. In examinations, the way marks are awarded may be different.

CONTENTS

Contents

INTRODUCTION

This book is to help you as you prepare for your final IB exams in either Standard or Higher Level Biology. It contains all the information that is covered in your syllabus in a clear and concise way. It will help you revise the key points and also help you to prepare for writing answers in the exams. All the Options are included but you should only revise the one you have been taught and will need for your exam.

At the start of each topic you will find a list of what it contains and the key information to revise. You can use this to check off each topic as you work through it. Each revision point is presented in the form of a question in the chapters. You might like to try to answer the question before and after reading the information so you can monitor how much you have understood and remembered.

Also, look out for diagrams which you may be asked to draw or label – these are clearly marked. Finally, don't forget to check your practical notes or text book to make sure you are confident about the experiments you have carried out during your studies.

Good luck!

General tips for revision

- Make sure you take lots of breaks when revising and be aware of yourself – stop if you are not taking anything in, do something else for a little while and then come back to your revision.
- Practise questions as well as learning material. There are some types of questions that come up regularly – learn the methods for doing these.
- Try to understand the topics – the more you can understand, the less you will have to learn by rote.
- You will not be allowed a calculator for Paper 1 (the multiple choice paper), so when you do past papers do them under timed conditions without a calculator.
- Do not learn mark schemes – use them as a guide to the type of answers required. You are unlikely to get an identical question to one in a past paper.

General tips for examinations

- Get a good night's sleep so that you are fresh for the exams!
- Be aware of time. Use the number of marks for each question as a guide to plan how long you should spend on each question. Always use the time you are given to read the questions carefully before you answer. Don't rush and remember that marks are not deducted for wrong answers so it's always worth trying to answer, even if you are not absolutely sure you're correct.
- Be aware of the number of marks for each question – if there are 3 marks available for a particular question then you should make sure that you make at least three points in your answer.
- Think carefully about your answers and try to make them concise and clear as possible – you do not have to write in complete sentences.

In your exam you will have three papers summarised in the table below.

Paper	% of mark	Standard Level	Higher Level	Type of questions
1	SL and HL 20	45 mins	1 hour	Multiple choice questions: 30 for SL and 40 for HL
2	SL 40 HL 36	1 hour 15 mins	2 hours 15 mins	**Section A:** Short answer questions. **Section B:** Longer response questions. One out of two for SL and two out of three for HL
3	SL 20 HL 24	1 hour	1 hour 15 mins	**Section A:** Short-answer questions based on experimental work. **Section B:** Questions from one of the options that you have studied.

HOW TO USE THIS BOOK: A GUIDED TOUR

Introduction – sets the scene of each chapter, helps with navigation through the book and gives a reminder of what's important about each topic.

1

CELL BIOLOGY

This chapter covers the following topics:

☐ The cell theory and cell size   ☐ Membrane structure   ☐ Origin of cells

☐ Ultrastructure of cells   ☐ Membrane transport   ☐ Cell division

Definitions – clear and straightforward explanations of the most important words in each topic.

DEFINITIONS

DIFFUSION is the passive movement of molecules such as oxygen, carbon dioxide or glucose down a concentration gradient.

FACILITATED DIFFUSION is a special case of diffusion across a membrane through specific protein channels.

OSMOSIS is the passive diffusion of water molecules from a region of higher concentration of water molecules to a region of lower concentration of water molecules.

ACTIVE TRANSPORT is the movement of substances against a concentration gradient. This process requires energy in the form of ATP.

Model answer – an example of an answer that would score full marks to show you exactly what an examiner wants to see.

☆ Model answer 6.1

Explain how the function of arteries, capillaries and veins is related to their structure. [8]

Arteries carry blood under high pressure, so their structure must withstand this pressure; they have thick muscular walls; elastic fibres that can recoil when blood has passed through them; and smooth lining to reduce friction.

Capillaries receive low-pressure blood; their function is to allow useful substances to pass from the blood into cells; structures that allow this are their very thin walls (one cell), so diffusion is easy, fenestrations or spaces which allow substances through, small diameter and large surface area that allow them to penetrate tissues and reach every cell.

Veins receive blood under low pressure from the capillaries; their role is to return it to the heart; walls are thin as there is no pressure to withstand; they contain valves so that blood does not flow backwards.

Annotated exemplar answer – a question with a sample answer plus examiners' comments about what was good and what could be improved. An excellent way to see how to snap up extra marks.

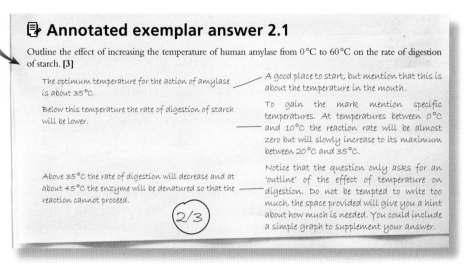

Annotated exemplar answer 2.1

Outline the effect of increasing the temperature of human amylase from 0°C to 60°C on the rate of digestion of starch. [3]

The optimum temperature for the action of amylase is about 35°C.

Below this temperature the rate of digestion of starch will be lower.

Above 35°C the rate of digestion will decrease and at about 45°C the enzyme will be denatured so that the reaction cannot proceed.

2/3

A good place to start, but mention that this is about the temperature in the mouth.

To gain the mark mention specific temperatures. At temperatures between 0°C and 10°C the reaction rate will be almost zero but will slowly increase to its maximum between 20°C and 35°C.

Notice that the question only asks for an 'outline' of the effect of temperature on digestion. Do not be tempted to write too much, the space provided will give you a hint about how much is needed. You could include a simple graph to supplement your answer.

Worked example 1.1

Stage	Number of cells
interphase	530
prophase	19
metaphase	24
anaphase	8
telophase	18

To calculate the number of cells in mitosis:
19 + 24 + 8 + 18 = 69
Total number of cells in the sample:
69 + 530 = 599
Mitotic index for this sample:
$\frac{69}{599} = 0.12$

Worked examples – a step by step approach to answering exam-style questions, guiding you through from start to finish.

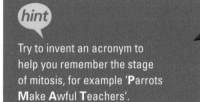

hint

Try to invent an acronym to help you remember the stage of mitosis, for example 'Parrots Make Awful Teachers'.

Hints – quick suggestions to remind you about key facts and highlight important points.

Test yourself questions – check your own knowledge and see how well you're getting on by answering questions.

TEST YOURSELF 1.1

What are the three key parts of the cell theory?

Nature of Science – these discuss particular concepts or discoveries from the points of view of one or more aspects of Nature of Science.

Nature of Science. Chemiosmosis theory was proposed by Peter Mitchell in 1961, but it took many years to be accepted because it was a radical departure from the accepted theory of the time. The chemiosmotic theory produced a paradigm shift in biochemistry.

ACKNOWLEDGEMENTS

The author and publisher acknowledge the following sources of copyright material and are grateful for the permissions granted. While every effort has been made, it has not always been possible to identify the sources of all the material used, or to trace all copyright holders. If any omissions are brought to our notice, we will be happy to include the appropriate acknowledgements on reprinting.

Artwork illustrations throughout © Cambridge University Press

Cover image: Tischenko Irina/Shutterstock; pp. 3 123 Dr Keith Wheeler/SPL; p. 6 K.R. Porter/SPL; p. 11 Michael Abbey/SPL; p. 71 John Mason/Ardea.com; p. 112 CNRI/SPL; p. 117 Dr Jeremy Burgess/SPL; p. 149 James Dennis/Phototake; p. 220 Manfred Kage/SPL

Key

SPL = Science Photo Library

CELL BIOLOGY

This chapter covers the following topics:

- ☐ The cell theory and cell size
- ☐ Ultrastructure of cells
- ☐ Membrane structure
- ☐ Membrane transport
- ☐ Origin of cells
- ☐ Cell division

1.1 The cell theory and cell size

Key information you should revise:

- What 'the cell theory' is and how it relates to single-celled organisms.
- How surface area to volume ratio limits cell size.
- How cell differentiation leads to specialised tissues in multi-cellular organisms.
- What emergent properties are and how they develop in multi-cellular organisms.
- What stem cells are and why they are so important in development.

What is the cell theory?

Key principles of the **cell theory** are:

- Living organisms are made of one or more cells.
- Cells are the smallest units of life.
- All cells come from pre-existing cells.

One cell can carry out all the functions of life and anything which cannot is not considered to be a cell. Viruses are not made of cells and are not considered to be living organisms.

Human red blood cells are sometimes suggested as an exception to the cell theory because they have no nucleus, but nuclei are present as they form, and red blood cells of other animals do have nuclei.

Are there exceptions to the cell theory?

The cell theory, like all scientific theories, is accepted until significant exceptions to it are found and a new theory is formulated. Remind yourself about what is meant by a scientific theory from your theory of knowledge (TOK) studies.

Many millions of different cells have been studied and the cell theory has been supported by these observations. A few examples have been found which do not fit it perfectly. These include:

- Fungal hyphae have many nuclei in their long threads.
- Skeletal muscle is made of fibres that are much larger than normal cells and contain many nuclei.
- Giant algae are uni-cellular but associate with other cells in a matrix.

At present these few exceptions have not led to a new theory.

TEST YOURSELF 1.1

What are the three key parts of the cell theory?

Cell biology

What functions do all cells carry out?

All cells must carry out these functions:

- metabolism
- homeostasis
- growth
- excretion
- reproduction
- nutrition.
- response (or showing sensitivity)

Some cells have additional functions such as the ability to move.

How do single-celled (unicellular) organisms live?

Paramecium is a unicellular aquatic organism and *Chlorella* is a unicellular photosynthetic organism.

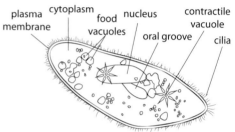

Figure 1.1 *Paramecium* carries out all the life functions within its single cell (×300).

Table 1.1 Life processes in *Paramecium* and *Chlorella*.

Function	Paramecium	Chlorella
respiration	by diffusion of gases large surface area to volume ratio	
growth and reproduction	binary fission	
response	surface sensitive to touch and chemicals	responds to light
homeostasis	excretory products diffuse out	carbon dioxide leaves by diffusion
nutrition	feeds using cilia	photosynthesis
movement	cilia propel the organism	floats in water

Why is surface area to volume ratio important in determining the size of cells and organisms?

Surface area to volume ratio is an important concept and relates to topics such as breathing and **absorption** of food where surface area is important.

Think about a simple cube.

- A cube with a side 1 cm long has a surface area of 6 cm² and a volume of 1 cm³ – a ratio of 6:1.
- A cube with a side 2 cm long has a surface area of 24 cm² and a volume of 8 cm³ – a ratio of only 3:1.

As the cube gets larger it has proportionately less surface area available. For a cell this means that it has less surface area to obtain the materials it needs through its surface and to dispose of waste. The rate of exchanging materials becomes limiting and cannot keep up with the needs of a cell, so beyond a certain size the cell could not survive.

Once you understand the concept of surface area to volume ratio you will be able to explain how living things solve the problem and are able to become larger.

Living things may develop structures, such as folds or villi on their cell surfaces but even so a single cell's size is limited. The cell must divide, so many organisms have become multicellular to overcome problems of the limited size of a cell.

A multicellular organism has many advantages, it can grow to a larger size and its cells can differentiate so that different cells do different jobs.

TEST YOURSELF 1.2

 What happens to the surface area to volume ratio of a cell as it grows larger?

DEFINITION

DIFFERENTIATION involves the expression of some genes in a cell's genome but not others.

In your body you have muscle cells and pancreatic cells, which do very different jobs. They both contain the same genome but differentiation means they have different functions in the body.

TEST YOURSELF 1.3

 Explain the importance of surface area to volume ratio in limiting the size of cells. [3]

> **hint**
>
> In Test yourself **1.3** you need to include three important points in your answer. This could be part of a short answer question or an essay.

What is an emergent property?

DEFINITION

EMERGENT PROPERTIES are new properties that appear in multicellular organisms as a result of interactions of the components of their cells.

Unicellular organisms must carry out all the functions of life but cells in a group with others can interact to perform a range of more complicated tasks. These are **emergent properties**. Cells form tissues and organs, which carry out functions such as breathing and reproduction in a different way. Use the analogy of a musical group to help you remember emergent properties. One instrument can play a simple tune but several instruments playing as a group produce a wider variety of sounds and effects.

📝 Annotated exemplar answer 1.1

Figure **1.2** shows a section through the root of a maize plant under a microscope.

a List two visible features of the photograph, which are common to the structure of all complex organisms. [2]

b Define the term 'emergent property'. [1]

c Outline two emergent properties shown by a root, which are not present in a unicellular plant. [2]

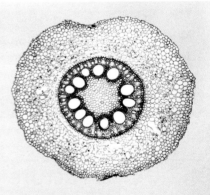

Figure 1.2

a 1. Cells   2. Tissues ———————— 'Tissues' is correct but it would be better to say 'Cells are specialised into tissues and have different functions within the stem'.

'Cells' is a correct answer, as all organisms have cells, but a better response would be 'The plant is multicellular'.

b New properties that are present in multicellular organisms.

Adding 'so that the organism can carry out a range of more complex tasks than an individual cell' would gain marks here.

c 1. Transport – some specialised cells transport water and others transport nutrients.   2. Structure.   (3/5)

It would be better to name the cell types xylem and phloem.

To make this a good answer, add 'specialised cells form the root hairs and cortex'.

What is special about stem cells?

Unlike differentiated cells, stem cells retain the ability to turn into a great many different cell types and they are:

- unspecialised
- can divide repeatedly to make large numbers of new cells
- can differentiate into several cell types.

Be prepared to put forward views from both sides of an ethical debate.

Embryonic stem cells come from the blastocyst (a ball of cells from a fertilised egg, which are all alike).

Adult stem cells, for example those found in bone marrow, are different and can only differentiate into a limited number of cell types.

Scientists must consider the ethics of any research involving living cells. Some people consider all stem cell research as unethical but different sources of stem cells have different properties and should be considered separately.

Medical uses of stem cells

To demonstrate your knowledge ensure that you can outline a few examples of stem cell use in treating medical conditions.

Here are a few important examples for each type of stem cell:

1 Stem cells from umbilical cord blood to treat certain types of leukaemia.
2 Embryonic stem cells have recently been used to treat Stargardts disease, which leads to macular degeneration and blindness.
3 Stem cells from bone marrow from living donors are used to treat leukaemia in carefully matched recipients.

TEST YOURSELF 1.4

 1 How do stem cells differ from other cells?
   2 Why do some people think that stem cell research is unethical?
      A Organisms can be produced from stem cells.
      B Stem cells are living organisms.
      C Use of stem cells involves growing modified cells.
      D Use of embryonic stem cells involves early-stage embryos.

Read multiple choice questions carefully before you make your selection. If you are not sure always make a calculated guess.

1.2 Ultrastructure of cells

Key information you should revise in this subtopic is:

- The detailed structure of a prokaryotic cell and a eukaryotic cell, including the structures inside these cells.
- How electron microscopes differ from light microscopes and how they have helped in our understanding of cell structure.
- How to draw a cell from a microscope image.

What are prokaryotic cells?

Prokaryotic cells are cells with no nucleus or internal membrane-bound organelles. They are smaller than eukaryotic cells. All bacteria are prokaryotes.

Study Figure **1.3** then try to redraw it from memory including all nine labels. You must remember the functions of all the structures too.

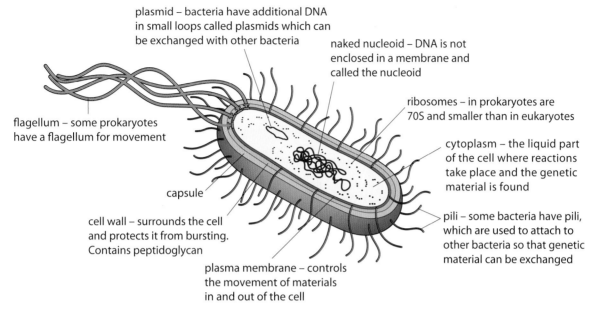

plasmid – bacteria have additional DNA in small loops called plasmids which can be exchanged with other bacteria

naked nucleoid – DNA is not enclosed in a membrane and called the nucleoid

ribosomes – in prokaryotes are 70S and smaller than in eukaryotes

flagellum – some prokaryotes have a flagellum for movement

cytoplasm – the liquid part of the cell where reactions take place and the genetic material is found

capsule

cell wall – surrounds the cell and protects it from bursting. Contains peptidoglycan

pili – some bacteria have pili, which are used to attach to other bacteria so that genetic material can be exchanged

plasma membrane – controls the movement of materials in and out of the cell

Figure 1.3 The structure of a prokaryotic cell.

How are eukaryotic cells different from prokaryotes?

Eukaryotes have structures, which prokaryotes do not. See Figure **1.4**.

Notice that the cell has internal structures that are 'compartments' or organelles with their own membranes.

DEFINITION

ORGANELLES are cell structures that have their own specific functions. Examples include ribosomes, nucleus and mitochondria.

TEST YOURSELF 1.5

 Which of the following is a characteristic of organelles?
  A They are only found in eukaryotic cells.
  B They are only found in prokaryotic cells.
  C They are subcellular structures.
  D They are all membrane bound.

Read multiple choice questions carefully. In Test yourself **1.5** think about the word 'only' in answers A and B.

TEST YOURSELF 1.6

 What is the function of the rough endoplasmic reticulum (RER)?

Plant cells have additional structures:

- Cell wall – made of cellulose that encloses the cell membrane and its contents.
- Chloroplasts – are the site of photosynthesis.
- Large vacuole – contains water and salts.

Drawings of cells should not have any shading. Use clear lines and a ruler for labels.

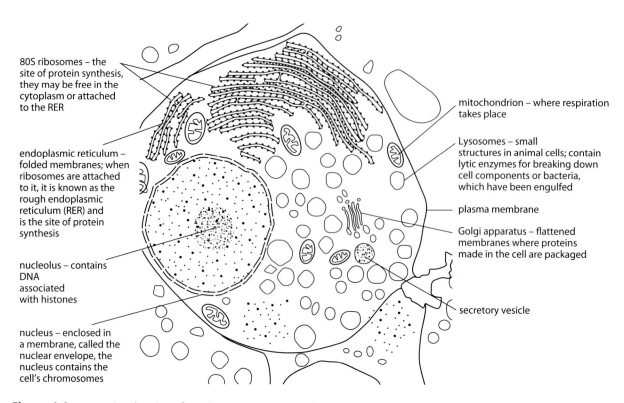

Figure 1.4 Interpretive drawing of an electron micrograph of an exocrine cell from the pancreas (×12 000) showing some of the cell structures that are visible.

Table 1.2

Structure	Eukaryotic cell	Prokaryotic cell
nucleus	surrounded by a nuclear envelope, contains chromosomes and a nucleolus	no nucleus, no nuclear envelope or nucleolus
mitochondria	present	never present
chloroplasts	present in plant cells	never present
endoplasmic reticulum	present	never present
ribosomes	relatively large, about 30 nm in diameter, or 80S	relatively small, about 20 nm in diameter, or 70S
chromosomes	DNA arranged in long strands, associated with histone proteins	DNA present, not associated with proteins, circular plasmids may also be present
cell wall	always present in plant cells, made of cellulose, never present in animal cells	always present, made of peptidoglycan
flagella	sometimes present	some have flagella, different in structure from those in eukaryotic cells

You must be able to draw a line diagram of a eukaryotic cell like the one in Figure **1.4** from an electron microscope image.

Exam questions may ask you to draw prokaryotic and eukaryotic cells and to label their structures. If you're asked to compare the cells, you can use a table like Table **1.2**

For Test yourself **1.7** you are asked only to name the structures, so you do not need to add any other information.

TEST YOURSELF 1.7

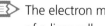 The electron micrograph here shows part of a liver cell.
  a Name the organelles labelled A and B. **[2]**
  b State the main function of these organelles. **[2]**
  c Calculate the magnification of the micrograph. **[2]**
  d Calculate the actual length of organelle A. **[2]**

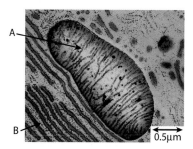

Figure 1.5

1.3 Membrane structure

Key information you should revise in this subtopic is:

- How membranes are constructed including the arrangement of the phospholipid layers and the fluid mosaic model which explains this.
- The range of proteins that membranes contain and their functions.
- The importance of cholesterol in animal membranes.

What are the important features of a membrane?

Can you explain what **hydrophilic** and **hydrophobic** mean?

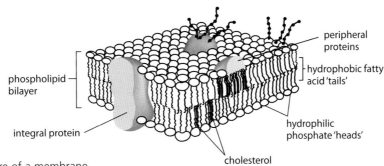

 hint

Figure **1.6** shows the structure of a membrane in three dimensions. You will only need to be able to draw a two dimensions version of this in an examination.

Figure 1.6 The structure of a membrane.

DEFINITIONS

HYDROPHILIC MOLECULES (the phosphate groups in the phospholipid) are 'water-loving' and can appear on the outside of the membrane where water is present.

HYDROPHOBIC MOLECULES (the fatty acids in the phospholipid) are 'water-hating' and are found on the inside of the membrane.

What is the fluid mosaic model and how does it explain a membrane's properties?

The **fluid mosaic model** is used to explain our understanding of membrane structure. The most up to date model is based on Singer and Nicolson's model, which was proposed in 1972. The membrane mosaic is formed of many small separate units, the phospholipids. Each one can appear in any area of the membrane and thus it is said to be fluid. The membrane can fold and form **vesicles**, which can rejoin the main structure at any point because the phospholipid units can fit into a new area anywhere in its structure.

The phospholipids form two layers with the hydrophilic heads on the outside and the hydrophobic tails on the inside. There is more information about phospholipids in Chapter **2**.

TEST YOURSELF 1.8

 What is meant by the term hydrophobic?

What are the functions of proteins and cholesterol?

Integral proteins are embedded in the bilayer and form protein channels for transport (see below). Peripheral proteins are attached to the surface and some of them have carbohydrates attached and act as hormone binding sites or for cell-to-cell communication. Some of the proteins embedded in a membrane are enzymes.

Cholesterol molecules are embedded between the non-polar fatty acid chains and make the membrane more rigid.

TEST YOURSELF 1.9

 What is the importance of cholesterol in a cell membrane?

1.4 Membrane transport

hint

Learn the definitions of transport shown here as you may need to explain them in an exam.

Key information you should revise in this subtopic is:

- How particles move across membranes by active transport, osmosis, simple diffusion and facilitated diffusion.
- How materials are taken in by endocytosis and leave by exocytosis.
- How vesicles move substances around inside a cell.

DEFINITIONS

DIFFUSION is the passive movement of molecules such as oxygen, carbon dioxide or glucose down a concentration gradient.

FACILITATED DIFFUSION is a special case of diffusion across a membrane through specific protein channels.

OSMOSIS is the passive diffusion of water molecules from a region of higher concentration of water molecules to a region of lower concentration of water molecules.

ACTIVE TRANSPORT is the movement of substances against a concentration gradient. This process requires energy in the form of ATP.

What are the key features of each method of transport across membranes?

These four methods of transport are vital to many life processes, including nerve impulses (Chapter **6**), absorption by plant roots (Chapter **9**) and gas exchange (Chapters **6** and **11**). Be sure you can describe each method.

Table 1.3 Four methods of transport.

Simple **diffusion**	• passive • needs a **concentration gradient** • occurs until particles of a substances are in equilibrium • important in the movement of oxygen, carbon dioxide • membrane must be fully permeable to the substance
Facilitated diffusion	• passive • needs a concentration gradient • important for polar substances (e.g. glucose and amino acids) • involves a carrier protein and a protein channel • allows faster diffusion to take place
Osmosis	• is the diffusion of water molecules • passive • needs a concentration gradient • occurs until there is equilibrium on each side of the membrane
Active transport	• requires energy from **ATP** • can move substances against the concentration gradient • specific proteins may act as carriers • many carriers are specific to a particular molecules

You should be able to explain what happens if plant or animal cells are bathed in very salty or sugary solutions and observed under a microscope.

TEST YOURSELF 1.10

 Distinguish between diffusion and osmosis. **[1]**

What are endocytosis and exocytosis and how do they work?

Endocytosis involves infolding of the **plasma membrane** to form a small vesicle within the cell. The vesicle may contain either liquid or solid items that the cell takes in from its external environment. For example, a white blood cell will engulf a bacterium by endocytosis so that it can be destroyed inside the cell.

Exocytosis is a method a cell uses to export something from within a cell. This may be an enzyme for digestion that the cell has made on the RER or a waste product, such as the digested remains of a bacterium. Vesicles formed inside the cell move towards the membrane and fuse with it, opening up so they can release their contents outside.

Remember both these process work because the membrane is a fluid mosaic, so vesicles can break away or rejoin the main membrane in any position.

hint

For Test yourself **1.10**, make sure that you include a comparative word in your answer to distinguish between the terms. **Whereas, on the other hand** and **but** are all suitable. Without comparative words you would score no marks even if you define the terms correctly.

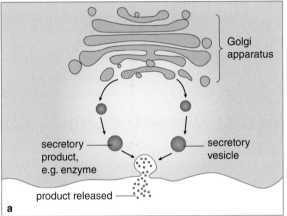 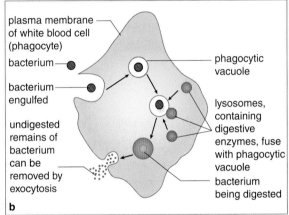

Figure 1.7 a Endocytosis and **b** exocytosis.

TEST YOURSELF 1.11

What is the function of proteins in passive transport?

  A to act as electron carriers in the membrane

  B to interact with hormones and influence cell processes

  C to act as channels for specific molecules to diffuse across the membrane

  D to release energy from ATP so that specific substances cross the membrane

1.5 Origin of cells

Key information you should revise:

- Cells form from the division of pre-existing cells.

- Non-living material must have given rise to cells long ago.

- **Endosymbiosis** explains the origin of eukaryotic cells.

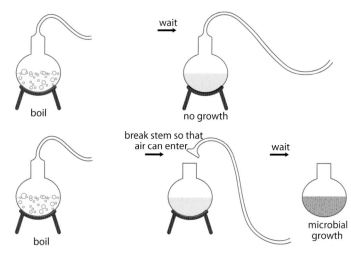

Boiling the flask kills any bacteria present in the broth. The curved neck of the flask prevents the entry of any new organisms from the atmosphere.

If the neck of the flask is broken it is possible for bacteria to enter the broth where they reproduce to produce more cells.

Figure 1.8 Pasteur's experiment demonstrating that living cells cannot 'spontaneously generate', but must originate from pre-existing living cells.

How are new cells formed and how did Pasteur demonstrate this?

Louis Pasteur used experiments to demonstrate that living cells cannot spontaneously generate (appear) and must be produced from existing cells, as shown in Figure **1.8**.

How did the first cells originate?

The first cells probably appeared about 3.5 billion years ago and must have arisen from chemicals present at that time. Certain steps must have occurred in the process.

- Organic molecules must have formed, and larger molecules been assembled from the basic organic molecules.
- Some molecules must have been able to reproduce themselves and have formed membranes from mixtures of larger molecules.

What is the endosymbiosis theory and how does the origin of eukaryotic cells depend on it?

DEFINITION

ENDOSYMBIOSIS THEORY suggests that some organelles, notably mitochondria and chloroplasts that are found inside eukaryotic cells, were once simple free-living prokaryotes.

Evidence to support the theory includes the observations that both chloroplasts and mitochondria:

- contain smaller 70S ribosomes that are found in prokaryotes
- contain small circular pieces of DNA rather like plasmids
- have their own membrane
- can replicate by binary fission.

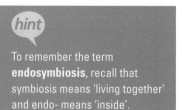

To remember the term **endosymbiosis**, recall that symbiosis means 'living together' and endo- means 'inside'.

This theory suggests that long ago simple prokaryotes were engulfed by larger cells and remained inside them. There are critics of the theory and because it is a scientific theory, if strong evidence is found to refute it then the theory will have to change.

TEST YOURSELF 1.12

 Why did Pasteur's experiment provide evidence for the cell theory?

1.6 Cell division

The cell division described here is **mitosis**. This is the type of division which produces two identical daughter cells. Do not confuse it with meiosis, which is the cell division that produces haploid gametes and is described in Chapter **3**.

Key information to revise in this sub topic:

- The stages of the cell cycle.
- The definition of mitosis.
- The stages of mitosis and what happens at cytokinesis.
- The role of cyclins.
- The development of primary and secondary tumours.

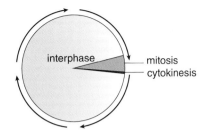

Figure 1.9 The cell cycle.

Try to invent an acronym to help you remember the stages of mitosis, for example 'Parrots Make Awful Teachers'.

What happens at each stage of the cell cycle?

- Interphase is the period when a cell carries out the tasks which it is programmed to do. It may produce protein and secrete enzymes. DNA is replicated during interphase ready for mitosis.
- Mitosis is division of the nucleus. There are four stages to mitosis that are described in Table **1.4.**
- **Cytokinesis** is the short period after mitosis when the cytoplasm divides.
- After mitosis the cytoplasm divides to separate the two new nuclei. In plant cells a cell plate forms first and this eventually becomes the new cell wall.

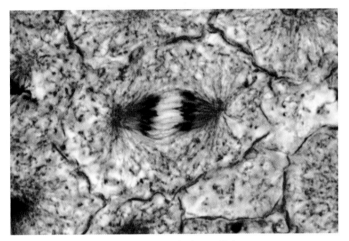

Figure 1.10 At anaphase microtubules pull the chromatids to opposite poles (× 900).

Table 1.4

Stage of mitosis	Observations
prophase	• chromosomes supercoil and become shorter, thicker and visible • two chromatids (produced during interphase) are joined at the centromere • nuclear envelope breaks down
metaphase	• chromosomes move into position and **sister chromatids** align on microtubules in the middle of the spindle attached by their centromeres
anaphase	• centromeres split and sister chromatids are pulled apart to opposite ends of the cell (they are now called chromosomes again)
telophase	• nuclear envelopes form around the separated chromosomes which uncoil

Memorise the four stages of mitosis and learn to recognise them in microscope photographs or diagrams.

TEST YOURSELF 1.13

List the stages of mitosis in the correct order.

What is the mitotic index?

When researchers study cells they count the proportion of cells undergoing mitosis. The **mitotic index** is the number of cells undergoing mitosis divided by the total number of cells in the sample. Mitotic index is used in cancer studies to predict the likely response of cancer cells to treatments.

TEST YOURSELF 1.14

What information do you need to calculate a mitotic index?

Worked example 1.1

Stage	Number of cells
interphase	530
prophase	19
metaphase	24
anaphase	8
telophase	18

To calculate the number of cells in mitosis:

$19 + 24 + 8 + 18 = 69$

Total number of cells in the sample:

$69 + 530 = 599$

Mitotic index for this sample:

$$\frac{69}{599} = 0.12$$

How is the cell cycle controlled and what can go wrong?

Cyclins and CDKs form enzymes that direct the cell cycle. **Tumours** are formed by an excessive growth of cells in a tissue. Some are benign but others are malignant (cancerous) and can form secondary tumours (metastasis).

hint

Use the key words mutagen, oncogenes, and metastasis to describe how secondary tumours form.

DNA mutations can be caused by mutagens such as X-rays, gamma rays and UV light. Some mutagens are said to be carcinogenic because they cause cancer.

Activated **oncogenes**, special genes that have the potential to cause cancer, can lead to tumours. Most cells undergo apoptosis (programmed death at a particular time), but activated oncogenes can block apoptosis so that cells grow out of control.

MOLECULAR BIOLOGY

This chapter covers the following topics:

- ☐ Molecules to metabolism
- ☐ Water
- ☐ Carbohydrates and lipids
- ☐ Proteins
- ☐ Enzymes

- ☐ Structure of DNA and RNA
- ☐ DNA replication, transcription and translation
- ☐ Cell respiration
- ☐ Photosynthesis

2.1 Molecules to metabolism

Key information you should revise:

- Carbon atoms are important because they form four covalent bonds and form many different stable compounds.
- Carbon compounds form the basis for life.
- Metabolism is defined as a series of reactions catalysed by enzymes that occur in a living organism.
- Macromolecules are built up from monomers during condensation reactions.
- Macromolecules are broken down to monomers during hydrolysis reactions.

What are the special properties of carbon that make it the building block of life?

Carbon atoms can form four covalent bonds. The simplest compound a carbon atom forms is methane, when it bonds with four hydrogen atoms, but it will bond to many other atoms to form a wide range of diverse, stable organic compounds.

DEFINITION

There are several possible definitions of an **ORGANIC COMPOUND**. One commonly used states that it is a compound that contains two or more atoms of carbon, while others say that it must contain one or more C–H bonds. A few carbon-containing compounds, such as carbonates and simple oxides or carbon dioxide and carbon monoxides, are considered inorganic.

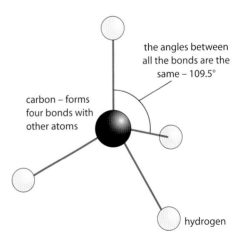

Figure 2.1 Carbon atoms can form four covalent bonds in four different directions so complex 3D molecules can be built.

Molecular biology

What are the most important organic molecules that build up living organisms?

Carbohydrates, lipids and proteins are the three key categories of molecules that are vital to life. All three contain carbon, hydrogen and oxygen atoms in different proportions and proteins also contain nitrogen.

Many organic molecules are very large but they are built up of simple units called **monomers** linked together to form **polymers** in a process known as polymerisation.

There is further detail about the properties and structure of carbohydrates and lipids in Section **2.3** and of protein in Section **2.4**.

Carbohydrates are built up of monomers of glucose.

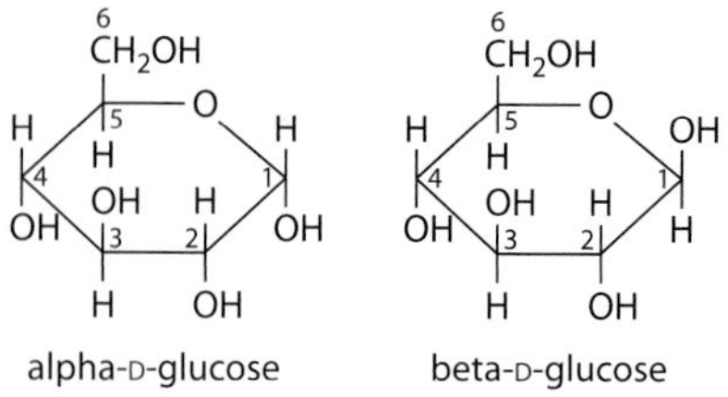

You must be able to recognise the two forms of glucose and show how they link to form carbohydrates. Look at the arrangement of H and OH groups at position 1 on each molecule to spot the difference. This affects the way the molecules form bonds with other molecules.

Figure 2.2

alpha-D-glucose   beta-D-glucose

> **DEFINITION**
>
> A single glucose molecule is called a **MONOSACCHARIDE**, two molecules linked together form a **DISACCHARIDE** and **POLYSACCHARIDES** are chains of monosaccharides linked together.

Lipids include triglyceride lipids, which are the fats and oils, and also a second group, the steroids, which includes several hormones, vitamin D and cholesterol. Lipids contain three **fatty acids** linked to a glycerol – hence the name triglyceride.

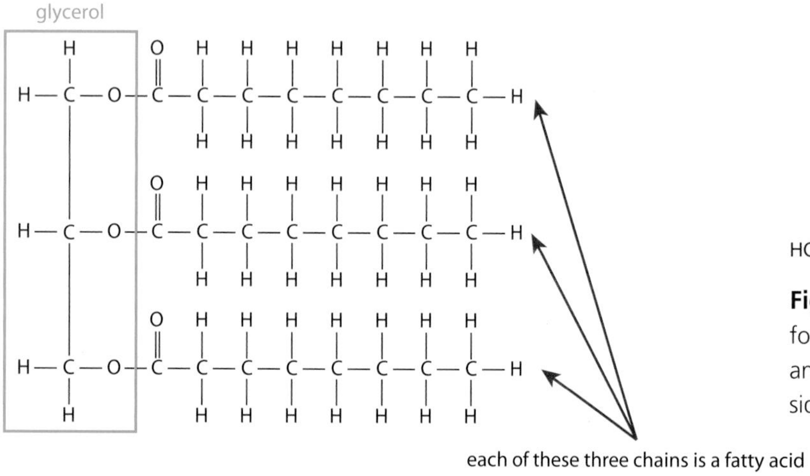

Figure 2.3 Triglyceride.

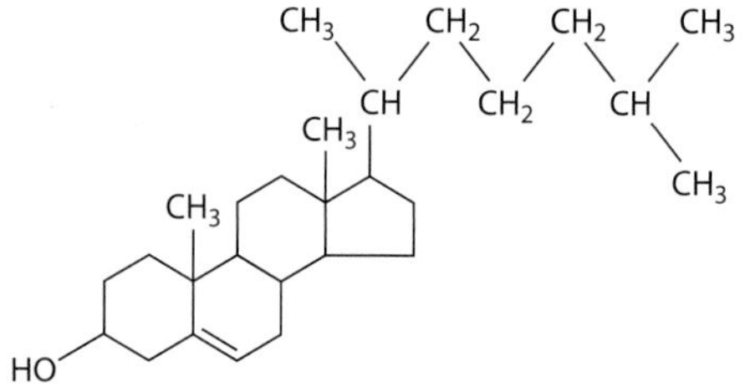

each of these three chains is a fatty acid

Figure 2.4 Like all steroids, cholesterol has four rings of carbon atoms. Vitamin D is another steroid. Other steroids differ in the side groups attached to them.

Proteins are built up of monomers called amino acids. Each has an 'R' group attached to the central carbon atom. Different **R groups** give the amino acids their different properties. The simplest R group is H. The amino group contains a nitrogen atom and there is a carboxyl group (COOH) at the other end of the molecule.

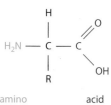

amino   acid

Figure 2.5 Amino acid.

> **hint**
>
> Make sure that you can recognise the monomers shown here.

Nucleic acids are found in all living cells. DNA and **RNA** are discussed fully in Chapters **3** and **7** but both molecules consist of long chains of nucleotides linked together. Each nucleotide contains a **pentose** sugar (ribose for RNA or deoxyribose for DNA) linked to a phosphate group and a base.

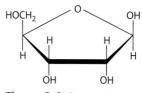

Figure 2.6 The pentose sugar ribose.

How are monomers linked together to form polymers?

Two molecules can be joined to form larger molecules in **condensation reactions**. Condensation links monomers to form macromolecules by forming covalent bonds between them. Each condensation reaction requires an enzyme and produces one molecule of water. Here are condensation reactions which form disaccharides, dipeptides and triglcerides:

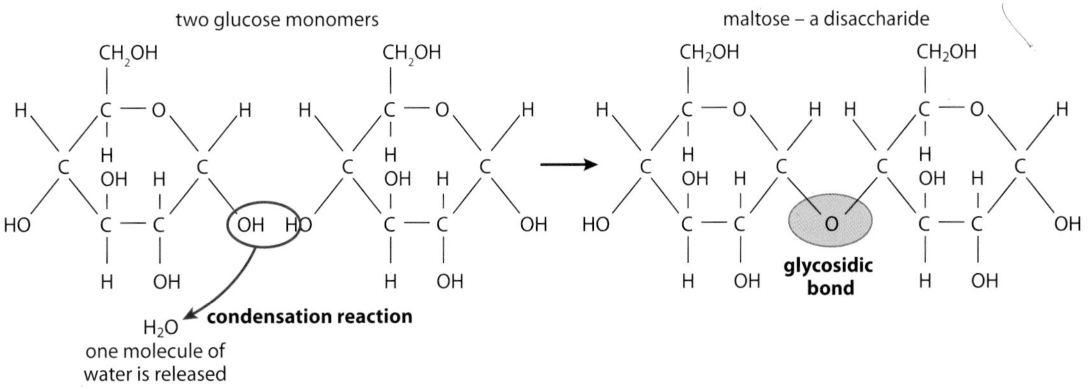

Figure 2.9 Monosaccharide subunits (glucose in this case) are joined in a condensation reaction, forming a disaccharide (maltose) and water. Glycogen is a polysaccharide, formed from long chains of glucose subunits.

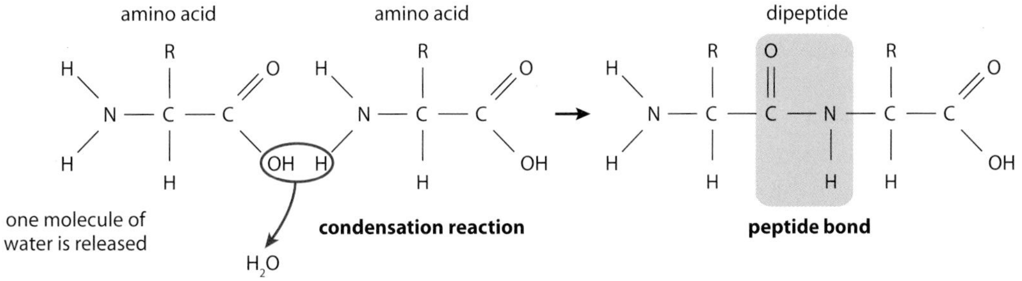

Figure 2.10 Two amino acids combine to form a dipeptide.

TEST YOURSELF 2.1

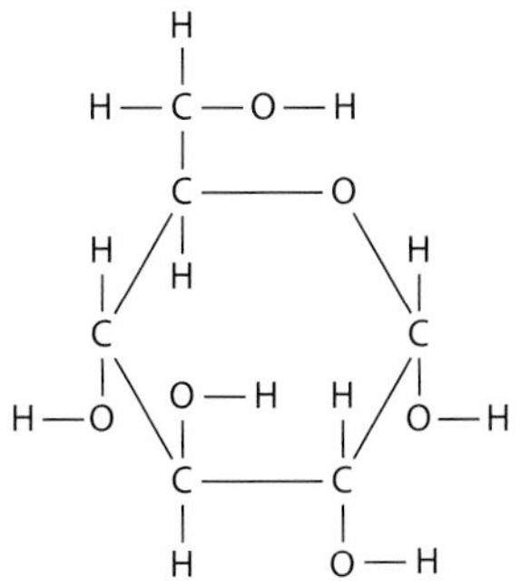

Figure 2.7

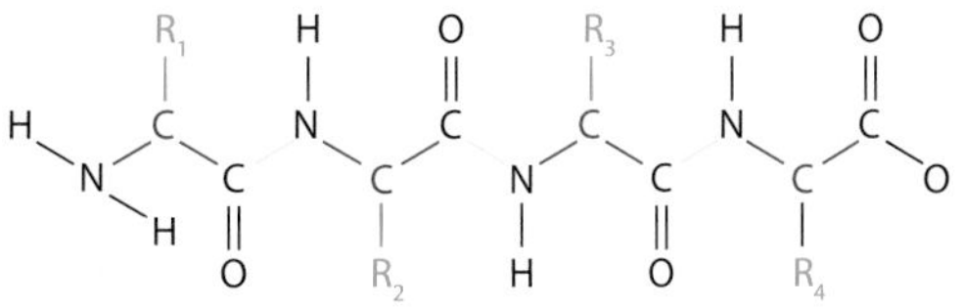

Figure 2.8

1 Identify the molecule in Figure **2.7**
2 Identify the molecule in Figure **2.8**
3 Name the type of bond used to link the monomers in Figure **2.8**.

What is the difference between condensation and hydrolysis reactions?

Condensation links monomers together using enzymes to form larger molecules and it produces water. Condensation is an example of anabolism – building new molecules.

Hydrolysis uses water and enzymes to break larger molecules apart and reduce them to monomers. Digestion is an example of a **hydrolysis reaction**. Hydrolysis and respiration (Sections **2.8** and **8.2**) are examples of catabolism – breaking up large molecules.

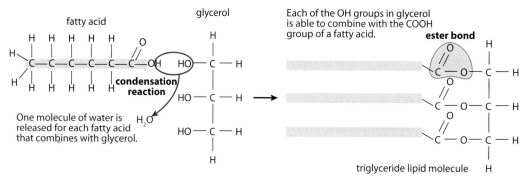

Figure 2.11 How a triglyceride lipid is formed from glycerol and three fatty acids in a condensation reaction.

Check that you can use these words with confidence:
monomer, polymer, condensation, hydrolysis, anabolism, catabolism, monosaccharide, disaccharide and dipeptide.

Table 2.1

Condensation of monomers	Produces the macromolecule	Hydrolysis of macromolecule produces
monosaccharides	carbohydrate	monosaccharides
fatty acids and glycerol	lipid	fatty acids and glycerol
amino acids	protein	amino acids

2.2 Water

Water is the main component of living things, most of our cells are 80% water and it provides the medium for most biochemical reactions in the body.

Key information you should revise:

- Water molecules are polar and hydrogen bonds form between them.
- Hydrogen bonding and polarity explain the cohesive, adhesive, thermal and solvent properties of water.
- Substances can be hydrophilic or hydrophobic.
- The properties of water have benefits to living organisms, for example water is a coolant in sweat.
- Thermal properties of water can be compared with those of methane, a similar molecule with very different properties.
- Modes of transport of glucose, amino acids, cholesterol, fats, oxygen and sodium chloride in blood are related to their solubility in water.

Make sure you can recognise diagrams of triglycerides, phospholipids and steroids and remember that they are all lipids.

What does polar mean and what are hydrogen bonds?

A water molecule H_2O has a small negative charge on the oxygen atom and a small positive charge on each of the two hydrogen atoms. It is known as a polar molecule because it has unevenly distributed electrical charges; there is a positive region and a negative region.

A **hydrogen bond** is a weak bond between the negative charge of one water molecule and the positive charge of another. Hydrogen bonds between large numbers of water molecules give water many of its properties.

What are the most important properties of water to remember?

Cohesion and adhesion

DEFINITIONS

COHESION is the force of attraction caused by hydrogen bonding between water molecules that enables them to form a lattice.

ADHESION is a force which attracts water molecules to a surface by hydrogen bonding.

Cohesion is important in holding molecules together as they are pulled up the xylem of a plant and also it causes surface tension. **Adhesion** is very strong in a narrow tube so water is 'held up' by this force in the xylem of a plant.

What are the thermal properties of water?

Cohesion holds water molecules together and it takes a lot of energy to break all of them apart. It is unusual for such a small molecule to be liquid at the normal range of temperatures. Three of water's most important thermal properties are shown in Table **2.2**.

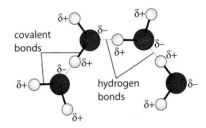

small negative charge
$\delta-$

$\delta+$ $\delta+$
small positive charges

In a water molecule, the two hydrogen atoms are found to one side of the oxygen atom. The oxygen atom pulls the bonding electrons towards it, which makes the oxygen slightly negatively charged. The hydrogen atoms have small positive charges.

Figure 2.12 The structure of a water molecule.

covalent bonds

hydrogen bonds

Figure 2.13 Hydrogen bonding in water.

Table 2.2

Property of water	Consequence for living things
high heat capacity – lots of energy is needed to break hydrogen bonds and change water's temperature	• organisms tend to remain at the same temperature. • blood or other fluids can carry heat around their bodies
high boiling point – many hydrogen bonds need a lot of energy to be broken	• water is liquid at most temperatures and is useful for metabolic reactions
evaporation requires a lot of heat energy	• sweating and transpiration enable organisms to lose heat • water acts as a coolant

TEST YOURSELF 2.2

Outline why water is good at cooling your body when you sweat. **[1]**

What are the solvent properties of water?

A water molecule has small negative charges in one area and a small positive charge in another.

Most inorganic ions dissolve well and so do polar (charged) organic molecules such as amino acids and sugars which are relatively small in size. These substances are called **hydrophilic** (water loving). **Hydrophobic** (water-hating) substances are usually uncharged and do not dissolve, examples include fats and oils and large proteins.

The solvent properties of water make it an excellent transport medium. It carries dissolved minerals through the xylem of plants and blood (which is mostly water) carries many dissolved solutes, such as glucose, in animals' bodies. (See Chapter **6**.)

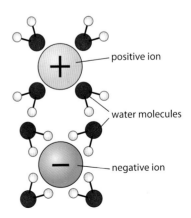

positive ion

water molecules

negative ion

Figure 2.14 The positive and negative charges of water molecules attract ions with negative or positive charges, which means that the ions dissolve.

DEFINITIONS

HYDROPHILIC means water loving, hydrophilic molecules are small and polar.

HYDROPHOBIC means water hating, hydrophobic molecules are uncharged and insoluble.

TEST YOURSELF 2.3

 1 Which feature of water determines its solvent properties?

    A ionic bonds   **C** hydrophobic interactions

    B polarity   **D** peptide bonds

  2 State the meaning of the term hydrophobic. **[1]**

  3 State two reasons why lipids are hydrophobic. **[2]**

How are substances carried in blood?

Table 2.3

Substance	Transported
sodium chloride	• as ions carried in plasma
amino acids	• some are more soluble than others, depending on their R groups, but all are soluble enough to dissolve in blood plasma
glucose	• freely soluble in plasma because it is a polar molecule
oxygen	• slightly soluble but it is not polar so most oxygen is carried bound to hemoglobin
fats	• fat molecules are hydrophobic. • they are carried inside lipoprotein complexes that have a single layer of phospholipid on the outside
cholesterol	• cholesterol is hydrophobic and is transported with fats in lipoprotein complexes

Methane CH_4 has very different properties to water, why is this?

Methane is the smallest, simplest hydrocarbon.

- Unlike water it does not have hydrogen bonding between its H atoms.
- Without these bonds very little energy is needed to separate methane molecules.
- This means it easily turns from liquid to gas (it boils at $-161\,°C$ compared with $100\,°C$ for water).
- Methane has a similar molecular mass to water but is liquid over a range of only $22\,°C$, whereas water is liquid over a range of $100\,°C$.

2.3 Carbohydrates and lipids

Key information you should revise:

- How monosaccharides are linked together by condensation reactions to form disaccharides and polysaccharides.
- The structure and function of starch, cellulose and glycogen.
- How triglyerides are formed by the condensation of three fatty acids molecules and a glycerol molecule.
- How lipids and carbohydrates are used for energy storage in humans.
- The differences between saturated, monounsaturated and polyunsaturated fatty acids molecules.
- How to distinguish *cis* and *trans* unsaturated fatty acids.

Which new molecules are produced by condensation reactions?

When two **monosaccharides** combine, one molecule loses an OH group and the other an H. The two monomers combine and water is released.

Two monosaccharides combine to form a disaccharide, examples include maltose (glucose + glucose) and sucrose (glucose + fructose)

Many **monosaccharides** combined together form polysaccharides. Starch, **glycogen** and **cellulose** are **polysaccharides** (see below).

Look back at Section **2.1** and practice drawing a condensation reaction between two glucose monomers.

What are the similarities and differences between starch, cellulose and glycogen?

All three are large carbohydrate molecules built up of glucose monomers.

Table 2.4

Starch	Cellulose	Glycogen
found in plants	found in plants	found in animals
used as an energy store	used as a structural molecule in cell walls	used as an energy store in liver and muscles
made of α glucose units linked by 1–4 glycosidic bonds.	made of chains of β glucose units with OH groups forming h bonds between chains	made of branching chains of glucose in a compact form
occurs in two forms: amylose is helical in shape; amylopectin has some 1–6 links which cause branching	straight chains with cross links form strong straight fibres	branched in form
amylose amylopectin Starch	Cellulose (fibre)	Glycogen

TEST YOURSELF 2.4

How does the shape of a cellulose molecule differ from that of other polysaccharides?

How are lipid molecules formed?

The most important group of lipids is the triglycerides, which are formed by condensation of three fatty acids and one glycerol molecule. Examples include the fat found in human adipose tissue and oils that are found in plants.

Each fatty acid is linked to one glycerol by a condensation reaction, which releases a total of three water molecules. You can see diagrams of this reaction in Section **2.1**.

TEST YOURSELF 2.5

What type of chemical reaction links monosaccharide units to form a disaccharide?

2 Molecular biology

How are lipid molecules used for energy storage in humans?

Lipids not carbohydrates are used for long-term energy storage in humans. Reasons for this include:

- Energy released by the respiration of lipids is about double that for the same mass of carbohydrate. Fat forms droplets inside cells with no water content but glycogen is associated with water, which makes it heavier to store.

- Lipid stores have other functions, such as providing heat insulation and as shock absorbers.

- Fat stores cannot be released quickly, so glycogen must be used for easily accessible, short-term energy storage.

What is the difference between a saturated, a monounsaturated and a polyunsaturated fatty acid?

You do not have to remember the names of specific fatty acids for your IB exams.

- A **saturated** fatty acid is a chain of carbon atoms with hydrogen atoms attached by single covalent bonds.

- A monounsaturated fatty acid is also a chain of carbon atoms with hydrogen atoms attached but it contains one double bond in the fatty acid chain.

- A polyunsaturated fatty acid contains more than one double bond.

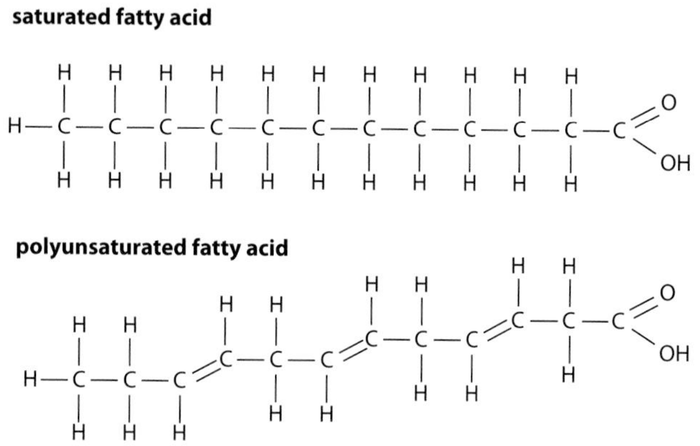

saturated fatty acid

every carbon atom in the hydrocarbon chain has the maximum number of hydrogen atoms bonded

polyunsaturated fatty acid

this hydrocarbon chain includes three double bonds, which means the carbon atoms do not have the maximum number of hydrogen atoms bonded

Figure 2.15 Saturated and polyunsaturated fatty acids.

What is the difference between a *cis* and a *trans* fatty acid?

Cis and *trans* forms of fatty acids are found in **unsaturated** fatty acid molecules. If two hydrogen atoms are absent from the same side of the molecule it will bend and form a *cis* fatty acid. Most oils are *cis* fatty acids and are liquid at normal temperatures.

If one hydrogen atom is missing from each side of the fatty acid, it is straight and known as a *trans* fatty acid. This is the form most commonly found in living things. *Trans* fatty acids can be produced artificially from vegetable or fish oils. They are used to produce margarine and some processed foods.

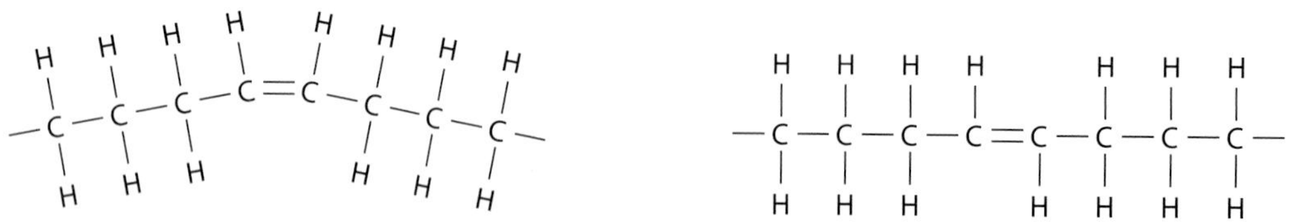

bent *cis* fatty acid – two hydrogen atoms are absent from the same side of the hydrocarbon chain

straight *trans* fatty acid – one hydrogen atom is absent from each side of the hydrocarbon chain

Figure 2.16 *Cis* and *trans* fatty acids.

What are some of the health issues related to fatty acids?

Many health claims have been made about saturated fat and also *trans* fats.

There seems to be a positive correlation between the amount of saturated fat in a person's diet and the likelihood that they will develop coronary heart disease (CHD). But heart disease is a complex issue and other factors such as genetics, sex and lifestyle are important.

Olive oil is a *cis* monounsaturated fatty acid and people with so-called 'Mediterranean' diets have lower rates of CHD. But genetics and other aspects of lifestyle may also have an influence on this.

Omega-3 group fatty acids are *cis* fatty acids found in salmon, pilchards and walnuts. They are used to synthesise long chain fatty acids in the nervous system. It has been suggested that a lack of this group could affect development of the brain and nervous system but more evidence is needed to prove the claim.

Observations without experiments cannot provide reliable scientific evidence. Ethically, it is very difficult to experiment on humans and their diets.

Nature of Science. If an exam question asks you to 'evaluate' health claims, check for the following: correlation and cause; other factors such as age, sex and lifestyle; sample size and if all groups are represented.

How are phospholipids formed?

Phospholipids are very important in the formation of membranes (see Section **1.3**)

A phospholipid is formed when a triglyceride combines with a phosphate group. The phosphate combines with one of the three OH groups of glycerol and two fatty acid chains as shown in Figure **2.17**.

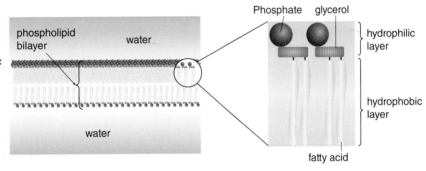

Figure 2.17 A phospholipid molecule includes a phosphate, glycerol and two fatty acids; this molecule is often simplified and shown as a circle with two tails.

2.4 Proteins

Key information you should revise:

- How amino acids are linked to form polypeptides and how different sequences can give many different polypeptides.
- That there are 20 different amino acids that are used to produce polypeptides on ribosomes.
- That amino acid sequences are coded for by genes so that every individual has a unique **proteome**.
- How proteins consist of single or several polypeptides.
- How amino acid sequence determines three-dimensional shape.
- That there are many different proteins with different functions.

Molecular biology

How are amino acids linked together to form polypeptides?

You should be able to draw a diagram like Figure 2.18 to show how this reaction takes place and water is released.

They are linked by condensation reactions that result in the formation of a **peptide bond**.

More amino acids can be added to each end of a dipeptide to form a **polypeptide**. Polypeptides can contain any number of amino acids and the genetic code determines the order in which they are added.

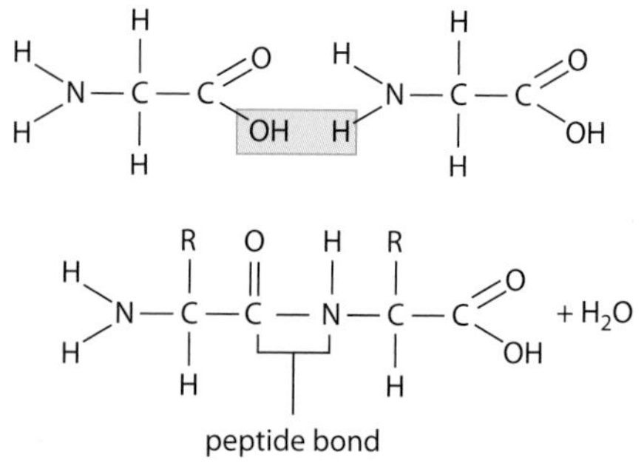

Figure 2.18 Formation of a peptide bond producing a dipeptide.

TEST YOURSELF 2.6

Name the bond and the type of reaction that links amino acids in a polypeptide.

How many different amino acids are there?

Twenty different amino acids are used to synthesise polypeptides on ribosomes. The R group on the side of an amino acid molecule determines the properties of each one and of the proteins they will become part of. Other amino acids do exist but these are formed by modification of the basic form. For example hydroxyproline is a modified form of the amino acid proline.

Nine of the amino acids (shown in bold in Table **2.5**) are known as essential amino acids because they must be included in a human diet. You can learn more about this in Option **D**.

Table 2.5 The 20 amino acids; essential amino acids shown in bold.

Abbreviation	Amino acid	Abbreviation	Amino acid
ala	alanine	**leu**	**leucine**
arg	arginine	lys	lysine
asp	aspartic acid	**met**	**methionine**
asn	asparagine	**phe**	**phenylalanine**
cys	cysteine	pro	proline
gln	**glutamine**	ser	serine
glu	glutamic acid	**thr**	**threonine**
gly	glycine	**trp**	**tryptophan**
his	**histidine**	tyr	tyrosine
ile	**isoleucine**	**val**	**valine**

How many different combinations of amino acids are possible?

Twenty amino acids are available so the possible combinations can be calculated. If a dipeptide is formed from any two amino acids the possible combinations are $20^2 = 400$

If we consider all 20 amino acids the possible number of combinations is enormous.

How do genes code amino acid sequences?

Most of the genes in our **genome** code for the amino acids that make up a polypeptide. The genetic code uses three bases for each amino acid. Genes also contain additional sequences that serve as 'punctuation' in the genetic code. Find out more about the genetic code and proteins in Section **2.7**.

A **GENOME** is all the genes in a cell, tissue or organism.

A **PROTEOME** is all the proteins produced by a cell, tissue or organism.

TEST YOURSELF 2.7

 How many different amino acids are used for polypeptide synthesis by ribosomes?

How are proteins formed from polypeptides?

A protein may consist of one polypeptide chain or several linked together. Some examples include:

- lysosome – found in tears and other secretions has **one** polypeptide chain

- collagen – a structural protein in tendons and ligaments and skin has **three** polypeptide chains

- hemoglobin – a respiratory pigment in red blood cells contains **four** polypeptides chains.

The chain of amino acids in a polypeptide folds and becomes a three-dimensional shape, which is determined by the R groups of the amino acids.

- Secondary structure is the way that the primary sequence folds into either an α helix or a β pleated sheet

- Tertiary structure is the three-dimensional shape, held together by ionic bonds and disulfide bridges.

- Quaternary structure forms as polypeptide chains associate together, for example in the four sub units of hemoglobin.

TEST YOURSELF 2.8

 What is meant by the tertiary structure of a protein?
A The sequence of amino acids
B The unique three-dimensional folding of the molecule
C Interaction of the protein with another subunit
D Interaction of a protein and a nucleic acid

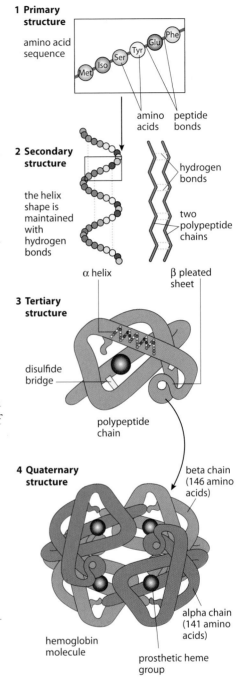

Figure 2.19 The structure of hemoglobin.

The amino acid sequence also determines other features of a protein.

- Soluble globular proteins have hydrophilic R groups on the outside of their molecules so that they can interact with water. Enzymes are one group of globular protein.

- Fibrous proteins have amino acid sequences that prevent their molecules from folding so they form long chains. Actin and myosin in muscles (see Chapter **11**) and collagen are examples of fibrous proteins.

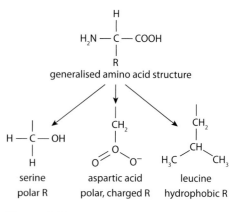

Figure **2.20**

 Figure **2.20** shows the structures of three different amino acids, which have different R groups.
Name the amino acid that is likely to be present on the outside of an insoluble protein.

What important roles do proteins have?

Different organisms synthesise many different proteins. You should be familiar with six examples, which show the range of different roles that proteins have in living organisms.

Table 2.6

Protein	Function
rubisco	an enzyme vital for the fixation of carbon dioxide during photosynthesis
immunoglobulin	antibodies which form the basis of our immunity to disease
collagen	a structural protein which forms skin, blood vessels and ligaments.
insulin	a hormone vital to the control of blood sugar levels.
rhodopsin	a visual pigment found in the retina which changes shape in the presence of light
spider silk	a strong, fine, slightly elastic fibre produced by web-building spiders

 Which of the following could be the function of a protein found in a membrane?

A storing energy   **C** taking in oxygen

B catalysing a reaction   **D** insulation

How does denaturation destroy a protein?

DEFINITION

DENATURATION is a permanent change to the shape of a protein caused by the breaking of stabilising bonds and interactions between R groups of their amino acids.

The shape and structure of a protein is complex and held together by peptide bonds, hydrogen bonds, ionic bonds and disulfide bridges. Anything that breaks these bonds will destroy the shape and thus the function of a protein. **Denaturation** can be caused by:

- heat which can disrupt secondary, tertiary and quaternary structure
- strong acids or alkalis which affect charges on R groups so that ionic bonds are broken.

Denatured proteins cannot return to their original shapes so the change is permanent. Denaturation can change the appearance of a protein – when an egg is cooked the proteins in the white (albumin) and yolk are denatured and solidify. The shape of an enzyme is altered by denaturation so that it can no longer act as a catalyst.

2.5 Enzymes

Enzymes are biological catalysts. They speed up reactions such as digestion and respiration but they remain unchanged at the end of the reaction and can be used over and over again.

Key information you should revise:

- Enzymes are globular proteins with an active site to which specific substrates bind.
- During enzyme-catalysed reactions molecules move and collide so that substrates reach the active site.
- The rate of enzyme action is influenced by pH, temperature and substrate concentration.
- Enzymes can be denatured.
- Immobilised enzymes are used in industry.

An **ENZYME** is a globular protein that functions as a biological catalyst.

The **ACTIVE SITE** is the region on the surface of an enzyme where substrate molecules bind and which catalyses a reaction involving the substrate.

What is an active site?

Enzymes are protein molecules with a three-dimensional shape. On the surface of every enzyme is a region with a special shape, known as the **active site**. The substrate for the enzyme binds to the active site to form an enzyme–substrate complex. It is in the active site that substrates are converted into products.

How do enzymes and substrates meet?

Most biological reactions take place in solution, so enzyme and substrate molecules move freely and eventually collide with one another. When a collision occurs in the correct orientation, the substrate molecule fits into the active site in a similar way to a key fitting into a lock.

Nature of Science. The lock and key hypothesis has been used as a 'model' or analogy to explain enzyme-substrate interactions. A second theory, the induced fit model has refined our understanding of the process. Models like these enable scientists to make predictions and describe the process in simple terms.

How do enzymes catalyse chemical reactions?

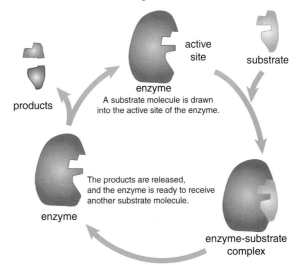

Figure 2.21 How an enzyme catalyses the breakdown of a substrate molecule into two product molecules.

Substrates undergo chemical reactions while bound to the active site. Two molecules may be bound together in an anabolic reaction, or a molecule may be separated into new products in a catabolic reaction. The best example of catabolism is digestion when enzymes break large molecules, such as starch or protein into small components that can be absorbed. In both types of reaction the products are released from the active site when the reaction has occurred.

What factors affect how quickly an enzyme works?

Temperature, pH and substrate concentration affect the rate at which enzymes catalyse reactions.

An enzyme works most efficiently at its optimum temperature. Below the optimum, the rate of reaction is slower but above it the rate decreases and eventually falls to zero as the enzyme is denatured. Temperature affects enzymes in two ways:

- Particles in liquids move more quickly as the temperature rises so enzyme and substrate molecules move faster and are more likely to collide.
- If an enzyme reaches a very high temperature the increase in kinetic energy causes bonds in the enzyme to move. If bonds are broken the enzyme may be denatured.

Most enzymes are found at temperatures where they work best e.g. human enzymes work best at 37 °C human body temperature.

Enzyme action is influenced by the pH of the surroundings. Different enzymes have a different optimum pH at which they work best. Stomach enzymes work well at pH 2, but most enzymes in the human body have an optimum of pH 7. Above or below the optimum the enzyme's active site may be altered so it is less efficient. At extremes of pH enzymes may be denatured.

Substrate concentration affects the potential of a substrate to bind to an active site. As substrate concentration rises from low to moderate there is more chance of collisions between the active site and the substrate, so the rate of reaction increases. At high substrate concentrations many active sites will be occupied, so the rate of reaction will not increase. The enzyme will be working at its maximum rate.

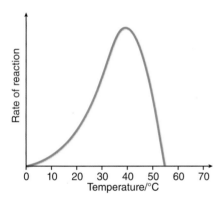

Figure 2.22 The effect of temperature on the rate of an enzyme-controlled reaction.

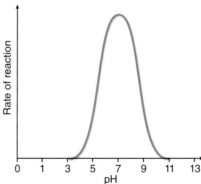

Figure 2.23 The effect of pH on the rate of an enzyme-controlled reaction.

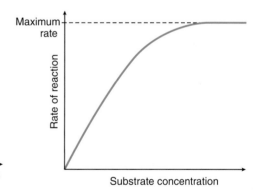

Figure 2.24 The effect of substrate concentration on the rate of an enzyme catalyzed reaction.

TEST YOURSELF 2.11

 Describe the change in rate of reaction when substrate concentration is increased and the amount of enzyme remains fixed.

How are enzymes used in industrial processes?

More than 500 enzymes are used commercially in processes such as brewing, baking and in biological detergents.

Lactose-free milk can be produced for lactose-intolerant people, using the enzyme lactase to convert milk sugar into glucose and galactose.

Proteases and amylases are used in detergents to remove stains that are protein or starch based.

Many enzymes are used in the biotechnology industry. One example is glucose oxidase, used in testing for glucose in blood samples.

For maximum efficiency industrial enzymes are often immobilised on a column of inert material, which holds them in place.

The substrate is poured through the column and products collected at the bottom. Advantages of immobilisation include:

- it is easy to separate enzyme and product
- enzyme can be reused, which increases the economic viability of the process
- production time can be extended
- enzymes can be kept in stable, optimum conditions.

What factors must be considered when designing experiments with immobilised enzymes?

Experiments must be reliable and accurate. Accuracy is improved by using the correct apparatus and taking readings carefully by:

- accurate measurement of substrates and enzyme with the correct-sized syringes
- careful reading of apparatus, such as stopwatches.

Reliablity is improved by minimising variation between the results. Reliability can be improved by:

- repeating the experiment to check readings
- taking an average of results
- rejecting any erroneous or outlying readings
- repeating the whole experiment for consistentcy.

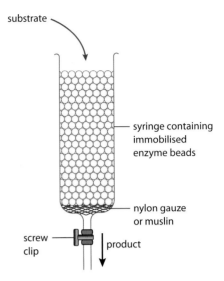

Figure 2.25 The alginate beads are enclosed in a 20 cm³ syringe in a laboratory demonstration, such as that shown here. An industrial process uses the same principles but on a much larger scale.

📑 Annotated exemplar answer 2.1

Outline the effect of increasing the temperature of human amylase from 0°C to 60°C on the rate of digestion of starch. **[3]**

The optimum temperature for the action of amylase is about 35°C.

> A good place to start, but mention that this is about the temperature in the mouth.

Below this temperature the rate of digestion of starch will be lower.

> To gain the mark mention specific temperatures. At temperatures between 0°C and 10°C the reaction rate will be almost zero but will slowly increase to its maximum between 20°C and 35°C.

Above 35°C the rate of digestion will decrease and at about 45°C the enzyme will be denatured so that the reaction cannot proceed.

> Notice that the question only asks for an 'outline' of the effect of temperature on digestion. Do not be tempted to write too much, the space provided will give you a hint about how much is needed. You could include a simple graph to supplement your answer.

(2/3)

2.6 Structure of DNA and RNA

Key information you should revise:

- DNA and RNA are polymers of nucleotides.
- There are three key differences between a DNA and an RNA molecule.
- DNA is a double helix with two antiparallel strands of nucleotides linked by hydrogen bonds.

What is a nucleotide?

A simple representation of a nucleotide is shown in Figure **2.26**. A nucleotide consists of three parts:

- a base
- a pentose sugar
- a phosphate group.

hint

You should be able to draw simple diagrams of DNA and RNA to show how nucleotides link to form a polymer.

How do DNA nucleotides differ from RNA nucleotides?

In DNA the pentose sugar is deoxyribose and in RNA it is ribose.

There are four different bases in both DNA and RNA.

In DNA they are: **A** (adenine), **G** (guanine), **C** (cytosine) and **T** (thymine). In RNA **T** is replaced by **U** (uracil).

How are the nucleotides linked to form DNA and RNA molecules?

In both molecules, the nucleotides are linked via their phosphate groups to form a chain of nucleotides.

In DNA hydrogen bonds form between the bases giving a double-stranded structure.

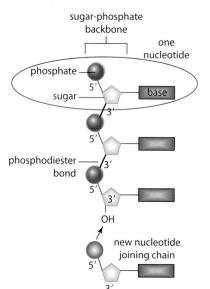

Figure 2.26 The structure of single nucleotide strand.

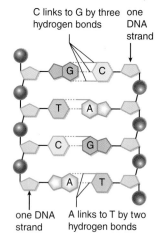

Figure 2.27 Part of a DNA molecule. Two DNA strands, running in opposite directions, are held together by hydrogen bonds between the bases.

hint

Exam questions often ask for comparisons between DNA and RNA. Remember to include a comparative term or present the differences as a table.

What are the differences between a DNA and an RNA molecule?

There are three key differences to remember:

1 DNA contains deoxyribose sugar while RNA contains ribose.

2 DNA is a double stranded molecule while RNA is single stranded.

3 DNA contains the bases A,CG,T while RNA has A,CG,U.

How are the two strands in a DNA double helix arranged?

Look carefully at Figure **2.27**. Notice the following points about DNA structure.

- Each strand has nucleotides which are covalently bonded to form a 'backbone'.
- The strands on each side run in opposite directions, they are antiparallel.
- The strands are held together by hydrogen bonds between their bases. A always bonds to T and C to G.
- The strands are wound around each other to form a double helix (this is not shown in the figure).

hint

Invent a mnemonic to help you remember base pairings. For example: **A**pple **T**art for A and T and **C**hocolate **G**ateau for C and G.

TEST YOURSELF 2.12

1 If a DNA molecule contained 350 adenine bases how many thymine bases would be present? **[1]**
2 Which DNA double helix do you think would be harder to separate into two strands: DNA composed mostly of AT base pairs or DNA composed mostly of GC base pairs? Outline the reason for your answer. **[2]**

☆ Model answer 2.1

a Figure 2.28 shows the formula of a molecule of an organic compound. Name the group of organic compounds that this substance belongs to. [1]

b Table 2.7 shows organic compounds found in a typical bacterial cell.

Table 2.7

Organic compound	% in cell (dry mass)	Different types of molecule present
DNA	3	1
glycogen	2.5	1
lipid	9	4
RNA	20	460
protein	55	1049

$$CH_3$$
$$H_2N — C — COOH$$
$$H$$

Figure 2.28

 (i) Glycogen and protein are both polymers. Outline what is meant by a polymer. [1]

 (ii) Explain why there is just one type of glycogen molecule, but many types of protein. [3]

(iii) Explain why there are many types of different RNA molecule found in this cell. [2]

a amino acid

b (i) A polymer is an organic molecule which contains many units called monomers linked together. Glycogen is made of glucose monomers, protein is made of amino acid monomers.

(ii) Glycogen contains only glucose monomers, which are linked in a specific way. Protein molecules may contain any number of the 20 different amino acids and each protein will have its own combination of amino acids. Amino acids can be linked together in any sequence giving a huge range of possible proteins.

(iii) Both mRNA and tRNA are present in a bacterial cell. Different molecules of mRNA will be transcribed from different sections of the bacterial genome and there are many different tRNA molecules present which correspond to different the 20 amino acids needed for the translation of mRNA.

2.7 DNA replication, transcription and translation

If you are studying HL, Chapter **7** contains more details about DNA replication, transcription and translation.

Key information you should revise:

- DNA replication is semi-conservative and depends on complementary base pairing.
- The enzyme **DNA helicase** unwinds the two DNA strands and **DNA polymerase** links nucleotides to form a new strands during replication.
- During transcription mRNA is synthesised from the DNA template by RNA polymerase.
- Translation is the synthesis of polypeptides on ribosomes.
- The sequence of amino acids in a polypeptide is determined by the genetic code and mRNA.
- What a codon is and how translation depends on complementary base paring between codons on mRNA and tRNA.

hint

Many students find this topic difficult. Separate your replication notes from the notes on transcription to keep the two concepts clear in your mind.

What is replication and how is DNA copied as a cell prepares to divide?

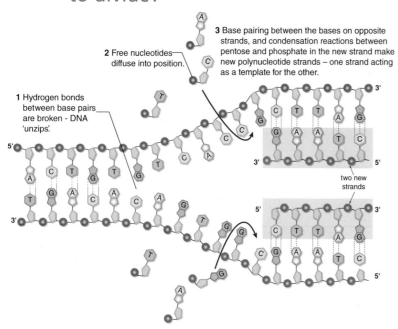

3 Base pairing between the bases on opposite strands, and condensation reactions between pentose and phosphate in the new strand make new polynucleotide strands – one strand acting as a template for the other.

2 Free nucleotides diffuse into position.

1 Hydrogen bonds between base pairs are broken - DNA 'unzips'.

two new strands

Figure 2.29 DNA replication.

Replication is the copying of the two strands of DNA to form two new double stranded molecules. It takes place as a cell prepares to divide. There are two key features of DNA replication; it is semi-conservative and it involves **complementary base pairing**.

DEFINITIONS

DNA replication is **SEMI-CONSERVATIVE**; that is, each of the original strands acts as a template for a new strand. Every new DNA molecule contains one original and one new strand.

COMPLEMENTARY BASE PAIRING – complementary bases pair only with each other. The pairs in a DNA molecule are A and T, and also C and G. If these pairs did not form then hydrogen bonding between the two strands could not occur. Complementary base pairing ensures that each new strand is exactly the same as the molecule that is being replicated.

Which enzymes are involved in DNA replication?

Two of the enzymes needed for DNA replication are:

- **DNA helicase** unwinds the two strands of DNA and then separates the two strands by breaking the hydrogen bonds between the bases
- **DNA polymerase** links new nucleotides together to form a new strand, using the original strand as a template.

Both of the original strands act as a template, so that two new strands are formed. DNA polymerase moves along each strand and adds one nucleotide at a time. DNA polymerase forms H bonds between the complementary bases and also covalent bonds between the sugar and phosphate groups of adjacent nucleotides.

If you are studying HL, you will need to know more detail about replication. You will find this in Chapter **7**.

What is the theory of semi-conservative replication and how did Meselson and Stahl obtain evidence to support it?

Nature of Science. In the 1950s two theories about DNA replication were suggested. The semi–conservative replication theory proposed that one of each of the original DNA strands of the double helix passed to each new cell at mitosis. The conservative theory suggested that two original strands passed to one of the two new cells and two copied new strands passed to the other. Meselson and Stahl's experiment involved labelling DNA with ^{15}N, they were able to follow the distribution of the isotope and their work supported the theory of semi-conservative replication.

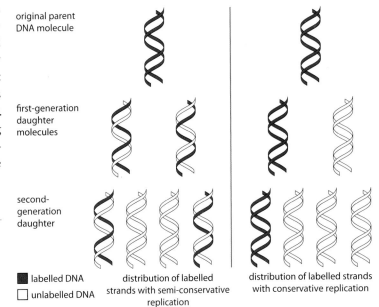

Figure 2.30 The distribution of labelled DNA in daughter molecules after replication, according to the semi-conservative theory.

TEST YOURSELF 2.13

 Which of these statements about DNA replication is or are correct?

   I It is a stage in protein synthesis.

   II It is semi-conservative.

   III It occurs during interphase.

     A I only   **C** II and III

     B II only   **D** I, II and III

What is transcription, how and where does it happen?

Do not confuse transcription with replication. Replication is needed before a cell can divide, but transcription (followed by translation) is needed for the cell to manufacture proteins using the DNA code.

DEFINITION

TRANSCRIPTION is the process which copies a sequence of DNA bases to mRNA. In a eukaryotic cell transcription takes place in the nucleus.

Transcription is the first stage in the synthesis of proteins in a cell. It involves copying a section of DNA (a gene) to form an intermediate molecule of **mRNA**. mRNA nucleotides are matched to just one strand of DNA by complementary base pairing.

   1 DNA is unzipped by the enzyme **RNA polymerase** so that the two strands uncoil and separate.

   2 Free RNA nucleotides move into place along the 'reference' strand and form H bonds with the bases of corresponding DNA nucleotides.

   3 RNA polymerase assembles the free nucleotides and links them to form a single strand of mRNA.

   4 Finally, the completed strand of mRNA detaches from the DNA and RNA polymerase zips up the two strands of DNA again.

Remember that RNA contains uracil not thymine, so that as mRNA is built up adenine pairs with uracil.

What is translation, how and where does it take place?

DEFINITION

TRANSLATION is the process that uses the coded information in mRNA to construct polypeptide chains, which in turn are used to build proteins.

The genetic code is written in sequences of three bases. Each triplet of bases on the mRNA molecule is called a **codon** and each one codes for an amino acid. Notice in Table **2.8** that some codons act as punctuation and indicate where translation should stop and start.

TEST YOURSELF 2.14

 1 Use Table **2.8** to work out the sequence of amino acids coded for by this mRNA sequence: AUG GAU UCC UGC
2 Name the codons for the proteins arginine (Arg) and tyrosine (Try).
3 Deduce the DNA sequence that was transcribed to produce the mRNA that codes for these proteins.

Table 2.8 Amino acids and their associated mRNA codons.

First base		Second base								Third base
		U		**C**		**A**		**G**		
U		UUU	phenylalanine	UCU	serine	UAU	tyrosine	UGU	cysteine	U
		UUC		UCC		UAC		UGC		C
		UUA	leucine	UCA		UAA	'stop'	UGA	'stop'	A
		UUG		UCG		UAG		UGG	tryptophan	G
C		CUU	leucine	CCU	proline	CAU	histidine	CGU	arginine	U
		CUC		CCC		CAC		CGC		C
		CUA		CCA		CAA	glutamine	CGA		A
		CUG		CCG		CAG		CGG		G
A		AUU	isoleucine	ACU	threonine	AAU	asparagine	AGU	serine	U
		AUC		ACC		AAC		AGC		C
		AUA		ACA		AAA	lysine	AGA	arginine	A
		AUG	methionine or 'start'	ACG		AAG		AGG		G
G		GUU	valine	GCU	alanine	GAU	aspartic acid	GGU	glycine	U
		GUC		GCC		GAC		GGC		C
		GUA		GCA		GAA	glutamic acid	GGA		A
		GUG		GCG		GAG		GGG		G

Important facts about translation are:

- It takes place in the cytoplasm on ribosomes.
- It involves a third nucleic acid called transfer or **tRNA**.
- Ribosomes have binding sites for both **mRNA** and tRNA.
- Each tRNA has an **anticodon**, which is complementary to a codon of mRNA (Figure **2.31** shows a tRNA, which has the anticodon for the amino acid methionine).

- Each tRNA collects an amino acid that corresponds to its anticodon.

- Ribosomes bind to mRNA and then draw in the tRNA with the anticodon that matches the mRNA codon.

- When two amino acids are in place in a ribosome a peptide bond forms between them.

- Once a dipeptide has formed the first tRNA molecule detaches and leaves to collect another amino acid.

- The next tRNA moves into position and the process is repeated.

How is the sequence of amino acids in a polypeptide determined?

The sequence is determined by the genetic code carried by DNA. A section of DNA is copied to the mRNA strand which in turn is translated to a polypeptide.

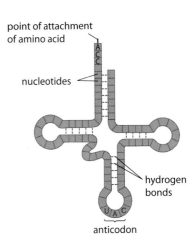

Figure 2.31 tRNA - a 'clover leaf' shape.

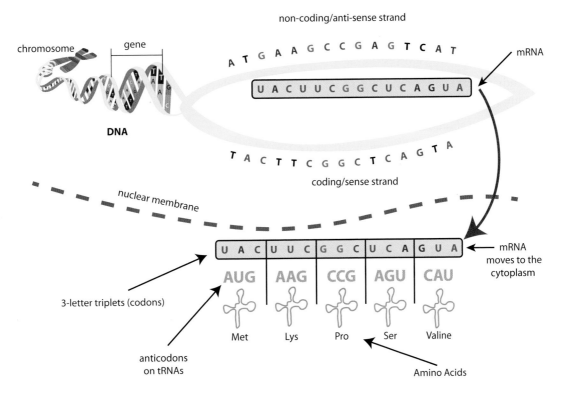

Figure 2.32 Transcription and translation. Transcription in eukaryotes takes place in the nucleus. mRNA is produced by complementary base pairing the non-coding strand of DNA. mRNA has the same base sequence as the sense strand. Translation happens in the cytoplasm. tRNA molecules carry amino acids matching mRNA codons to the ribosomes (not shown).

Why are codons important in the formation of polypeptides by mRNA and tRNA?

A codon and its corresponding anticodon pair perfectly. The tRNA anticodon decides which amino acid is brought into position on a ribosome and therefore the pairing of codons and anticodons decides the sequence of amino acids in a polypeptide.

hint

If you are asked to work out the amino acid specified by a codon or anticodon you will be given a section of Table **2.8** to help you. Take your time as you do this. It is easy to misplace a letter and lose your marks.

hint

Test yourself **2.15** question 2: two marks are indicated so make sure you include two relevant points in your answer.

TEST YOURSELF 2.15

1 Draw and label a simple diagram of an RNA nucleotide containing uracil. **[1]**
2 Compare the difference in structure of a tRNA molecule and a DNA molecule. **[2]**
3 Table **2.9** shows the mRNA codons for some amino acids:
   a Write the DNA sequence for cysteine that corresponds to the mRNA codon. **[1]**
   b Name the amino acid coded by the tRNA anticodon UCA. **[1]**

Table 2.9

Codon	Amino acid
CUA	leucine
GCU	valine
ACG	threonine
UGC	cysteine
GCU	alanine
AGU	serine

2.8 Cell respiration

If you are studying HL, you should also revise Chapter **8**, which contains more details about the process of respiration and photosynthesis.

Key information you should revise:

- Cell respiration is the controlled release of energy from organic substances to produce ATP.
- ATP is an immediately available source of energy for a cell.
- Aerobic respiration releases a large yield of ATP from glucose.
- Anaerobic respiration releases a small amount of ATP from glucose.

How is respiration defined?

DEFINITION

CELL RESPIRATION is the controlled release of energy in the form of ATP from organic compounds in a cell.

Organic compounds that can be used in respiration include glucose (the most familiar source of energy), fats and protein.

Aerobic respiration is summarised in the equation:

$$C_6H_{12}O_6 + 6O_2 \rightarrow 6H_2O + 6CO_2 + energy$$

(glucose + oxygen → water + carbon dioxide + energy)

Energy = about 38 useable molecules of ATP

Scientists disagree about exactly how many ATP molecules are produced but this is a good approximation.

Do not confuse respiration with 'breathing', respiration is a cellular process whereas breathing simply means exchanging oxygen and carbon dioxide with the air via the lungs.

What is ATP?

Adenosine triphosphate (ATP) is the immediately available energy source for a cell. It is made in mitochondria. ATP is broken down to ADP (adenosine diphosphate) and organic phosphate. This conversion releases energy. Once energy has been used ATP is reformed during respiration so the process is cyclical.

During aerobic respiration 38 molecules of ATP are produced but **anaerobic respiration** produces only 2 molecules of ATP.

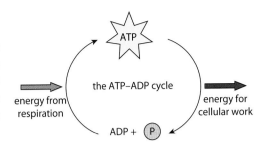

Figure 2.33 The ATP–ADP cycle.

What are the main stages in the process of respiration? Where does each one take place?

The first stage of respiration is always glycolysis which takes place in the cytoplasm.

 • Glycolysis produces two molecules of ATP.

During aerobic respiration:

 • this is followed by the link reaction, and

 • the Krebs cycle which take place inside mitochondria.

During anaerobic respiration reactions continue in the cytoplasm.

How are aerobic and anaerobic respiration different from one another?

Anaerobic respiration in microorganisms is also known as fermentation and is very useful in food production. Beer, wine and bread are all produced by microorganisms that respire anaerobically.

Table 2.10

Aerobic	Anaerobic
occurs in the cytoplasm and mitochondria	occurs in the cytoplasm
produces 38 ATP molecules	produces only a small yield of ATP
requires oxygen	no oxygen is used
produces carbon dioxide and water as waste products	in animals, lactate is a waste product in yeast ethanol and carbon dioxide are produced

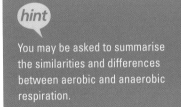

hint

You may be asked to summarise the similarities and differences between aerobic and anaerobic respiration.

Molecular biology

What is a respirometer and how is it used?

Respirometers are used to measure the rate of respiration of invertebrates or germinating seeds by measuring the rate of oxygen consumption.

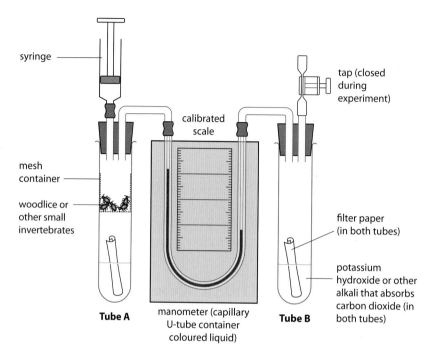

Figure 2.34 A simple respirometer

Worked example 2.1

The graph shows the readings taken from three respirometers containing germinating peas, dry peas and glass beads over a 20 minute period.

a What was the respiration rate of the germinating peas?

To calculate a respiration rate you must divide the oxygen consumption by the time that the readings were made. In this case the y-axis shows that 3 ml oxygen were consumed in the 20 minute period shown on the x-axis. Thus the respiration rate is 3/20 = 0.15 ml min^{-1}

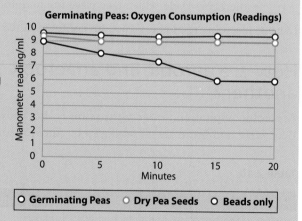

Figure 2.35

b Why were measurements for glass beads also taken?

The beads act as a control to show that changes in the respirometer readings are due to the peas and not the apparatus itself.

c Explain the difference between the readings for dry and germinating peas.

Dry peas did not cause any change in the respirometer reading so they are not removing oxygen from it. This indicates that they are not respiring. Only the germinating peas are using oxygen and so we can say that they are respiring.

Figure **2.36** possible pathways for the breakdown of glucose in different types of cell.
1 Name the substances A, B, C and D. **[4]**
2 Name the processes R and Q. **[2]**
3 Where exactly in a cell does the process R take place? **[1]**

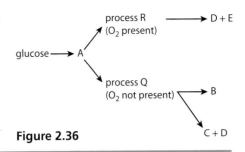

Figure 2.36

2.9 Photosynthesis

Key information you should revise:

- How photosynthesis uses light energy to make carbon compounds.
- Light energy from the sun contains a range of wavelengths.
- Chlorophyll, the main photosynthetic pigment, absorbs mainly the red and blue wavelengths of light.
- Photosynthesis releases oxygen as a result of splitting water molecules.
- Energy is needed to fix carbon dioxide.
- Temperature, light and carbon dioxide concentration affect the rate of photosynthesis and can be **limiting factors**.

How is photosynthesis defined and what are the important inputs and outputs?

In terrestrial plants carbon dioxide enters leaves via the stomata on the underside of each leaf and the roots absorb water. Aquatic plants may have stomata on their upper surfaces. You can read more about the structure of plants in Chapter **9**.

Light energy from the Sun is the driving force for photosynthesis and provides the energy for the chemical reactions that take place.

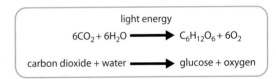

Figure 2.37

Glucose produced in the leaves of a plant is distributed to all parts via the phloem, usually in the form of sucrose. It is then used to make other carbon compounds within plant cells. Oxygen is a waste product and leaves the plant via the stomata.

Remember that the equation here is a summary of a much more complex series of chemical reactions. If you are studying HL there is more detail about these processes in Chapter **8**.

How are the wavelengths of visible light used in photosynthesis?
Visible light consists of a range of wavelengths between 400 and 700 nm long. These wavelengths can be separated using a prism to produce the familiar rainbow of colours. Plants contain **chlorophyll**, which is a green pigment that reflects green light but is able to absorb other wavelengths well.

Red and blue light are absorbed better than other colours and provide the energy needed for photosynthesis.

What is an absorption spectrum and how is it different from an action spectrum?
Chloroplasts contain a number of different pigments that can absorb light. Figure **2.38** shows the **absorption spectrum** for two types of chlorophyll, a and b, and also for carotenoids which are pigments found in many plants. Notice that the three pigments absorb mostly the blue and red wavelengths of light.

> **hint**
> Make sure you can recall practical techniques to separate leaf pigments. You have probably carried out experiments using chromatography to do this in your practical studies.

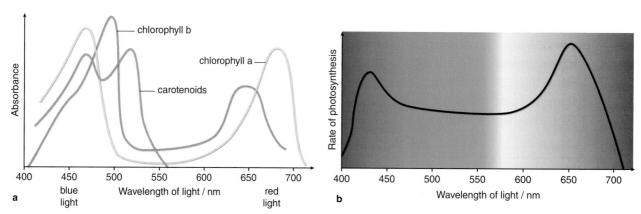

Figure 2.38 a Absorption spectra of chlorophylls a and b, and carotenoid pigments. **b** Photosynthetic action spectrum. These graphs show the wavelengths (colours) of light absorbed by plants and the rate of photosynthesis that occurs at each wavelength.

An action spectrum shows the wavelengths of light that permit the highest rates of photosynthesis. Notice how the action spectrum is very similar to the absorption spectrum and shows that the best wavelengths for photosynthesis are the red and blue ranges.

TEST YOURSELF 2.19

 Which colours (wavelengths) of light do green plants absorb most effectively?

How are leaf pigments separated by chromatography?

Chloroplasts contain several pigments and these can be extracted and separated by paper chromatography or thin layer chromatography. The steps are as follows:

Step 1. Grind leaf pieces in a pestle and mortar. Add a little propanaone and continue to grind. Cover and leave until the liquid has turned dark green. Decant or filter the liquid.

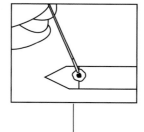

Step 2. Use a capillary tube to apply the extract to chromatography paper or a thin layer strip. Repeat until a small dark spot is formed.

Step 3. Place the chromatography strip into a narrow glass tube containing a little chromatography solvent. Leave until the solvent front has moved to the top and separated the pigments.

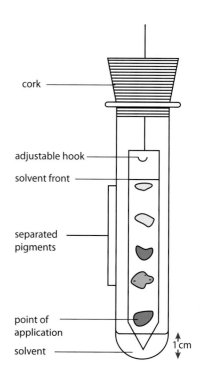

Figure 2.39 Chromatography.

What are the main stages in the process of photosynthesis?

The complex reactions of photosynthesis are usually separated into two stages:

1 The light dependent reactions:

   • require light energy

   • light energy is absorbed by chlorophyll

   • light energy is used to split water molecules in a process called photolysis

   • photolysis produces ATP, hydrogen ions and electrons for use in the light independent reactions.

2 Light independent reactions:

   • carbon dioxide from the environment is combined with hydrogen and ATP in a process called **carbon fixation**

   • these reactions produce glucose and a range of other organic molecules for the plant.

DEFINITION

CARBON FIXATION is the conversion of carbon atoms into a combined organic form. In this case carbon becomes fixed in glucose molecules that become other organic compounds.

HL students must study these chemical reactions in more detail. This is covered in Chapter **8**.

TEST YOURSELF 2.20

 Outline three differences between the light-dependent and light-independent reactions of photosynthesis.

How do we measure the rate photosynthesis?

Chemical processes can be estimated by measuring either inputs or outputs of the reaction. The rate of photosynthesis can be estimated by:

   • measuring the uptake of carbon dioxide in a period of time

   • measuring the output of oxygen in a period of time

   • indirectly by measuring the increase in plant biomass over a period of time.

Aquatic plants release oxygen into their surroundings as they photosynthesise. Bubbles of oxygen can be collected and the volume measured in a fixed period of time.

Aquatic plants absorb carbon dioxide from the water, and over a period of time this causes the pH to rise slightly, so pH change can be used to estimate photosynthesis.

You may be asked how an experiment could be used to measure the rate of photosynthesis at different light intensities or temperatures; or how the variables are controlled.

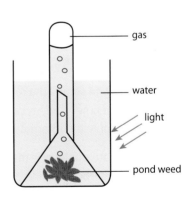

Figure 2.40

 hint

Remind yourself how light, temperature and pH can be controlled and remember that photosynthesis is controlled by enzymes, which are affected by these variables.

What are the factors that can limit photosynthesis?

DEFINITION

A **LIMITING FACTOR** is a resource that influences the rate of photosynthesis if it is in short supply.

In an exam you may be asked to define a limiting factor and interpret different graphs which show how combinations of factors affect the rate of photosynthesis.

The rate of photosynthesis depends on factors in a plant's environment. The most important factors are:

- light intensity: shows how the rate of photosynthesis increases as light intensity increases but fails to increase further after a certain point. This may be because temperature or carbon dioxide are limiting the reaction (Figure **2.41**)

- temperature: shows how the rate of photosynthesis changes with increasing light intensity at different temperatures (Figure **2.42**)

- concentration of carbon dioxide: shows how the rate of photosynthesis is influenced as carbon dioxide concentration is increased at either low or high light intensity. Notice that the temperature is kept the same (Figure **2.43**).

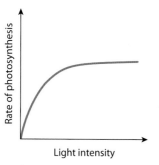

Figure 2.41

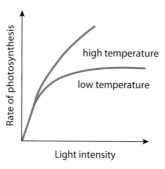

Figure 2.42

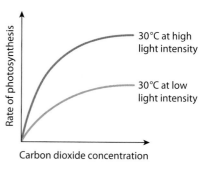

Figure 2.43

If any one of these factors is in short supply then the rate of photosynthesis will slow down even if there is an abundance of the others. The factor which is in short supply is said to limit the rate of reaction.

TEST YOURSELF 2.21

 Figure **2.44** shows the results of two experiments on the rate of photosynthesis in dim and bright light. The experiments were carried out at 19 °C and the plants had been kept in identical conditions.

1 Use only the information in the graph to:

    a State one factor that is limiting the rate of photosynthesis at carbon dioxide concentrations less than 0.02 %. **[1]**

    b Suggest one factor that limits the rate of photosynthesis in the experiment conducted in bright light at concentrations of 0.14–0.16 %. **[1]**

2 Describe two ways in which the data in the graph might be useful to farmers who grow tomatoes in greenhouses. **[3]**

3 Define a limiting factor for photosynthesis and explain why plants cannot always increase their rate of photosynthesis in increasing intensities of light. **[3]**

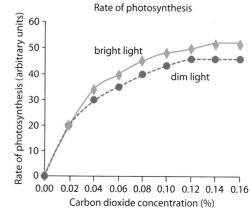

Figure 2.44

GENETICS

This chapter covers the following:

- ☐ Genes
- ☐ Chromosomes
- ☐ Meiosis
- ☐ Inheritance
- ☐ Genetic modification and biotechnology

3.1 Genes

Key information your should revise:

- What a gene is and how each gene can influence a characteristic.
- That a gene is found in a specific place on a chromosome.
- What an allele is and how alleles differ from one another.
- How mutations can happen and what their effect on an allele may be.
- How a mutation causes sickle cell anemia.
- What the human genome project achieved and exactly what a genome is.

hint

Learn the key definitions in this section – gene, allele, mutation, genome. They are often asked for in exams.

What is a gene?

DEFINITION

GENES are heritable factors that consist of a section of DNA which codes for the formation of a polypeptide. Each gene influences a specific characteristic.

- DNA is a double stranded molecule with chains of nucleotides linked together via their bases (adenine, cytosine, guanine and thymine).
- Sections of DNA, known as **genes**, that consist of particular bases, code for specific polypeptides when they are transcribed and translated (transcription and translation are described in Section **2.7**).
- When a gene is transcribed, the section of DNA containing the gene is copied to a corresponding molecule of RNA.
- RNA is then translated to make a chain of amino acids, which forms a polypeptide when it is complete.

Make sure you can recall how DNA code in the nucleus becomes a polypeptide. Check Sections **2.6** and **2.7** if you need to.

TEST YOURSELF 3.1

 Transcription is the:

- **A** Copying of DNA nucleotide sequence to form a duplicate DNA strand.
- **B** Reading of DNA nucleotide sequence to form an mRNA strand.
- **C** Reading of a DNA nucleotide sequence to form a polypeptide chain.
- **D** Movement of mRNA from the nucleus to the cytoplasm.

Genetics

Where exactly is a gene on a chromosome?

A gene for a characteristic always occupies the same place, or **locus**, on the same **chromosome**. For example the gene that codes for the beta subunit of hemoglobin protein is found at the end of chromosome 11 and people with cystic fibrosis inherit a defective gene that is found on chromosome 7.

How do genes influence characteristics?

The polypeptides and proteins produced by translation of genes influence and control all aspects of an organism's life. For example, the proteins made include hemoglobin proteins, hormones such as insulin (which controls our blood sugar) level and pigments which give hair and fur their colour. Proteins build skin, muscles and blood and all are coded for by different genes.

What is an allele?

DEFINITION

An **ALLELE** is the specific form of a gene which occupies the same position on a chromosome as other alleles of the gene, but differs from other alleles by small variations in its base sequence.

Organisms which reproduce sexually have paired sets of chromosomes, one of each pair comes from each parent. Equivalent chromosomes are called homologues (or **homologous chromosomes**) and they contain the same genes. But the exact version of a gene each chromosome carries can be slightly different – these different versions are called **alleles**.

For example, the type of earlobes you have, either attached or not, is determined by the alleles you have. If you inherit one 'free earlobe' allele (G) from either parent you will have free earlobes. To have attached earlobes you must inherit two copies of the slightly different 'attached' version (g) of the allele.

What are mutations?

DEFINITION

A **GENETIC MUTATION** is a change in the sequence of bases in a gene.

When DNA is copied mistakes sometimes happen. A nucleotide can be missed out or an extra one added in. Sometimes a nucleotide that is already present can be changed to one with a different base, such as A to G, errors are called **mutations**. Sometimes they are caused by the copying process but they can also be due to environmental factors called **mutagens** (Section **1.6**) such as UV light or X-rays.

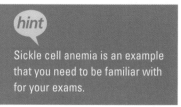

hint

Sickle cell anemia is an example that you need to be familiar with for your exams.

What is an example of a condition caused by a base substitution mutation?

Sickle cell anemia is caused by a base substitution mutation in the DNA of chromosome 11.

What is sickle cell anemia?

- A blood disorder caused by a change in just one base in a gene.

- It leads to anemia because part of the hemoglobin molecule is not formed correctly.

- The two beta chains in hemoglobin are the wrong shape, so hemoglobin cannot carry oxygen properly.

- Between 10 and 40% of people of African origin have a copy of the faulty allele and are carriers of the disease about 1% have two copies and are badly affected by it.

- Symptoms of the disease are caused by sickle-shaped red blood cells that obstruct capillaries and restrict blood flow. This causes pain; organs can be damaged or parts of them may die due to lack of blood and oxygen. The spleen is often affected and blood cells break down at a faster rate.

What causes sickle cell anemia?

The triplet **GAG** is changed by mutation to **GTG** in the allele that codes for the beta he-moglobin chain. The result is that the amino acid valine is included in the hemoglobin molecule instead of glutamic acid. This small change deforms the shape of red blood cells so they are sickle shaped instead of round.

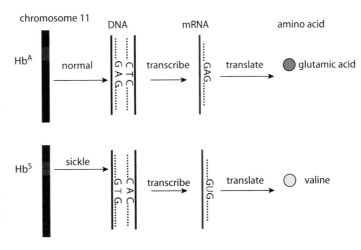

Figure 3.1 In sickle cell anemia the base sequence in the allele of DNA is decoded via transcription and translation to insert valine instead of glutamic acid into hemoglobin molecules.

What is a genome and why was the Human Genome Project so important?

DEFINITION

A **GENOME** is the whole genetic information of an organism.

The Human Genome Project, completed at the end of the 20th century, sequenced all the bases in a human genome and was the first step in understanding the genome. Now comparative genomics is used to compare genomes from different species as well as our own. Genomes of mice, fruit flies, bacteria, yeast and many other microorganisms have been sequenced.

Genomics is used to:

- compare genomes so that evolutionary relationships can be worked out
- identify the location of genes
- work out the functions of genes and non-coding regions of DNA.

TEST YOURSELF 3.2

 Suggest two benefits of the study of genomics (sequencing genomes). [2]

3.2 Chromosomes

Key information you should revise:

- Prokaryotes have one circular chromosome while eukaryotes have linear chromosomes which carry different genes.
- Prokaryotes may also have plasmids but eukaryotes do not.
- Eukaryotes have histone proteins associated with the DNA of their chromosomes.
- Each species has a specific number of chromosomes in its cells.
- One set of chromosomes is called the haploid number; two sets is the diploid number.
- Homologous chromosomes make up matching pairs and carry the same genes.
- Karyograms are pictures, which show chromosomes arranged in pairs according to their size.
- **Sex chromosomes** (X and Y in humans) determine sex and the other chromosomes are called **autosomes**.

Eukaryotic **CHROMOSOMES** are long threads of DNA and protein that carry the genetic material of the cell. In prokaryotes the DNA in a chromosome is not associated with proteins.

What are the key features of prokaryotic and eukaryotic DNA?

Table 3.1

Prokaryotic	Eukaryotic
circular chromosome also called a nucleoid	linear chromosomes enclosed in a nucleus
cells contain additional DNA as small circular **plasmids**	no plasmids
DNA is naked and not associated with other proteins	DNA is associated with histone proteins
cell contains just one chromosome	cell contains two or more chromosome types

Look at Chapter **6** and remind yourself about the importance of DNA in plasmids for transferring antibiotic resistance between bacteria.

DEFINITIONS

A **DIPLOID** nucleus contains two copies of each chromosome in homologous pairs.

A **HAPLOID** nucleus contains one chromosome of each homologous pair.

A **HOMOLOGOUS PAIR** is a pair of matching chromosomes that carry the same genes but not necessarily the same alleles of those genes.

A **SOMATIC CELL** is a body cell that is not a gamete.

A **GAMETE** is a haploid sex cell, for example, sperm, ovum or pollen.

You don't have to remember the chromosome numbers for different species but don't be surprised if they are given in an exam question.

Short answers with the important facts are all that are needed in questions like Test yourself **3.3**. Don't waste time writing too much.

Make sure you can compare pairs of terms in this chapter: prokaryote and eukaryote; karyogram and karyotype; diploid and haploid.

Which cells are diploid and which are haploid?

Human **somatic cells** are diploid and contain 46 chromosomes (23 homologous pairs). Human gametes are haploid and contain only one of each chromosome, a total of 23 single chromosomes.

How many chromosomes do organisms have?

Every organism has its own characteristic number of chromosomes, here are some examples of the diploid numbers of different species:
domestic dog–78, chimpanzee–48, human–46, rice plant–24, fruit fly–8.

TEST YOURSELF 3.3

 1 A plant has 30 chromosomes in its leaf cells, what is this number called?
2 How many chromosomes would the plant have in its gametes?

What is genome size and how is it measured?

- Genome size is measured as the number of base pairs in a single genome.
- The complexity of an organism is not proportional to its genome size, many organisms have more DNA than humans.
- Genome size is not proportional to the number of genes either because some organisms have a lot of non-coding DNA.
- A human genome has 3200×10^6 base pairs, and the marbled lungfish has $130\,000 \times 10^6$ base pairs, the largest known vertebrate genome.

What is used to measure genome size?

What's the difference between a karyogram and a karyotype?

A **karyogram** is a picture organised to show chromosomes arranged in their pairs according to their size. Chromosomes are stained with dyes to show their banding patterns. The various banding patterns are influenced by the proportions of the different base pairs present in a region of DNA and by the histone proteins that are associated with it.

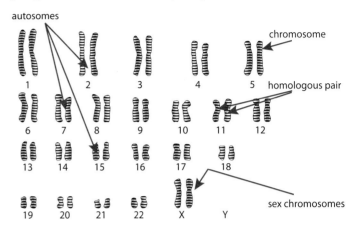

Figure 3.2 A karyogram of human chromosomes. This karyogram has two X chromosomes and is therefore from a female.

DEFINITION

A **KARYOTYPE** is the number and types of chromosomes in the nucleus.

TEST YOURSELF 3.5

1 Give two reasons why the karyogram in Figure **3.2** could not show chromosomes from a bacterium.
2 State the number of autosomes in the karyogram.

⧉ Annotated exemplar answer 3.1

The diagram below shows the chromosomes of a male. Study the diagram and answer the questions that follow.

a What is the name given to this type of diagram? [1]

b How can you be sure that this diagram is from a male? [1]

c The male has a genetic condition which is shown by a chromosome abnormality. What is the condition and the abnormality? [2]

d Explain how this abnormality occurs. [4]

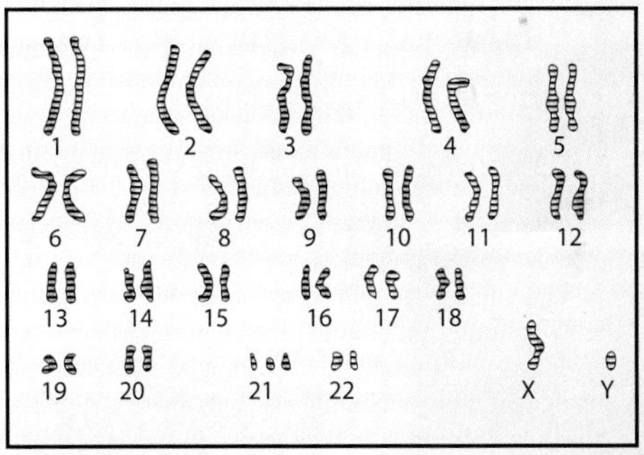

Figure 3.3

a The diagram is called a karyogram. —————— Do not confuse this with karyotype.

b There is one X and one Y chromosome in the diagram therefore it is from a male.

c The condition is called Down syndrome and ———— is caused by having an extra chromosome.

Include the term 'trisomy' and state that chromosome 21 is involved to gain both marks.

d The abnormality is caused by an error in the division of the cell during meiosis. ————

Chromosomes fail to separate properly during meiosis

So half the gametes contain two chromosomes (of number 21 in this case) and the other half have none

Here there are 4 marks to be gained and the command term is 'explain' so you must give a full answer that includes at least four points. This answer would score 3 but could be improved by adding:

The fusion of the first type of gamete with a normal gamete produces a zygote with 3 chromosomes instead of 2. Or, a trisomy gives people with Down syndrome their characteristic appearance.

3.3 Meiosis

Do not confuse **meiosis** with **mitosis** that you studied in Chapter **1**.

Key information you should revise:

- When a diploid cell divides by meiosis four haploid cells are produced.
- Haploid gametes are important for sexual reproduction, when they fuse the diploid number is restored.
- Meiosis has a number of stages, but DNA replication happens before meiosis, so all chromosomes are made up of two chromatids.
- In the first division of meiosis the chromosome number is halved, crossing over takes place.
- Genetic variation is increased in three ways: crossing over, random orientation of chromosomes on the spindle and fusion of gametes from different parents.
- Non-disjunction occurs when chromosomes don't separate properly during meiosis. It produces cells with too few or too many chromosomes.
- Down syndrome is caused by a trisomy of chromosome 21.

What happens during meiosis?

DEFINITION

MEIOSIS is the type of cell division that takes place in ovaries and testes of animals, and in the anthers and ovaries of plants to produce haploid gametes for sexual reproduction.

You will need to be familiar with the stages of meiosis and especially where **crossing over** causes alleles to be exchanged or when chromosomes don't separate properly and errors occur. Remember that chromosomes replicate during interphase, so at the start of meiosis they consist of two identical **chromatids**. (Interphase is the period when a cell carries out the tasks, which it is programmed to do. For example it may produce protein and secrete enzymes.)

Here is a summary of the stages of meiosis and what happens at each stage:

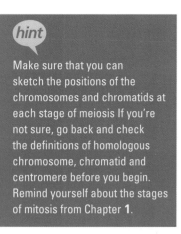

hint

Make sure that you can sketch the positions of the chromosomes and chromatids at each stage of meiosis If you're not sure, go back and check the definitions of homologous chromosome, chromatid and centromere before you begin. Remind yourself about the stages of mitosis from Chapter **1**.

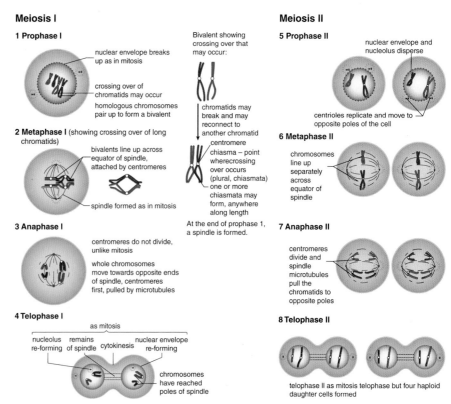

Figure 3.4 The stages of meiosis in an animal cell showing just two homologous pairs of chromosomes.

Table 3.2

Stage	Process	Important things that happen at each stage
interphase (before meiosis begins)	cell carries out protein production chromosomes replicate	chromosomes replicate so they consist of two identical chromatids
prophase I	chromosomes consisting of two identical chromatids super coil and homologous pairs line up side by side	crossing over may happen if chromatids become entangled new combinations of allele can form (see Figure **3.5**)
metaphase I	chromosomes line up on the spindle at the centre of the cell and attach by their **centromeres** the way they align is random, so maternal and paternal chromosomes can be on either side of the equator for each pair	a centromere is the point where the two chromatids are joined. The spindle is made of microtubules because the alignment is random, more genetic variation is produced in the gametes
anaphase I	microtubules contract towards opposite poles homologous chromosomes are separated but sister chromatids remain together	this stage is the reduction division when the number of chromosomes is halved
telophase I	spindles break down and a new membrane forms round each new nucleus cytokinesis divides the cytoplasm and two new cells are formed	each new cell contains only one chromosome of the homologous pair. Each is made of two chromatids
prophase II	each new cell produces new spindle microtubules. Chromosomes recoil and the nuclear envelope breaks down	
metaphase II	individual chromosomes line up at the equator of the cell spindle fibres attach at the centromeres	
anaphase II	sister chromatids are separated as the centromere splits, spindle fibres pull the chromatids to opposite ends of the cell	
telophase II	nuclear envelopes form around the four new haploid nuclei and the chromosomes uncoil a second cytokinesis divides the cytoplasm	four haploid gametes are produced at the end of meiosis

TEST YOURSELF 3.6

1 After meiosis I, the chromosomal makeup of each daughter cell is:
   A diploid, and the chromosomes are each composed of a single chromatid
   B diploid, and the chromosomes are each composed of two chromatids
   C haploid, and the chromosomes are each composed of a single chromatid
   D haploid, and the chromosomes are each composed of two chromatids
2 Meiosis II is similar to mitosis in that:
   A sister chromatids separate during anaphase
   B DNA replicates before the division
   C the daughter cells are diploid
   D the chromosome number is reduced

What is non-disjunction and when does it happen?

Non-disjunction is when homologous chromosomes don't separate properly during meiosis. It can happen at anaphase 2 or sometimes at anaphase 1.

Gametes produced contain either one too few or one too many chromosomes.

Those with too few seldom survive but sometimes a gamete with too many does.

TEST YOURSELF 3.7

Name the stage when:

1 The nuclear envelope breaks down.

2 Reduction division occurs.

3 Homologous chromosomes separate.

What is a trisomy?

After fertilisation a gamete with an extra chromosome will produce a zygote with a particular chromosome having three chromosomes instead of two. There is said to be a **trisomy** in that chromosome. Trisomy in human chromosome 21 produces a baby with 47 chromosomes instead of 46. This is known as Down syndrome.

Trisomy of chromosome 21 produces children that survive because the chromosome is small and has few genes. Trisomies of most other chromosomes lead to the zygote failing to survive.

How meiosis leads to variation

- Each chromosome in a homologous pair contains different alleles so gametes formed when they separate are different.

- Different homologous pairs line up independently on the spindle and separate independently, so gametes contain different combinations of chromosome pairs.

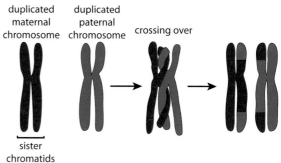

- Crossing over means that genetic material is exchanged and produces new combinations (see Figure **3.5**).

- At fertilisation, gametes from different parents fuse and produce more variation among offspring.

Figure 3.5 The process of crossing over.

> **hint**
>
> Variation is a favourite topic with examiners, so check you can remember the ways it is increased shown in this list.

3.4 Inheritance

In this section you will be asked to work out allele combinations and their effects on the appearance or characteristics of an organism. Practice using Punnett grids and check the hints that are given here and in the exam questions.

Key information you should revise:

- Mendel worked out the principles of inheritance using pea plants.

- Haploid gametes fuse at fertilisation to form a diploid zygote.

- **Dominant alleles** mask the effect of recessive alleles.

- Co-dominant alleles have combined effects.

- **Recessive alleles** on autosomes account for many genetic disorders in humans.

- Some disorders are linked to sex chromosomes and their pattern of inheritance is different.

- Mutation rate is increased by radiation and chemicals, which can lead to cancer or genetic disease.

Some important definitions

DEFINITIONS

GENOTYPE is the alleles an organism possesses (in genetics problems an allele is represented by a pair of letters, e.g. TT or Tt).

PHENOTYPE refers to the characteristics of an organism, such as flower colour or blood group.

A **DOMINANT ALLELE** is an allele (shown as a capital letter) which has the same effect on a phenotype whether the organism has one copy or two (e.g. TT or Tt).

A **RECESSIVE ALLELE** is an allele, which only affects the phenotype when two copies are present. It is always shown as a small letter (e.g. tt).

CO-DOMINANT ALLELES are pairs of alleles that both affect the phenotype, for example human blood groups are affected by both alleles A and B. These are represented in genetics questions in exams as I^A and I^B.

HOMOZYGOUS means two identical copies of an allele are present (e.g. TT or tt).

HETEROZYGOUS refers to two different alleles are present (e.g. Tt).

A **CARRIER** is an individual who has one copy of a recessive allele that causes a genetic disease if two copies are present in an organism.

PURE-BREEDING refers to an organism that is homozygous for a specified gene or genes. If a pure breeding individual is crossed with another pure breeding individual they produce offspring, which also have the same phenotype.

> *hint*
>
> This is a theoretical section. Before you begin check the special terms used in analysing inheritance.

Who was Mendel and what did he do?

Mendel was a monk who lived in the 19th century in what is now the Czech Republic.

He didn't know about DNA (which hadn't been discovered), but he studied plant breeding and how characteristics are inherited in the pea plants, which he grew for many generations over a number of years.

Mendel used what we call a monohybrid cross, studying just one pair of characteristics, to follow the inheritance of features, such as plant height, petal colour and seed shape.

Mendel proposed that 'factors', which we would now call alleles, are transmitted to offspring in gametes.

He also described how dominant and recessive characteristics are inherited in predictable ratios.

An example of a cross that Mendel made

A Punnett grid is a diagram that shows the possible gametes in a cross. Where a row and column intersect it shows the **genotype** of the offspring produced by the two gametes being united in a zygote. Always use a Punnet grid for these diagrams and add a key to show the alleles and the ratio of **phenotype** in the offspring.

Upper and lower case letters represent alleles. R and r would be a good choice but Y and y look too similar, especially when they are hand-written. The labels P = parents, F_1 = first generation and F_2 = second generation are used in genetics problems.

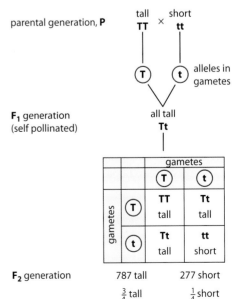

Figure 3.6 Diagrams to show Mendel's crosses of tall and short pea plants, with modern knowledge of alleles included.

🖾 Worked example 3.1

Suppose that a single gene controls hair length in guinea pigs. Long hair is dominant to short hair. A guinea pig that is homozygous for long hair was crossed with a short-haired guinea pig. Work out the possible genotypes and phenotypes of their offspring.

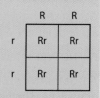

	R	R
r	Rr	Rr
r	Rr	Rr

Figure 3.7

1 To begin, choose a suitable letter. Long hair is dominant to short so let R = long hair and r = short hair.

2 If the long-haired guinea pig is homozygous it must have the genotype RR and the shorted-haired animal can only be rr (because if an R were present the animal would have long hair).

3 Set out the cross and Punnett grid for the F_1 generation as shown in Figure **3.7**.

Parents' phenotypes	long-haired	short-haired
Parents' genotypes	RR	rr
Gametes	R and R	r and r

The Punnett grid Figure **3.7** shows that all the offspring will be phenotypically long-haired and their genotype will be Rr.

4 Write out the cross between two of these long-haired offspring (Rr). State the phenotypes of the offspring and ratio between them. The answer is shown in Figure **3.8**.

	R	r
R	RR	Rr
r	Rr	rr

three of the offspring have long-hair
The ratio is 3:1.

one is short-haired

Figure 3.8

What are co-dominant and multiple alleles?

- Co-dominant alleles are alleles that both have an influence on an organism's phenotype.
- One example of co-dominance is the ABO system of classifying human blood groups.
- There are three alleles: I^A, I^B and i and each person has only two of the three alleles.

Table 3.3 Human blood groups and their genotypes must be written in this format.

Genotype	Phenotype or blood group
$I^A I^A$	A
$I^A i$	A
$I^B I^B$	B
$I^B i$	B
$I^A I^B$	AB
ii	O

🖾 Worked example 3.2

Mary is blood group A and her husband Ivan is blood group B. Their daughter Sally is blood group O. Determine the genotypes of Mary and Ivan.

1 The alleles are represented by I^A, I^B and **i**.

2 To be blood group A, Mary could have genotype $I^A I^A$ or $I^A i$.

To be blood group B, Ivan could have genotype $I^B I^B$ or $I^B i$.

To be blood group O, Sally could **only** have the genotype **ii**.

3 Each of Sally's two alleles have come from her parents, so she must have received one **i** from her mother and one **i** from her father, as shown in the Punnett grid.

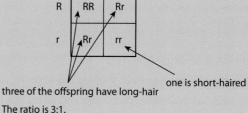

		Gametes from Ivan	
		I^B	i
Gametes from Mary	I^A	$I^A I^B$	$I^A i$
	i	$I^B i$	ii Sally group O

4 Mary is blood group A so must have the genotype $I^A i$ and Ivan's genotype has to be $I^B i$.

What are sex chromosomes and how are they inherited?

Humans have one pair of chromosomes, which determine sex.

- Females have XX.
- Males have XY.

The Y chromosome is smaller than the X and the X carries more genes than the Y.

Sex chromosomes are inherited in the same way as other chromosomes so that there is always a 50% chance that a baby will be a boy and a 50% chance that it will be a girl.

Sex chromosomes and genes: what is sex linkage?

DEFINITION

SEX LINKAGE is the way that genes for characteristics located on the X chromosome are inherited. Certain conditions, such as hemophilia and red–green colour blindness are said to be sex-linked because genes, which control them, are found on the X chromosomes.

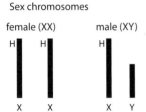

Figure 3.9 Male and female sex chromosomes. The female has two copies of the H allele but the male has only one.

- Females have two X chromosomes and so have two copies of all the alleles on those chromosome.
- Females can be **heterozygous** for conditions, such as red–green colour blindness and hemophilia, which do not usually affect women.
- Males have only one X chromosome.
- Males, who have only one copy of these alleles, will always be affected by these conditions if they have the recessive allele.

hint

Notice how the alleles for sex-linked characters are written. It's similar to the way co-dominant alleles for blood groups are written.

Hemophilia is a sex-linked condition that affects blood clotting. The genes controlling the production of factor VIII protein, which helps blood to clot, are on the X chromosome.

A female who is $X^H X^h$ is a carrier of the condition but does not suffer from it but a male who has one recessive allele $X^h Y$ will be a hemophiliac.

It is rare for a female to have hemophilia because she would have to be the daughter of a male hemophiliac and a female carrier. Today, hemophiliacs are treated with the clotting factors they cannot produce. These may be made using gene technology.

Red–green colour blindness leaves a person unable to tell the difference between red and green properly. It is inherited in a similar way to hemophilia. Check that you understand this in Worked example **3.3**.

⊠ Worked example 3.3

A woman who is homozygous for normal vision married a man who is red–green colour blind. Determine the possible types of vision inherited by their two children, one girl and one boy.

1 Standard letters are always used for these alleles – normal vision is X^B and colour blind is X^b. The X must always be included.

2 The woman is homozygous for normal vision so her genotype must be $X^B X^B$.

Since the man is colour blind, his genotype must be $X^b Y$.

3 Set out the diagram as shown.

The Punnett grid shows that a daughter will have normal vision, but be a carrier for red–green colour blindness. A son will have normal vision.

		Gametes from father	
		X^b	Y
Gametes from mother	X^B	$X^B X^b$	$X^B Y$
	X^B	$X^B X^b$	$X^B Y$

If the daughter of the couple in Worked example **3.3** married a colour-blind man, what is the chance that **a** their sons and **b** their daughters would be red–green colour blind?

What examples are there of other genetic diseases?

There are many genetic diseases, most are caused by single mutations to a gene and most are on the autosomal chromosomes (not X and Y chromosomes).

Remember you can't catch a genetic 'disease' like other diseases; they are inherited from parents.

Here are some examples of the more common ones:

- Cystic fibrosis (carried by 1 in 25 Caucasians) – chromosome affected is number 7.
- Beta thalassemia (most common in Asia and the Middle East) – allele for hemoglobin production on chromosome 11 is affected.
- Sickle cell anemia (most common in people of African origin) – caused by a single mutation in the beta hemoglobin alleles on chromosome 11.
- Huntington's disease (HD) – unusual as it is a dominant mutation of the HD gene on chromosome 4; only 1 in 20 000 people are affected.

Notice that genetic diseases are not evenly distributed. Different conditions affect populations in different parts of the world to a greater or lesser extent.

What causes mutations and how often do they happen?

Mutations are spontaneous, permanent changes in the base sequence of DNA, which can occur at any time in any organism.

DEFINITION

The **MUTATION RATE** is the frequency of mutation, which is usually very low.

Mutation rate is increased by ionising radiation, for example from nuclear plants, UV light, X-rays and chemicals, such as formaldehyde, benzene and tobacco tar.

Mutations that affect body cells, such as skin cells or lung cells, are not usually inherited but can cause cancer. Only mutations in gamete-producing cells are likely to be passed on.

 Huntington's disease is a disorder caused by the repetition of the amino acid glutamine in the protein huntingtin. What type of disease is it?

A an inherited disease

B a nutritional disease

C a sexually transmitted disease

D a sex-linked disease

hint

To answer a question like Test yourself **3.8**, start by drawing a Punnett grid like the one in Worked example **3.1** to check your answers.

hint

If a question asks for the 'chance' of a characteristic appearance you can use either a percentage or a ratio. But check carefully – if a percentage is asked for and you give a ratio you will lose marks.

☆ Model answer 3.1

Cystic fibrosis is a genetic disease in humans. The disease is inherited and caused by a single gene, which is found as two alleles.

Two healthy parents have three children. The first two did not have CF but the third did.

a Define the term 'allele'. [1]

b Is the CF allele dominant or recessive? [1]

c Explain your answer to b. [2]

d What was the genotype of the two parents? [2]

e Use a Punnett grid to deduce what the chance would be of a fourth child having CF. [3]

a An allele is the form of a gene, which occupies the same position on a chromosome as another allele of the gene, but differs from it by small variations in base sequence.

b The faulty CF allele is recessive.

c Because neither parent nor two of the three children has the condition. The third child must have received two copies of the recessive allele to suffer from CF.

d Both parents were heterozygous for the faulty CF allele.

e The dominant allele is G the recessive allele is g.

	G	g
G	GG	Gg
g	Gg	gg Child with CF

The chance of a fourth child having cystic fibrosis is 1 in 4 or 25%

hint

In an exam, if asked to define a term, give the definition clearly and concisely.

hint

In a Punnett grid, add the phenotypes (characteristics) if there's space, as shown in here. If not, put them underneath to support your answer and make it clear.

📋 Annotated exemplar answer 3.2

Albinism is an autosomal, recessive condition in which the skin pigment melanin does not form. The pedigree chart shown below is of a family that has several members with albinism.

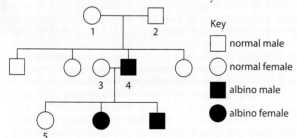

Key

□ normal male

○ normal female

■ albino male

● albino female

a Give the genotypes of the parents 1 and 2, the female 3 and the male 4, who has albinism. [4]

b What is the probability that female 5 is a carrier of albinism? [1]

c How many members of the family are definitely heterozygous for this allele? [1]

Figure 3.10

a Parents 1 and 2 must be heterozygous because they have produced children both with and without albinism.

If A is the normal allele and a is the recessive allele, both 1 and 2 must be Aa.

Female 3 does not have albinism but her husband (male 4) does.

b Female 5 must be a carrier because she has one a allele from her father and one A allele from her mother. She must be Aa.

c Individuals 1 and 2 are definitely heterozygous and individuals 3 and 5 are definitely heterozygous.

(3/6)

This is good. As you answer the questions always use the correct terms – heterozygous in this case.

This part of the answer does not give the genotype of female 3 or male 4 but only mentions their phenotypes. For full marks, the answer should say 'Male 4 must be aa, but as the couple have children with and without albinism, female 3 must be Aa because her second daughter and son have albinism.'

Many students would write this answer. The content is correct but the question asks 'How many' so the answer must include the fact that four members of the family are heterozygotes.

3.5 Genetic modification and biotechnology

Key information you should revise:

- How gel electrophoresis works and how it is used with the polymerase chain reaction to build genetic profiles.
- How DNA profiling is used to compare samples of DNA.
- How genes are transferred between species during genetic modification (GM).
- What a clone is and how some clones occur naturally.
- How cloning is used to reproduce plants and animals.
- How clones can be made by breaking up embryos and also by using differentiated cells.
- What some of the risks and benefits associated with gene technology are.

What is DNA profiling?

DNA profiling involves comparing samples of DNA from different sources. It is the correct term to describe taking and separating samples of DNA by electrophoresis and staining them so that patterns of bands unique to that sample can be seen.

The arrangement of the bands can be compared with other samples to see which bands are the same. DNA profiling is used to identify closely related organisms, parents and children and in forensic investigations.

DNA fingerprinting is a less accurate term for DNA profiling. It is used in forensic science, especially in crime investigations because it can identify suspects just as a fingerprint can.

What are the stages used to make a DNA profile?

How do the bands appear during electrophoresis?

The distance each fragment can travel depends on its sise. Small fragments move more easily, larger ones are left behind. After the fragments have been separated in the gel they are stained and produce the bands we see in a DNA profile.

How a DNA profile is made

- Sample collection: The sample of tissue containing DNA is collected. This can be blood, hair, skin or certain body fluids. The sample can come from a crime scene or a living person.

- DNA extraction and amplification: As the amount of material is usually quite small, DNA is copied in the PCR (polymerase chain reaction). DNA strands are separated and mixed with nucleotides so that new DNA strands are synthesised. After about 20 cycles of this process there is enough DNA to proceed.

- DNA cutting: The DNA is in long strands so they are cut into pieces with restriction enzymes which snip the DNA at very precise points.

- Electrophoresis: The smaller fragments are placed on a gel plate and gel electrophoresis is carried out. Fragments of DNA move in an electric field through the gel.

- Bands are stained so they are clear and permanently visible.

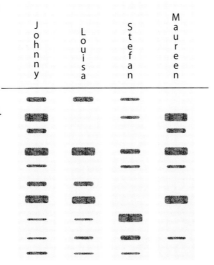

Figure 3.11 A DNA profile showing four samples and their banding patterns.

Which sections of DNA are used?

DNA from different organisms or people varies in the quantity of repeated sequences it has. **Restriction enzymes** cut out these sections, which are used to make the profile.

TEST YOURSELF 3.10

 What is the outcome of a polymerase chain reaction?

What is gene technology and genetic modification (GM)?

Gene technology is also called **genetic modification**. It involves the transfer of genes from one species to another. This is done to produces new varieties of organism with useful or desirable characteristics. Some examples include:

- The transfer of genes from eukaryotes to bacteria. This has been done to produce human insulin.

- Genes from spiders have been transferred to goats so that they produce spider silk (an extremely strong protein) in their milk.

What techniques are used in gene technology and transfer?

There are many different ways of getting new genes into an organism but the basic steps are:

1 Obtain the required gene in the form of a piece of DNA.

2 Attach this DNA to a vector, which can carry it into a host cell (the cell which the DNA is needed in). Bacterial plasmids are one type of vector used to do this. Plasmids containing DNA from another organism are called recombinant plasmids.

3 Culture or reproduce the cell with the new DNA in its nucleus.

In step 1, DNA may be obtained as **RNA** at first and converted by reverse transcriptase back into DNA (known as cDNA). This means that only useful regions of DNA are transferred.

In step 2, restriction enzymes are used to open up a plasmid and make a matching link with the DNA to be inserted.

In Step 3, **DNA ligase** enzymes join the fragments of DNA and plasmid to produce recombinant plasmids.

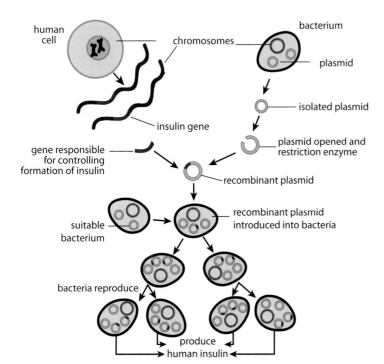

Figure 3.12 Production of human insulin using gene technology.

When human insulin is produced plasmids are inserted into the bacteria which are cultured on an industrial scale in a fermenter, Figure **3.12**. (There is more information about fermentation in Option **B**.)

TEST YOURSELF 3.11

 1 What are the two enzymes needed to make a recombinant plasmid?
2 How is DNA ligase used in gene transfer which involves plasmids?
  A opens bacterial cells and releases the plasmid
  B cuts DNA at a target sequence
  C links sections of DNA together
  D produces sticky ends

hint

You may be asked to give an example of a GM organism in an exam. So learn some examples so that you can use them when needed.

How many GM organisms are there and what are they used for?

More than 100 plant species have been modified to make them resistant to herbicide, stay fresh longer or produce high levels of important nutrients. Some examples include:

• Golden rice, which contains beta carotene that can be converted to vitamin A.

• Glyphosate-resistant maize, which means that fields can be sprayed with the herbicide glyphosate without killing maize plants. This has led to reduced herbicide use.

GM animals have also been farmed to produce proteins, such as blood clotting factors to treat hemophilia. These proteins are usually collected from the animals' milk.

TEST YOURSELF 3.12

 Which of the following techniques causes DNA fragments to move in an electric field?
  A the PCR (polymerase chain reaction)   **C** reverse transcription
  B genetic modification   **D** gel electrophoresis

What are the risks and benefits associated with GM?

Some people feel strongly about gene technology and it is important to consider both sides of the discussion. Some risks and benefits of GM crops are given in Table **3.4**.

Table 3.4

Benefits	Risks
• new varieties are resistant to herbicides so fewer chemical need to be used	• including genes for toxins to kill insects may lead to resistance in insects that will become more difficult to kill
• GM crops can be resistant to disease so yields could increase	• the cost of GM seeds may be too high for some farmers
• some GM crops are more tolerant of drought or salinity so can be grown in more areas	• genes for herbicide resistance in crop plants could spread to wild plants and weeds
• less insecticide needs to be used if pest-resistant crops are developed, protecting beneficial insects	• genes containing insect-killing toxins in crop plants could kill other non-pest insect species
• many GM varieties decay more slowly so they remain fresher for longer and there is less waste in the food chain	• GM crops could mutate and cause unexpected problems
• crops can be modified to contain vitamins, vaccines or their nutritional value can be increased	• long-term effects of GM are not known

What is a clone? How are plants and animals cloned?

DEFINITION

A **CLONE** is a group of genetically identical organisms or a group of cells produced from a single parent.

Cloning is not a new idea, identical twins and triplets are natural clones and cloning has been used by gardeners and horticulturalists for many years to propagate plants from cuttings of roots, stems and leaves.

A stem cutting can be placed in soil or compost and it will develop roots and new shoots so it turns into a plant that is genetically identical to the original plant.

Clones of farmed animals can be produced from early embryos, which are divided into two or more parts in a Petri dish soon after fertilisation. The embryos are then implanted into the uterus of a mother animal where they develop normally. In this way farmers can produce more animals with desirable characteristics, such as high milk yield or meat production.

Dolly the sheep was the first cloned animal produced from a somatic (body) cell not a fertilised egg. The stages of cloning from an adult animal are:

1 Select a suitable somatic cell from the animal to be cloned (in Dolly's case this was a mammary gland cell) and remove the nucleus.

2 Take an unfertilised ovum from another female and remove the nucleus.

3 Insert the donor nucleus from step 1 into the enucleated, unfertilised ovum.

4 Allow the ovum to divide to become an embryo.

5 Implant the embryo into a surrogate mother, who will give birth to a clone of the first animal.

Remember, each of these steps is very complex and must be carried out at the right stage of the cell cycle. The procedure is known as 'somatic–cell nuclear transfer'.

TEST YOURSELF 3.13

 What is one feature of the genetic code that means it can be transferred from one species to another? Think about what you know about the genetic code from Chapter **2**.

4
ECOLOGY

This chapter covers the following topics:

☐ Species communities and ecosystems   ☐ Carbon recycling

☐ Energy flow   ☐ Climate change

4.1 Species communities and ecosystems

Key information you should revise:

- What is meant by a species.
- Definitions of key ecological terms: community, population, abiotic environment and ecosystem.
- How species may be defined as autotrophs or heterotrophs depending on their method of nutrition.
- How heterotrophs may be divided into different groups: consumers, detritivores and saprotrophs.
- How some ecosystems have the potential to be indefinitely sustainable.

How do biologists define a species?

hint

The concept of a species is key to our understanding of ecology and evolutionary relationships. Be sure you can explain it fully in an exam question.

A species is a group of organisms that are able to interbreed and produce **fertile** offspring. If long distances separate members of a species, they may form separate populations. But as long as they are still able to interbreed when they do meet they are still members of the same species. Lions are a species because they interbreed and produce more lions. But if lions are separated from one another by long distances and exist in separate populations they remain members of the same species as they retain the potential to interbreed.

If populations remain separated for many generations, they may evolve differences so that they can no longer breed. In this case new species may evolve. This is covered in Chapter **5**.

Notice that it is the number of generations that is key here rather than the length of time. Consider the generation time of a bacterium and an elephant and you will get an idea of the significance of generations.

DEFINITIONS

A **POPULATION** is a group of organisms of the same species which live in the same area at the same time.

A **COMMUNITY** is a group of populations living and interacting with each other in the same environment.

ABIOTIC FACTORS are non-living aspects of the environment, such as water pH, amount of sunlight or type of soil.

An **ECOSYSTEM** is a community of organisms together with its abiotic environment.

What is the difference between an autotroph and a heterotroph?

Species are divided in two groups based on their method of obtaining food. Autotrophs are species, which can make their own food from simple **inorganic** materials; this group includes all photosynthetic species that use light as a source of energy.

Heterotrophs are consumers, which feed on organic matter. This group includes herbivores, which feed on plant material, and carnivores, which are meat eaters. A few unusual organisms such as *Euglena* are able to feed as both autotrophs and heterotrophs.

What are the other main groups of heterotrophs?

Detritivores and saprotrophs are two other important groups of heterotrophs. Detritivores are organisms, such as worms, woodlice and millipedes, which feed on dead organic matter such as fallen leaves or the bodies of dead animals. Saprotrophs are bacteria and fungi, which secrete enzymes on to organic matter and absorb pre-digested food. These organisms are vital to the recycling of inorganic material in an ecosystem. They break down organic compounds and release simple substances into the soil so that autotrophs have a supply of nitrates, phosphates and other raw materials to build their bodies and start food chains (See Section **4.2**). Figure **4.1** shows how these groups are related in an ecosystem.

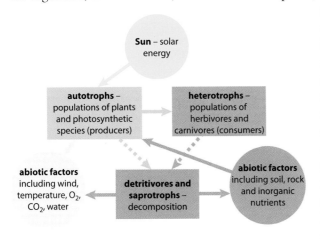

Figure 4.1 The components of an ecosystem.

> **hint**
>
> To identify an autotroph ask yourself whether the organism builds up simple inorganic substances or breaks down complex organic ones to build its body.

> **hint**
>
> Make sure you can describe the type of food which provides nutrients for each group.

What is a mesocosm and can a big ecosystem really keep going forever?

A mesocosm is a small-scale, self-sustaining system, which is set up, usually in a laboratory, so that ecologists can study how ecosystems work. Closed bottle gardens, growth chambers and aquariums are all mesocosms. Even though these systems do not have inputs, apart from light, they can keep going for a certain period of time because the mesocosm **community** recycles inorganic materials when organisms die and are broken down.

In the natural world an ecosystem has the potential to remain stable and self-sustaining just as a mesocosm does, but in reality, external events such as storms, floods, fires or human interference can disrupt an otherwise stable system. For a system to be sustainable it must be robust enough to resist human activities, such as fishing or harvesting without being harmed.

What can ecologists study in a mesocosm?
- How **abiotic** factors such as light affect living things.
- What effect a change in temperature has on the system.
- How feeding relationships such as competition for limited resources affect the ecosystem.

Ecologist can use the results to predict how these changes may affect larger ecosystems, for example how climate change may affect the world.

TEST YOURSELF 4.1

What is the role of saprotrophic bacteria in an ecosystem?
- **A** to recycle energy in dead organic material
- **B** to digest dead organic material and release nutrients from it
- **C** to produce dead organic matter by killing organisms
- **D** to feed on dead organic matter and prevent it from building up in the ecosystem

4.2 Energy flow

Key information you should revise:

- How light energy from the Sun forms the basis of life on Earth.
- How chemical energy in carbon compounds passes through food chains.
- Why energy is lost at each trophic level as animals feed.
- How these energy losses restrict the biomass of organisms at the end of food chains and also the length of food chains.

Why is the Sun so important?

The sun provides the energy which autotrophs can capture and store as chemical energy as they photosynthesise. Plants combine carbon dioxide and water during photosynthesis to produce glucose. The chemical bonds between the carbon, oxygen and hydrogen atoms in a glucose molecule are formed from the conversion of light energy to chemical energy. Autotrophs are also able to take in other raw materials such as nitrates and phosphates and produce all the other substances they need.

What is a food chain?

A food chain is a way of describing feeding relationships in an ecosystem. Every organism needs food to survive but will eventually be eaten themselves. A food chain shows the sequence of feeding relationships between organisms.

For example:

grass   ⟶   grasshopper   ⟶   meerkat   ⟶   eagle

autotroph   ⟶   heterotrophs

How are food webs formed?

It is very rare for an organism to feed on only one type of food. For example the meerkat will eat other small invertebrates as well as grasshoppers and the eagle will take other items of prey as well as meerkats. In this way a network or food web of feeding relationships is built up.

hint

Remember when answering an exam question about ecology that the arrows in a food chain or web must point towards the organism that is feeding.

A simple food web:

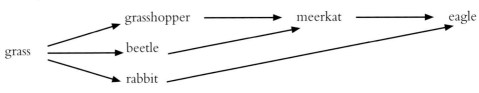

TEST YOURSELF 4.2

 Try to construct a food web using the following organisms: sparrow, wheat seeds, fox, cat, hawk, mouse.

What are trophic levels?

Trophic level is another term ecologists use to explain feeding relationships in an ecosystem. Trophic means feeding and every member of a food chain is on a particular tropic level.

- Trophic level 1 includes all the green plants (autotrophs), which are the 'producers' at the start of a food chain.

- Trophic level 2 are the herbivores, the first consumers in a food chain. In the example above, the grasshopper is at trophic level 2.
- Trophic level 3 includes the next consumers in the chain, in our example this is the meerkat.

Trophic levels above this are named from the number of further links in the food chain.

All the different terms used in describing feeding relationships can be confusing Table **4.1** may help you remember them. It uses the food chain above as an example:

Table 4.1

	Organisms	Trophic level	Example
autotrophs (producers)	green plants	1	grass
heterotrophs (consumers)	herbivores – primary consumers	2	grasshopper
	first carnivores – secondary consumers	3	meerkat
	second carnivores – tertiary consumers	4	eagle

What do you notice about the trophic level of the eagle in the simple food web above? What does this tell you about trophic levels?

TEST YOURSELF 4.3

 Food chains in aquatic ecosystems are often longer than those on land. Suggest two reasons for this.

How does energy flow in a food chain?

The arrows in a food chain show the flow of energy and nutrients from one organism to the next. As an animal feeds it obtains energy and nutrients to fuel its life and build its body. But not all the energy that an animal takes in can be assimilated into its body. At every trophic level energy is lost and does not pass on to the next level.

Energy is lost in three ways:

1 Not consumed: Energy in one level may not be consumed, for example a grasshopper does not eat all parts of a grass plant, so does not take in all the energy the grass has stored.

2 Not assimilated: Food which is eaten may not be assimilated into the trophic level; it may pass through an animal's gut undigested and be lost in feces. The animal may die and the energy in its body may pass, not to the next trophic level, but to decomposers.

3 Used for respiration: Animals use the food they eat for respiration to fuel cell activities. Heat is a waste product of this and is lost into the atmosphere, so it cannot be passed on.

TEST YOURSELF 4.4

 At which trophic level is there most energy available in an ecosystem?
  A primary consumers   **C** top consumers
  B saprotrophs   **D** producers

Why can't food chains be longer than about five links?

Every time food is eaten and transferred along a food chain energy is lost. By the end of the chain there is little energy left to pass on and a predator will have to spend more time hunting and catching its prey than it gains from eating it. Only about 10% of the energy in one trophic level is passed on to the next.

A famous biological question is 'Why are big fierce animals rare?' You should be able to answer this question using the information above.

What are pyramids of energy?

A pyramid of energy is simply a diagram that shows the feeding relationships and energy losses in a food chain or web in a visual form.

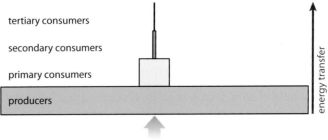

Figure 4.2 A generalised energy pyramid.

What happens to the nutrients in food an animal eats?

hint

Be prepared to compare the way energy and nutrients move through an ecosystem. It is a popular exam question.

hint

Questions like Test yourself **4.5** are likely to form part of an essay question on Paper **2**. Check the command term, in this case 'outline', and the number of marks. Try to include six good relevant points in your answer.

hint

When illustrating the carbon cycle make sure that you label arrows which show photosynthesis, feeding, death, decay, fossilisation, combustion and respiration.

Energy passes along food chains and is dissipated as heat during respiration whenever it is transferred from one organism to the next. Heat cannot be used as a source of life and is lost to living things. However, nutrients such as nitrates and phosphates are continually recycled in an ecosystem. A nitrogen atom may be absorbed as nitrate from the soil and incorporated into a plant, then used to make an amino acid. This may pass to an animal when the plant is eaten and then back into the soil as urea during animal excretion.

You can find out more about the role of saprotrophic bacteria and fungi in recycling nutrients in Section **4.3**.

TEST YOURSELF 4.5

 Outline the flow of energy between trophic levels in a food chain. **[6]**

4.3 Carbon recycling

Key information you should revise:

- How to draw and explain the carbon cycle.
- Where carbon dioxide occurs in the atmosphere and aquatic environments.
- How carbon dioxide is converted to compounds by autotrophs.
- How carbon dioxide eventually re-enters the atmosphere, both during respiration and when organic material is burned.
- Why methane is important and how it is produced in anaerobic conditions.
- How peat, oil and gas are formed.
- That calcium carbonate is found in shells or skeletons and can form fossils in limestone.

What should a diagram of the carbon cycle include?

If you are asked to draw the carbon cycle you can make your diagram simple, but it is important to include key labels to show you understand the processes which move carbon atoms from one part of the cycle to the next.

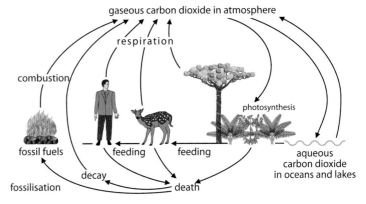

Figure 4.3 The carbon cycle.

Where is carbon dioxide found and how does it enter living things?

- Carbon dioxide is found as a gas in the atmosphere and in solution in aquatic environments where it is present as hydrogen carbonate ions and carbonate ions.
- Carbon dioxide gas diffuses into the cells of plants.
- Carbon dioxide is converted to complex organic compounds during photosynthesis.

Which processes return carbon dioxide to the atmosphere or water to restart the carbon cycle?

When living organisms respire they return carbon dioxide to the air or water. Large amounts are also produced during combustion. As biomass (for example wood), and fossil fuels (for example oil or coal), are burned, carbon dioxide is released from complex organic compounds and enters the environment as gas.

hint

Don't forget that plants respire *and* photosynthesise

TEST YOURSELF 4.6

 Name two processes that remove carbon from the atmosphere.

What happens if an organism does not decay completely when it dies?

In most cases plants and animals are broken down into the inorganic materials that made them and returned to the environment, but sometimes they do not decay.

In waterlogged, wetland soil only anaerobic bacteria can survive because there is so little oxygen. These bacteria break down organic matter very slowly, releasing methane. Over thousands of years, the organic matter gradually becomes peat.

Some partly decayed bodies of plants and animals from past geological eras have become compressed and fossilised over millions of years. These remains become fossil fuels – coal, gas and oil. Carbon in both fossil fuels and peat is locked out of the carbon cycle for long periods of time and only re-enters it as carbon dioxide when the fuels are burned.

Try using a table like Table **4.2** to revise where stores of carbon-containing compounds may be.

Table 4.2

Substance	Formed from	Where	Timescale
coal	ancient forests	anaerobic layers compressed on land	millions of years
oil and gas	bodies of ancient marine organisms	under the sea compressed and heated by layers of sediment	millions of years
peat	partially decayed plant remains	in waterlogged soils	1000–5000 years
fossils of organisms such as corals and molluscs	calcium carbonate – containing shells, bones and solid parts of animals	trapped in sediments and fossilised in limestone	millions of years

TEST YOURSELF 4.7

 State the biological origins of coal, oil and limestone.

What are the stages in peat formation?

Methanogenic bacteria break down organic material in wetlands and produce methane as a by-product. Other bacteria that live in the moss in the peat bog break down most of the methane. It is oxidised to carbon dioxide and water, so carbon dioxide re-enters the carbon cycle.

In some areas peat begins to form when:

- Water levels are low and aerobic bacteria feed on decaying vegetation.
- Over time this layer is covered over by more and more vegetation and conditions underneath become anaerobic.
- The part-decayed, wetter lower levels are preserved and don't change much over long periods of time. They become peat.

The type of peat varies from place to place depending on the plants in the area. Heather, sphagnum moss and sedges are typical plants found in peat bogs.

Peat is used as a fuel in some parts of the world. It is not classified as a renewable form of energy because it can take up to 5000 years to form and people extract it at a much faster than it forms.

What is carbon flux and why is it important?

Carbon is found in different forms and different places, known as 'pools'. For example as carbon dioxide in the air; organic molecules in the bodies of living things; dissolved gas in the ocean; and in organic molecules in fossil fuels and peat.

DEFINITION

CARBON FLUX is the flow of carbon from one pool to another. It is the net difference between carbon removal and carbon addition.

Carbon is removed by	Carbon is added by
• photosynthesis and plant growth • mineral formation • dissolving in the ocean	• respiration • burning fossil fuels • volcanic activity

Studying carbon flux is useful for monitoring changes and disturbances in the carbon cycle.

TEST YOURSELF 4.8

1 Outline the effect of human activity on the amount of carbon stored in carbon 'sinks' such as peat, coal and oil.
2 Outline the stages in the formation of peat. **[3]**
3 Why peat is not regarded as a renewable source of energy. **[1]**

hint

Before you start revising this section, make sure you understand the difference between the terms 'climate change' and 'global warming'. Climate change is the better term to describe how our climate is becoming different; not all of the world will become warmer.

4.4 Climate change

In this section you should revise:

- What the most significant greenhouse gases are.
- How greenhouse gases lead to warming of the atmosphere.
- How levels of greenhouse gases have changed since the Industrial Revolution.
- How levels of greenhouse gases are correlated with increased use of fossil fuels.
- The potential effects of climate change on ecosystems.

What are greenhouse gases and how do they increase atmospheric temperature?

DEFINITION

GREENHOUSE GASES absorb wavelengths of long wave (heat) radiation that are reflected from the surface of the Earth. The heat is retained in our atmosphere and keeps the Earth warm.

The two most significant greenhouse gases present in the atmosphere are carbon dioxide and water vapour. They ensure that the Earth is able to retain heat from the Sun that would otherwise be reflected back into space. This is known as the 'greenhouse effect'.

Oxides of nitrogen are also greenhouse gases but they have less impact because their concentration in the atmosphere is much lower.

Is methane a greenhouse gas?

Yes it is and it has the potential to cause warming of the atmosphere in the same way as carbon dioxide does (Section **4.4**) but methane is present in much smaller amounts.

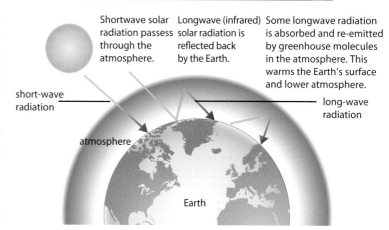

Figure 4.4 Greenhouse gases trap heat, warming the atmosphere.

Methane is produced by ruminants (cows and similar animals) as a result of their digestion and from rice paddy fields. It is also released from the ocean and when fossil fuels are extracted.

TEST YOURSELF 4.9

 Scientists recommend reducing carbon dioxide emissions. Less carbon dioxide in the atmosphere would be expected to:

A reduce the rate of climate change   C reduce destruction of the ozone layer

B increase the rate of climate change   D help protect rain forests

What about ozone?

Many students are confused about ozone. It is not a greenhouse gas and does not affect the temperature of the atmosphere. The ozone layer protects us from incoming UV light. The ozone layer has been damaged by refrigerants, such as CFCs released into the atmosphere.

How have levels of greenhouse gases changed over the last two centuries?

Carbon dioxide forms only about 0.04% of the Earth's atmosphere but is a significant greenhouse gas. Levels of carbon dioxide have been rising over the last two centuries as the world's human population has increased and the demand for energy for industry, transport and domestic use has risen. The increase in use of fossil fuels began in the mid 1800s when coal was first used to drive machines, a period known as the start of the Industrial Revolution. More greenhouse gases have led to a warmer Earth.

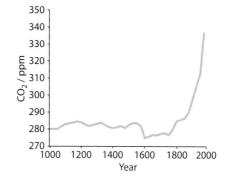

Figure 4.5 Graph to show the increase in carbon dioxide concentration in the atmosphere since the Industrial Revolution.

For your exams you should be able to interpret a graph showing the level of CO_2 (the most significant greenhouse gas) over the past 200 years. Levels are often shown as ppm or parts per million in the atmosphere.

4 Ecology

Why do some people doubt that carbon dioxide is causing climate change?

Nature of Science. There is a clear correlation between rising carbon dioxide levels and the increase in average global temperature. However, some people argue that correlation does not indicate cause with absolute certainty.

Data can be difficult to collect but clear evidence of climate change can be seen from melting ice caps and glaciers. Records also show that some species have moved from areas, which are warmer or drier than they used to be. Climatologists have used computer models to predict that weather patterns worldwide may change, so that many places will experience greater extremes of climate than they have done previously.

Table 4.3 The atmospheric CO_2 levels monitored at the Mauna Loa laboratory in Hawaii since 1959. The percentage change since 1959 continues to rise (source: NOAA Earth System Research Laboratory).

Year	CO_2 concentration / parts per million (ppm)	% increase from 1959
1959	316	
1970	326	3.2
1980	339	7.3
1990	354	12.0
2000	369	16.8
2004	378	19.6
2008	386	22.2

📝 Annotated exemplar answer 4.1

This graph Figure **4.6** shows changes in atmospheric carbon dioxide on the island of Mauna Loa in the Pacific Ocean.

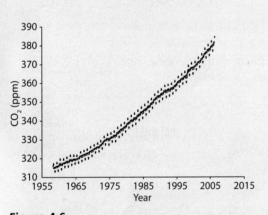

Figure 4.6

Source: National Oceanic and Atmospheric Administration and Scripps Institute of Oceanography

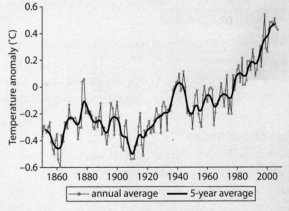

Figure 4.7

Figure **4.7** shows annual and 5-year average global temperatures. Note that temperature anomaly is the difference between the long-term average temperature (the expected temp) and the temperature that is recorded. A positive anomaly means that the temperature was warmer than normal; a negative anomaly indicates the temperature was cooler than normal.

hint

Data interpretation is an important skill. Read the graphs carefully and use a ruler to take measurements from them.

a Suggest why Mauna Loa is considered to be a good site to measure concentrations of carbon dioxide? **[2]**

b Calculate the percentage increase in carbon dioxide between the years 1985 and 2005. Show your working. **[2]**

c Explain what is meant by the 'greenhouse effect'. **[4]**

d Outline two reasons why climatologists prefer to use the 5-year average figure for global temperature rather than the annual average. **[2]**

a Mauna Loa is remote and far away from any sources of carbon dioxide from industry. (1)

There are two marks, so include two separate statements. A second statement could be:

The atmosphere in the middle of the Pacific Ocean is likely to be representative of the Earth as a whole.

b 1985 level = 340ppm, 2005 level = 375ppm

Difference = 35

$$\% \text{ change} = \frac{35 \times 100}{340} = 10.3\%$$

The marks are awarded for working and answer, you get a mark for the working even if the answer is wrong.

c The greenhouse effect is the term given to the way that carbon dioxide and other gases trap heat in the Earth's atmosphere.

This gains 1 mark.

Without an atmosphere, Earth would be very cold at night and very hot during the day.

True, but this is not an explanation of the greenhouse effect

The term greenhouse effect is used because the gases work in a similar way to the glass in a greenhouse which keeps warm air inside.

This gains 1 mark, with and has a good use of analogy here.

Two more marks are available. For full marks you should add:

d Over a long period of geological time the Earth's climate has had many fluctuations due to factors such as sun spots or volcanic eruptions.

Long wave radiation (heat) falls on the Earth and is reflected back from its surface and

Climatologists can get a more accurate picture of what is happening to the Earth's temperature by taking an average of 5 years' values to smooth out these fluctuations.

Carbon dioxide and methane in the atmosphere prevent this long wave radiation being reflected back into space.

7/10

A good answer, which scores both marks. The 5-year figures allow climatologists to discount unusual years.

5 EVOLUTION AND BIODIVERSITY

This chapter covers the following topics:

☐ Evidence for evolution   ☐ Classification of biodiversity

☐ Natural selection   ☐ Cladistics

5.1 Evidence for evolution

Key information you should revise:

- Evolution takes place when heritable characteristics of a species change.

- Evidence for evolution has come from fossils.

- Humans use selective breeding to produce domesticated animals and plants, and this too shows that artificial selection can cause change.

- Evolution of homologous structures by adaptive radiation explains similarities in structure when there is a difference in function.

- Populations of a species can gradually diverge into new species.

- Continuous variation across the geographical range of related population supports the idea of gradual divergence.

What is evolution?

DEFINITION

EVOLUTION is a cumulative change in the heritable characteristics of a population.

The differences or **variation** between individuals of any species result from genetic and environmental factors. If genetically determined variations confer an advantage on an individual it may survive better and produce more offspring. The characteristics of these individuals will be passed on to succeeding generations, so that as changes accumulate over generations, we can say that a species has evolved.

What evidence is there for evolution?

Fossils are the preserved remains of organisms that lived long ago. Although the fossil record is incomplete and fossils are rare, they do show how present-day organisms might have evolved from species that existed hundreds or thousands of million years ago.

- The age of fossils can be determined by the radioactivity present in them. The sequence of fossils at various geological eras matches our expectations of **evolution** so that the blue-green bacteria (cyanobacteria) are present in the oldest fossils, followed by simple invertebrates and finally vertebrates in younger rocks.

- Some organisms have changed little; horseshoe crabs today resemble fossils specimens from 1 million years ago as there has been little selection pressure on them. But fossil ancestors have been found of other groups, such as horses that show links with other possible groups. The modern genus *Equus* has fossil ancestors that show they are related to rhinoceroses and tapirs.

Why do some organisms found today look very similar to their fossil ancestors that are millions of years old, while other fossils have no modern day equivalent?

> **hint**
>
> In Test yourself **5.1** you are required to explain why some organisms have evolved and some have not.

How does selective breeding help us to understand evolution?

Humans have bred plants and animals for thousands of years. By choosing which domestic animals or plants to breed, humans have shown that artificial selection can cause changes in species.

For example, modern varieties of wheat, barley and rice now produce higher yields and are more pest-resistant than their wild ancestors of long ago. These characteristics have been selected for over time. Domestic chickens have been bred from jungle fowl from South East Asia and many different breeds of cattle now exist, each with its own characteristics, such as high milk yield or meat production.

Evidence from artificial selection shows how changes in domestic species can be achieved over a relatively short period of time. It shows that selection causes evolution of a plant or animal but it does not prove that evolution of a new species has occurred.

> **hint**
>
> The command word in Test yourself **5.2** is 'explain', so be sure to include what the term means and some examples of how humans use artificial selection.

 Explain the term 'artificial selection'. **[3]**

What are homologous structures and what evidence do they provide?

HOMOLOGOUS STRUCTURES are anatomical features with similarities in shape but not necessarily in function and are found in different species. They indicate a common ancestry between the species and show they have evolved from a common ancestor.

ADAPTIVE RADIATION is the term used to describe how organisms diverge from a common ancestor.

Homologous structures suggest that the species which have them are closely related and share a common ancestor.

For example, all vertebrates have a **pentadactyl** limb with similar arrangements of bones, but each group uses the limb for different functions.

Bats' wings, human arms and forelimbs of a whale all have the same bones present even though the limbs are used in very different ways.

Adaptive radiation can happen if the environment changes. The pentadactyl limb demonstrates adaptive radiation in vertebrates and Darwin's finches (see Section **5.2**).

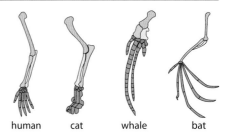

human   cat   whale   bat

Figure 5.1 The vertebrate forelimb, or pentadactyl limb, is an example of a homologous structure.

 What uses do the bones equivalent to the human fingers have in the cat, whale and bat forelimbs shown in Figure **5.1**?

> **hint**
>
> Notice you are only asked about the human finger bones. There's no need to write about other bones.

What is continuous variation and how does it help us understand that species diverge gradually from one another?

Species may be separated over a wide area with slight differences between individuals at the extremes of the range. If two **populations** are separated, for example by a physical barrier such as a mountain range, they may evolve in different ways. Speciation can also occur if part of a population is isolated, for example if it moves to an island habitat, and no longer interbreeds with the original population. New selection pressures act on the population and it may evolve into a new species.

You can read more about speciation in HL Section **10.3**.

5.2 Natural selection

This section covers the basic ideas put forward by Charles Darwin to explain how evolution might have taken place.

Key information you should revise:

- That genetic variation is required for natural selection.
- Variation is caused by mutation, meiosis and sexual reproduction.
- Adaptations make some individuals more suited to the environment than others.
- There is a struggle for survival between individuals that compete for resources.
- Better adapted individuals tend to survive and reproduce and pass their heritable characteristics on to their offspring.
- Natural selection increases the frequency of well-adapted individuals in a population and therefore leads to changes in a species.

As you revise this section, notice that natural selection acts on *individual* members of a population, but that the *population* is changed so that the frequency of well-adapted individuals increases and less well-adapted individuals decreases. Changes in the population can eventually lead to changes in a species.

Darwin's theory of evolution by means of natural selection was based on a series of observations that noted variation, over-production of offspring, competition for resources and inheritance of favourable characteristics in species.

Why is variation important?

Members of a population of any species are all slightly different from one another, for humans we see slight variations in height, skin colour and so on and the same is true for all species. Without this variation one individual could not have an advantage over the others and natural selection could not take place.

What causes variation between members of a species?
Variation is caused by three factors:

- Mutations – new alleles are produced if DNA is altered and this may produce new variations.
- Meiosis – new combinations of alleles are produced during meiosis because of independent alignment of chromosomes (metaphase 1) and crossing over (prophase 1).
- Sexual reproduction means that different alleles from different parents are brought together at fertilisation and produce more variation.

You can review these three factors in Sections **3.1**, **3.3** and **10.1**.

TEST YOURSELF 5.4

What are the three ways in which variation can arise in a population? **[3]**

How do adaptations provide an advantage to survival?

Members of a species are all slightly different, for example, in a snail population, shells will vary in shape and colour. In a stable environment small differences may make little difference but it is likely that some individuals will be better camouflaged than others and so will be less likely to be seen and eaten by predators. The individuals with this adaptation will survive to pass on their genes to the next generation.

It is said that there is a struggle for survival between members of a species, which compete for food, mates and territories. Slight variation between individuals means that some are better competitors than others. They have adaptations that give them an advantage.

Remember that the adaptations that are important do not need to be the physical strength of an individual. Plumage, mating display, loudness of calls, camouflage and many other features can all be vital to survival.

How does the struggle for survival lead to changes in a population?

The individuals with advantageous characteristics in an environment survive and out-compete their rivals. These survivors are the individuals that mate and reproduce, passing their favourable characteristics to the next generation. Gradually, over many generations, the proportion of favourable genes increases in the population as a whole. This is the process of natural selection.

> **hint**
>
> Note the three examples listed here and be ready to answer questions about them.

How does natural selection lead to changes in a species?

Natural selection increases the frequency of well-adapted individuals in a population. We can see how this can happen relatively quickly in changing conditions.

Examples of natural selection in action are:

- Darwin's finches on the Galapagos Islands whose beak shapes changed in response to a change in food availability.

- The response of the peppered moth population to pollution of their habitat with soot in the air.

- Emergence of new antibiotic resistant strains of bacteria following the introduction of antibiotics.

Figure 5.2 Light and melanic forms of peppered moths on light tree bark.

TEST YOURSELF 5.5

The diagram shows five species of finch from the Galapagos Islands. These are volcanic islands about 500 km west of South America.

> **hint**
>
> Note the command words used in Test yourself **5.5**. 'State' requires a simple answer with no details. 'Outline' requires a brief account or summary and 'describe' requires a more detailed answer.

Figure 5.3

1 State the main difference between the five species shown here? **[1]**
2 Outline how the differences might be related to the habits of the finches? **[1]**
3 It has been suggested that the finches probably diverged from a common ancestor.
4 Describe how the diversity of finches could have arisen. **[3]**
5 The different finches on the island do not interbreed. State what this suggests about the different finches. **[1]**

5.3 Classification of biodiversity

Key information you should revise:

- What is meant by the binomial system for naming species.
- How new species are given two-part names.
- The order of the hierarchy of eight taxa.
- The characteristic features of members of the three domains.
- That taxonomists reclassify species when evidence shows new evolutionary relationships.
- Biological classification helps to identify new species and predict shared characteristics of species within a group.
- Biological keys are used as a tool to help in identification of species.

What is the binomial system of naming species?

The binomial system of naming species was started by Linneaus in the 1700s to make it easier for scientists all over the world to discuss and classify organisms. International conventions are held regularly to ensure that all biologists use the same system of names. Every species is given a two-part name in Latin. Latin is used because it is an unchanging language. The first part of the name is the genus that the species belongs to and the second part is the species. There are rules which are used when names are written or printed.

DEFINITIONS

GENUS indicates a group of species that are closely related and share a common ancestor.

SPECIES is a group of individuals that are capable of interbreeding to produce fertile offspring.

- The species name of a Polar bear is *Ursus maritimus.*
- The genus has a capital (upper case) letter and the species a lower case letter.
- In printed text a binomial name is always italicised. When it has been used once it can be abbreviated, for example *U. maritimus*

What is the hierarchy of taxa used in biological classification?
Species are classified into groups called taxa (singular taxon), which form a hierarchy. As you go up the hierarchy the groups include larger numbers of species that share fewer features.

What are the three domains?
Classifications change as new discoveries are made, but at present organisms are divided into three domains.

- Eubacteria (bacteria) includes cyanobacteria and true bacteria.
- Archaea includes methanogens, halophiles and thermoacidophiles – often known as extremophiles.
- Eukaryota (also called eukarya) includes plants, animals, fungi and dinoflagellates.

What are the main groups used to classify members of the domain Eukaryota?
These are domain, kingdom, phylum, class, order, family, genus and species. To remember them try making up a mnemonic such as: **D**aring **K**ing **P**hilip **C**ame **O**ver **F**or **G**reat **S**andwiches.

Taxon	European mole	Dandelion
domain	Eukaryota	Eukaryota
kingdom	Animalia	Plantae
phylum	Chordata	Angiospermata
class	Mammalia	Magnoliopsida
order	Soricomorpha	Asterales
family	Talpidae	Asteraceae
genus	*Talpa*	*Taraxicum*
species	*europeae*	*offininale*

hint

For your exams you must remember the classification of one plant and one animal from kingdom to species. Two examples are shown here but you may find it easier to recall others. All animals and plants are in the domain Eukaryota.

What is a natural classification?

A natural classification is one in which the genus and higher taxa contain all the species that are thought to have evolved from a common ancestor. This means that all members of a genus (or higher taxon) should have a common ancestor and we can expect them to share many characteristics.

Sometimes it is difficult to work out which groups of species share common ancestors and this is why classifications can change over time as more detailed information becomes available.

An example of a non-natural or artificial classification might be bats, birds and insects because they can all fly. It is artificial because flight evolved in different ways in the different groups and they do not share a common ancestor.

Why do classifications change?

New evidence can come to light and show that members of a group do not share a common ancestor. In recent years this evidence has mainly come from the analysis of DNA or proteins. Evidence can show that groups can be more closely related than their physical appearance suggests. Species can be moved from one genus to another when this information is used. (See more about this in Section **5.4**.)

TEST YOURSELF 5.6

Why do taxonomists keep different breeds of dog, such as the Chihuahua and the Boxer, in the same species?

Constructing a dichotomous key

A key is an organised series of steps which is used to identify unknown organisms. At each step the key prompts you to decide whether or not a specimen has an observable feature that helps to distinguish it from organisms.

hint

You must be prepared to construct and use a dichotomous (branching) key so that an individual can be identified.

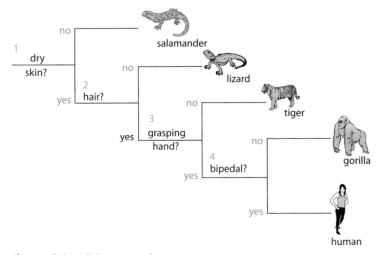

Figure 5.4 A dichotomous key.

Some points to remember:

- At each branching point there must be only two options so that the group is separated into two smaller groups.
- Features used for questions must be biologically relevant and easily visible.
- Size and colour can be used carefully but remember that juvenile forms are usually smaller and may differ from adults, so these characteristics can be misleading.
- Keys can be written as a series of questions or shown as diagrams, see Figure **5.4**.

Evolution and biodiversity

What are the main groups of plants and animals you should recognise?

All plants are in one kingdom, the phyla you should remember are shown in the summary Table **5.1**. There are more than 30 phyla of animals, there are seven shown in Table **5.1** that you should make sure you are familiar with. Check your notes or other sources of reference for full details.

Table 5.1 Key features of the main groups of plants and animals.

Plant groups	Animal groups
• Bryophyta: mosses and liverworts, have no true roots and only simple stems and leaves • Filicinophyta: ferns that have roots, stems, leaves and internal structures. Reproduce using spores, found in clusters under the leaves • Coniferophyta: conifers, such as pine, fir and cedar, have pollen and produce seeds in cones. Many have needle-like leaves • Angiospermophyta: flowering plants which reproduce using pollen and ovules produced in flowers, and seedsthat are dispersed within fruits or nuts	• Porifera: sponges which have some different types of cell but no tissues and no clear symmetry, all are aquatic. Some produce a skeleton of calcium carbonate or silica • Cnidaria: sea anemones, corals and jellyfish; are marine animals with cells and tissues organised into two layers • Platyhelminthes: flatworms with bilateral symmetry and ribbon-shaped bodies. Do not have blood or gas exchange systems • Mollusca: slugs, snails, squid and octopus;have mouth, anus and shells of calcium carbonate. Use a rasping organ called a radula to feed and a muscular foot for movement • Annelida: segmented worms, bristleworms and leeches; found in water or in the soil. Have a simple gutand an internal body cavity, which is kept firm with fluid under pressure • Arthropoda: crustaceans, such as crabs and lobsters, insects, spiders and scorpions; all have an exoskeleton ofchitin, segmented bodies and jointed limbs • Chordata: this phylum includes humans and other vertebrates with a dorsal nerve cord, a notochordofcartilage supporting the nerve cord, a post anal tail and pharyngeal slits Remember that not all chordates are vertebrates. The phylum also includes tunicates (sea squirts and salps).

TEST YOURSELF 5.7

 Is the classification of our food plants into fruit and vegetables a natural or an artificial classification?

5.4 Cladistics

Key information you should revise:

• How to define a clade.

• How evidence from base sequences and amino acids is used to place a species in a clade.

• That differences in base sequences accumulate so that there is a positive correlation between the number of differences in a gene in two species and the time they diverged from a common ancestor.

• Characteristics can be either homologous or analogous.

• Cladograms are diagrams showing clades.

• Evidence from **cladistics** has shown that groups classified according to their structure do not correspond with their evolutionary origins.

What is a clade and what is a cladogram?

DEFINITION

A **CLADE** is a group of organisms that have evolved from a common ancestor.

Species change over time and new species are formed. This can happen many times so that a large group of present-day species may be derived from a common ancestor. Evidence to identify members of a **clade** can be found by looking for characteristics which the group shares. Birds are a group that clearly share a common ancestor and form a clade, but sometimes a clade is not so obvious so DNA and **amino acid** sequences must be examined. Closely related species will have fewer differences between their DNA and amino acid sequences.

DEFINITION

A **CLADOGRAM** is a branching diagram which shows the most likely sequence of divergence of clades. It is based on similarities and differences between the species in the clade.

Most cladograms are based on evidence from DNA or amino acid sequences. Branching points are called nodes and diagrams may be presented like either of the diagrams in Figure **5.5**. They may also be drawn horizontally.

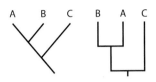

Figure **5.5** shows that A, B and C share a common ancestor but that A and B are more closely related to each other than they are to C.

Figure 5.5

How is evidence from DNA and amino acids used to place species in a clade?

We examine sequences of DNA bases or amino acids in polypeptides to build up clades. We can deduce that species with the most similar sequences are likely to be most closely related. Genetic changes (mutations) that are not harmful are likely to remain in an organism's genome and differences in DNA accumulate over time. Species with the most similarities are placed together. We also expect that closely related organisms will have the same molecules doing the same jobs in their bodies, so proteins (polypeptides) from different species are used to compare the sequences. Cytochrome c, chlorophyll and hemoglobin have been used to do this.

TEST YOURSELF 5.8

 A cladogram built up by studying the morphology of turtles and lizards suggests they are not a clade. How could you test whether this is true?

How is the evidence used to show how long ago species diverged?

Differences in DNA accumulate over time at an approximately even rate, so the number of differences between genomes can be used as an approximate evolutionary clock. More differences indicate that there has been more time for DNA mutations to accumulate.

What is the difference between homologous and analogous characteristics?

The pentadactyl limb (see Figure **5.1**) is an example of a homologous structure. As new species have evolved from a common ancestor, the arrangement of bones in the limb has become adapted to different situations.

Analogous structures have the same function in different species, but are structurally very different. An example is the wing of an insect and the wing of a bat. They have not evolved from a common ancestor.

Homologous structures are useful in establishing relationships but analogous structures are not.

TEST YOURSELF 5.9

 1 Suggest why Latin names are used to names organisms. **[1]**

2 Are the eyes of a bee and the eyes of a lion analogous or homologous structures? Outline the reasons for your answer. **[2]**

3 A new plant is found which has no roots and only simple leaves. In which phylum should it be placed? **[1]**

There are only two marks for question 2, so keep your answer short. Do not describe the structure of the two eyes. For question 3 use the correct scientific terminology. If you forget, it is better to write the common name than nothing at all.

Why has cladistics led to changes in classification?

Until it was possible to sequence DNA and proteins, species were placed in groups by studying their appearance (morphology). Modern cladograms show some groups were wrong. Some groups have been merged and some species moved into different groups.

Plant scientists have recently reclassified the figwort family (Scrophlariaceae) which had been in existence since the 18th century. The plants in the old group look very similar and there were 275 genera and 5000 species. Now the group has been reclassified into five clades with some genera being moved to completely new families and two families being added to the figwort family based on DNA evidence.

Nature of Science. Reclassification of the figwort family is a good example of how one theory has been superseded by another as a result of new evidence being used.

 hint

Test yourself **5.10** may confuse you with different styles of cladogram but take time and check the positions of the branching points to find the answer.

TEST YOURSELF 5.10

 1 Why are analogous structures not used to establish evolutionary relationships?

2 Study the four cladograms in Figure **5.6**.

    a State which cladogram shows an evolutionary history that is different from the others. **[1]**

    b Explain your answer. **[2]**

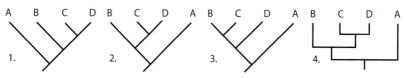

Figure 5.6

📑 Annotated exemplar answer 5.1

Outline the differences between the processes of selection and speciation. **[4]**

This question has four marks available so would be part of a longer, essay style question. Identify four clear facts about differences between the two terms to gain maximum marks. You can present answers to questions like this in a table. Make sure you highlight the differences by presenting them together. Do not simply define the terms.

Possible responses:

Selection occurs as a result of the environment acting on an individual, whereas speciation occurs when groups of individuals are separated from other members of their species and develop differences.

> *This is a reasonable answer but could be improved by mentioning survival and reproduction. The first statement should include 'better adapted individuals are more likely to survive than others'. Adding, 'which prevent them from interbreeding with the original group.' would also gain extra marks.*

Selection results in the survival of some individuals and the death (or failure to reproduce) of others. Speciation on the other hand results in the formation of two new breeding groups.

> *This is good, a clear distinction has been made.*

Selection may be natural (caused by the environment) or artificial (caused by people), the processes may be long term or much shorter, (e.g. the development of antibiotic resistant bacteria).

(3/4)

> *This answer is correct but it does not outline any differences between selection and speciation. To gain the mark, add 'but speciation is always a natural process and tends to occur over a long period of time'.*

HUMAN PHYSIOLOGY

This chapter covers the following topics:

☐ **Digestion and absorption**

☐ **The blood system**

☐ **Defence against infectious disease**

☐ **Gas exchange**

☐ **Neurons and synapses**

☐ **Hormones, homeostasis and reproduction**

6.1 Digestion and absorption

Key information you should revise:

- The main structures of the digestive system.
- Enzymes digest macromolecules into monomers for absorption.
- That enzymes are secreted from the pancreas into the small intestine.
- How contractions of the muscles in the intestine move food along and mix food with enzymes.
- The lining of the small intestine is folded into villi, which increase the area for absorption.
- Villi absorb minerals, vitamins and monomers produced by digestion.
- Different nutrients are absorbed using different methods of transport.

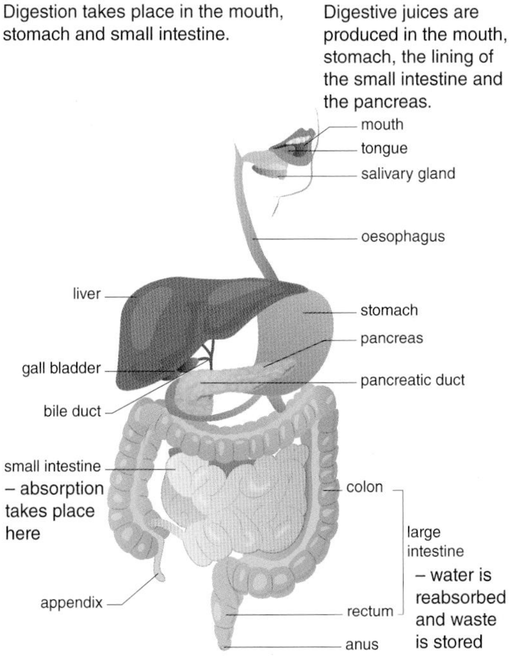

Digestion takes place in the mouth, stomach and small intestine.

Digestive juices are produced in the mouth, stomach, the lining of the small intestine and the pancreas.

- mouth
- tongue
- salivary gland
- oesophagus
- liver
- stomach
- pancreas
- gall bladder
- pancreatic duct
- bile duct
- small intestine – absorption takes place here
- colon
- large intestine – water is reabsorbed and waste is stored
- appendix
- rectum
- anus

Figure 6.1 The human digestive system.

What are the main parts of the human digestive system?

What is digestion?

DEFINITION

DIGESTION is a series of biochemical reactions that convert large ingested food molecules into small, soluble molecules that can be absorbed into the body.

Digestion is an example of a hydrolysis reaction (see Section **2.1**). It is speeded up by the presence of digestive enzymes, which make it fast enough to make sure that we can absorb enough nutrients to supply our needs.

 hint

Practise labelling a diagram like Figure **6.1** and be ready to draw and annotate a simple version of it in an examination.

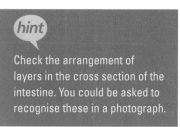

What sequence of organs does food pass through as it moves through the intestine?

A mouth → stomach → pancreas → small intestine → liver → large intestine → anus

B mouth → stomach → small intestine → pancreas → liver → large intestine → anus

C mouth → oesophagus → stomach → small intestine → large intestine → anus

D mouth → oesophagus → stomach → large intestine → small intestine → anus

What types of enzymes are found in digestive juices?

Different enzymes are released in different sections of the digestive system and each one is specific for one food type. Table **6.1** summarises those you should be familiar with.

Table 6.1

Enzyme type	Example	Source	Substrate	Products	Optimum pH
amylase	salivary amylase	salivary glands	starch	maltose	7
	pancreatic amylase	pancreas	maltose	glucose	7–8
protease	pepsin	gastric glands	protein	polypeptides	2
	endopeptidase	pancreas	polypeptides	amino acids	8
lipase	pancreatic lipase	pancreas	trigylcerides	fatty acids and glycerol	7–8

Revise the optimum conditions for enzyme activity in Section **2.5**.

How is food moved along the intestine?

Food passes from the oesophagus to the stomach and along the small and large intestines by a process called **peristalsis**. Longitudinal and circular muscles help to push food along. Longitudinal muscles run the length of the intestine and circular muscles encircle it. Remember muscles work in pairs as one set contracts the other relaxes.

> **hint**
>
> Check the arrangement of layers in the cross section of the intestine. You could be asked to recognise these in a photograph.

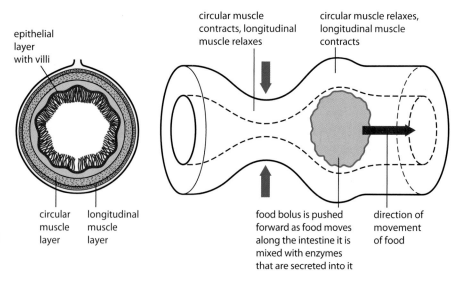

Figure 6.2 The actions of longitudinal and circular muscles in the intestine help to push food along, in a processes called peristalsis.

epithelial layer with villi

circular muscle layer   longitudinal muscle layer

circular muscle contracts, longitudinal muscle relaxes

circular muscle relaxes, longitudinal muscle contracts

food bolus is pushed forward as food moves along the intestine it is mixed with enzymes that are secreted into it

direction of movement of food

Where is endopeptidase produced?

What are villi and how do they help the absorption of food?

The lining of the small intestine is folded into tiny creases called **villi**. Each one contains capillaries and a lacteal to carry away digested food.

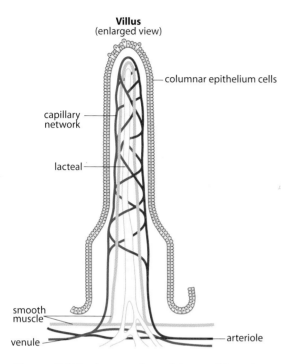

Villus
(enlarged view)

— columnar epithelium cells

capillary network —

lacteal —

smooth muscle —

venule —

— arteriole

Figure 6.3 The inner surface of the small intestine is highly folded, with millions of finger-like villi. Each epithelial cell is covered in minute microvilli, so the total surface area for absorption is vast.

Villi have features which make them good at absorption.

- They produce a very large surface area for absorption.
- Their epithelial layer is very thin.
- The blood vessels inside them carry away digested food quickly and maintain a good concentration gradient.

TEST YOURSELF 6.3

 Protein we eat is in the form of macromolecules, name the monomer produced after it has been digested.

Food is absorbed as monomers (see Table **6.2**). Monomers pass through the wall of the intestine in one of four ways:

- Diffusion – small molecules can pass through the hydrophobic part of the plasma membrane.
- Facilitated diffusion – hydrophilic monomers, such as fructose, move through protein channels if there is a concentration gradient.
- Active transport – molecules that do not have a high concentration gradient (e.g. glucose, mineral ions, and amino acids) can all be absorbed in this way.
- **Pinocytosis** – draws in small drops of liquid as vesicles.

Table 6.2 Large food molecules (macromolecules) are broken down in digestion into small molecules (monomers), which can be absorbed.

Type of molecule	Form of the molecule in ingested food	Monomers produced by digestion
carbohydrates	monosaccharides, disaccharides, polysaccharides (e.g. starch, glycogen)	monosaccharides (e.g. glucose)
proteins	proteins	amino acids
lipids	triglycerides	fatty acids and glycerol
nucleic acids	DNA, RNA	nucleotides

What is dialysis tubing?

You will probably have used dialysis tube in experiments on absorption. It is made of cellulose and acts as a partially permeable membrane. It allows small molecules, such as glucose, to pass through it but not larger polymers like starch.

Nature of Science. Using models to demonstrate life processes.

hint

Questions on absorption through membranes feature regularly in exam papers. Revise Section **1.4** again if you need to. You'll need the knowledge to explain gas exchange too.

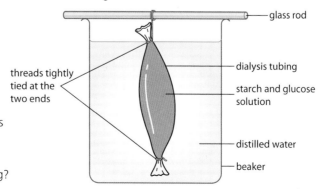

— glass rod

threads tightly tied at the two ends

— dialysis tubing

— starch and glucose solution

— distilled water

— beaker

Figure 6.4 Modelling absorption in the intestine using dialysis tubing. Water molecules are also able to pass through dialysis tubing by osmosis. What effect will this have on the appearance of the dialysis tubing bag?

TEST YOURSELF 6.4

 Which of the following correctly explains the functions of parts of the digestive system?

	Stomach	Small intestine	Large intestine
A	digests protein	absorbs fibre	absorbs water
B	absorbs water	digests carbohydrates	digests protein
C	digest lipids	digest protein	absorbs water
D	digests protein	absorbs glucose	absorbs water

6.2 The blood system

Humans have a closed blood system that has three parts: blood, tubes (blood vessels) to carry the blood and a heart to pump the blood through the blood vessels.

Key information you should revise:

- The structure and function of arteries, **veins** and capillaries.
- The role of capillaries in the exchange of materials in tissues.
- The return of low-pressure blood in capillaries to the heart via veins.
- The importance of valves in veins and the heart.
- The double circulation of blood in humans.
- The initiation and propagation of the heart beat in the heart.
- The variation of heart rate in response to activity by nerves or hormones.

What are the three main types of blood vessel and how do they differ from each other?

The three types of vessel are arteries, veins and capillaries. Table **6.3** compares their important differences.

Small artery

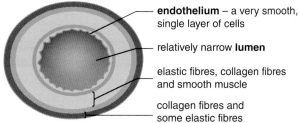

- endothelium – a very smooth, single layer of cells
- relatively narrow **lumen**
- elastic fibres, collagen fibres and smooth muscle
- collagen fibres and some elastic fibres

Figure 6.5 Diagram of transverse section of an artery.

Table 6.3

Arteries	Veins	Capillaries
carry blood under high pressure from the **ventricles**	carry blood at low pressure to the heart	carry blood under low pressure; link small arteries and veins
have strong muscle and and elastic fibres in their walls	contain fewer muscles or elastic fibres	walls are only one cell thick to allow plasma to seep out
valves not present except in the pulmonary **artery** and aorta	valves present in some veins to prevent back flow where pressure is very low	no valves
large arteries have thick walls and narrow lumen, diameter greater than 10 mm	thin walls but wide lumen, diameter of largest vein up to 30 mm	very thin wall, diameter approximately 5 μm

 hint

Questions on arteries, veins and capillaries feature regularly in exams.

 hint

Use A for artery which leads AWAY from the heart; and IN for the veINs that carry blood INTO the heart to help you remember.

What is a double circulation?

Humans have a double circulation, which means in any journey round the body blood passes through the heart twice.

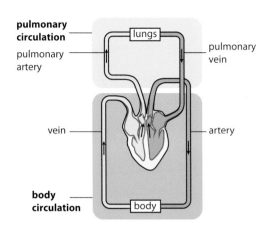

Figure 6.6 Diagram to show the double circulation of blood through the heart.

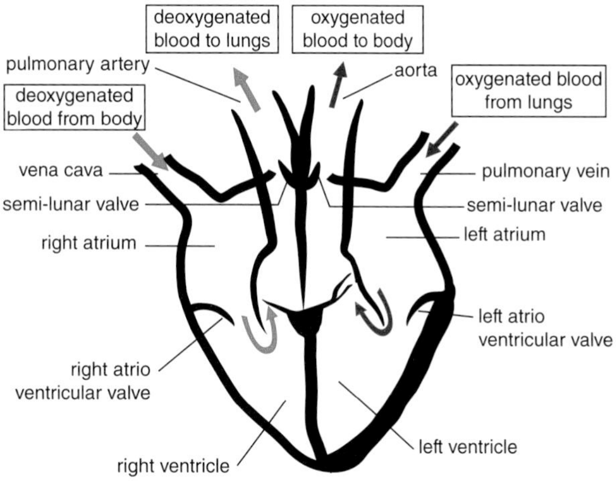

Figure 6.7 The heart.

What structures should I recognise in the heart?

You must be able to name the four chambers of the heart and all the main arteries and veins shown in Figure **6.7**.

Remember that ventricles have thicker walls than atria because they must pump blood further and also that the left ventricle has a thicker wall than the right ventricle for the same reason. Oxygen is present in the blood that is brought to the left hand side of the heart from the lungs, while the right hand side carries de–oxygenated blood destined for the lungs.

You can revise how oxygen is carried in the body in Section **6.4**.

What is the pacemaker, where is it and how does it control heartbeat?

Heart beat is initiated by a small area of specialised muscle tissue in the right atrium called the SAN (sinoatrial node) or pacemaker.

What changes the heart rate as we exercise or rest?

Heart rate can be increased or de-creased by nerves from the medulla of the brain which connect to the SAN. The rate increases when we are active and decreases when we sleep or rest. The medulla monitors blood pressure and carbon dioxide levels in the blood and adjusts heart rate automatically.

Emotions, such as anxiety, can also cause an increase in heart rate. At these times the adrenal glands release **epinephrine** (adrenalin), which travels in the blood and stimulates the SAN to increase heart rate.

1 Each cardiac cycle begins in the right atrium in a small patch of muscle tissue in the right atrium wall, called the **sinoatrial node (SAN)**. The SAN is the **pacemaker** because it sets the pace at which the whole heart beats.

2 The SAN produces an electrical impulse which passes through all of the muscle in the atria of the heart. This impulse stimulates the atrial walls to contract.

5 The ventricles then relax, and the SAN sends another impulse so that the whole sequence is repeated.

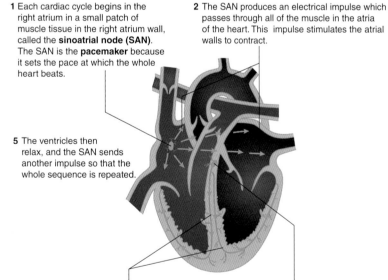

4 The impulse passes along the bundle of his to the **Purkinje fibres**. The impulse arrives at the base of the ventricles and stimulates them to contract.

3 The impulse travels to another patch of calls called the **atrioventricular node (AVN)** which delays the impulse for a fraction of a second, before it travels down into the ventricles. This delay means that the ventricles receive the signal to contract after the atria.

Figure 6.8 How electrical impulses move through the heart.

How does pressure change in the heart through the cardiac cycle?

The **CARDIAC CYCLE** is the sequence of events that takes place during one heart beat.

The graph here shows the changes in pressure and volume in the heart during one cycle.

SYSTOLE is contraction of the muscles of a chamber of the heart.

DIASTOLE is relaxation of the muscles.

Notice that as the ventricles contract (systole) their volume decreases as blood is forced out, as they relax and fill again, their volume rises. Blood pressure in the ventricles rises during systole as it is squeezed by the contraction. Eventually it is so great that the semi-lunar valves are forced open and blood enters the arteries.

TEST YOURSELF 6.5

1 Use Figure **6.9** to explain when the pressure in the aorta is highest and why. **[2]**

2 State when the atrio-ventricular valve closes. **[1]**

3 When is the volume of blood in the ventricles at a minimum and which valves are open and which are closed at this time? **[3]**

(hint)

Heart sounds 'lub' and 'dub' are caused by valves snapping shut.

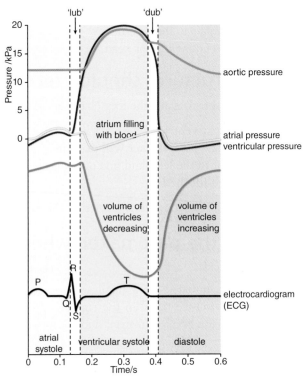

Figure 6.9 Pressure and volume changes in the heart during the cardiac cycle, with an electrocardiogram (ECG) trace. An ECG trace records the rhythm and electrical activity of the heart via electrodes attached to the chest.

☆ Model answer 6.1

Explain how the function of arteries, capillaries and veins is related to their structure. [8]

Arteries carry blood under high pressure, so their structure must withstand this pressure; they have thick muscular walls; elastic fibres that can recoil when blood has passed through them; and smooth lining to reduce friction.

Capillaries receive low-pressure blood; their function is to allow useful substances to pass from the blood into cells; structures that allow this are their very thin walls (one cell), so diffusion is easy, fenestrations or spaces which allow substances through, small diameter and large surface area that allow them to penetrate tissues and reach every cell.

Veins receive blood under low pressure from the capillaries; their role is to return it to the heart; walls are thin as there is no pressure to withstand; they contain valves so that blood does not flow backwards.

6.3 Defence against infectious disease

Key information you should revise:

- How the skin and mucous membranes act as the first line of defence.
- How cuts in the skin are sealed by clotting, which involves a cascade of reactions, involving platelets and blood proteins.
- How phagocytic **leucocytes** give non-specific immunity.
- Lymphocytes produce antibodies and provide specific immunity.
- Antibiotics block bacterial processes but not those in human cells.
- How some strains of bacteria have evolved resistance to antibiotics.
- AIDS is a worldwide pandemic caused by the HIV virus.

DEFINITION

PATHOGENS are living organisms or viruses that cause disease. Most pathogens are bacteria and viruses but fungi and parasitic worms can also be pathogenic.

What are the first stages in fighting off an infection?

Our first line of defence is our skin. Unbroken skin prevents pathogens entering the body but they may enter through openings, such as the eyes, ears and nose. These openings are protected with mucous membranes, which also line the intestine, urinary and reproductive tracts. Tears, mucus, saliva all contain enzymes that attack bacteria. The acid in our stomach also kills bacteria.

What happens if the skin is cut?

A cut provides an entry point for pathogens. Cuts are quickly sealed by blood clots. A sequence of events involving **platelets** and clotting factors goes into operation; it is summarised in Figure **6.10**. Fibrin entangles red blood cells to form a clot.

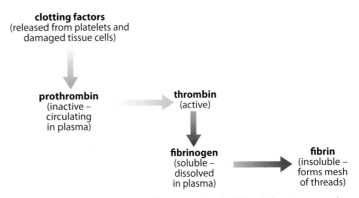

Figure 6.10 The sequence of reactions in the blood-clotting cascade.

TEST YOURSELF 6.6

 The two plasma proteins prothrombin and fibrinogen (shown in Figure **6.10**) circulate in their inactive form in the blood. Why must they be inactive until the skin is cut?

What is the difference between specific and non-specific immunity?

Non-specific immunity is a general response to invading pathogens. **Phagocytes** respond in the same way to any pathogen and attempt to engulf them by **phagocytosis**.

Specific immunity involves the production of antibodies in response to an antigen (antibody-generating substance).

DEFINITIONS

An **ANTIGEN** is a protein found in the membrane or cell wall of a bacterium that enables the body to recognise the pathogen.

ANTIBODIES are protein molecules produced by lymphocytes in response to antigens. There are many different antibodies and each one works to destroy a specific pathogen.

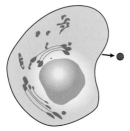 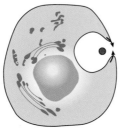 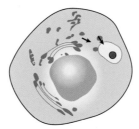 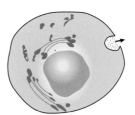

1 Phagocytic leucocyte detects a becterium and moves towards it. The bacterium attaches to receptors on the cell's plasma membrane.

2 Bacterium is engulfed by phagocytosis into a vacuole.

3 Lysosomes inside the cell fuse with the vacuole and release hydrolytic enzymes.

4 Bacterium is destroyed and any chemicals that are not absorbed into the cell are egested.

Figure 6.11 Phagocytosis of a pathogen.

What triggers antibody production?

Antigens on a pathogen stimulate cell division of the lymphocytes that produce the correct **antibody**. A clone of these lymphocytes called plasma cells is produced and secretes antibodies that will kill the pathogen.

How do antibodies kill pathogens?

- Some antibodies cause bacterial cells to clump together and make them easier for phagocytes to engulf them.
- Some antibodies cause cell walls to rupture.
- Some prevent viruses attaching to their host cells.

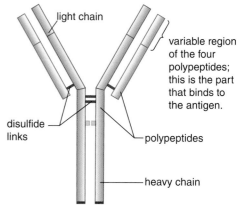

Figure 6.12 The basic structure of an antibody molecule. Variable regions bind to specific antigens and make them recognisable to phagocytes or prevent viruses attaching to cells.

How do we build up immunity to infections we have had before?

Antibodies last for a few weeks in the blood but some of the lymphocytes that were activated by antigens become memory cells. These memory cells remain in the blood and are available to give protection against the same infection later on.

Vaccination is based on the ability of the lymphocytes to produce antibodies and memory cells. HL students can learn more about this in Section **11.1**.

What is an antibiotic and how do antibiotics work?

Antibiotics kill or block the growth of bacteria. The first antibiotic to be discovered was penicillin in 1928. Different antibiotics work in different ways:

- some block protein synthesis inside bacteria
- some prevent bacteria producing a new cell wall as they divide
- some rupture the bacterial plasma membrane
- some inhibit bacterial enzymes.

Why don't antibiotics kill viruses?

Antibiotics disrupt metabolic processes of bacteria, but viruses do not have their own **metabolism** so are unaffected. Viruses use their human host's metabolism to build new viruses. Antibiotics do not affect these processes.

Which of these statements about antibodies is true?

A antibodies are produced in bone marrow   **B** antibodies are composed of polypeptides
C antibodies can kill bacteria but not viruses   **D** antibodies are pathogenic substances

How have some bacteria become resistant to antibiotics?

When antibiotics are used, there will always be a few bacteria in a population that are more resistant than others. Resistant forms may survive antibiotic treatments longer than susceptible forms and can pass on resistance to other bacteria via their plasmids (see Section **1.2**). As more antibiotics are used the risk that resistance will develop becomes greater. In some cases a stronger dose or a different antibiotic will kill resistant forms but there are now several strains of bacteria that have multiple resistance to several antibiotics. The best known of these are MRSA (methicillin resistant *Staphylococcus aureus*), which can infect hospital patients, and MDR-TB (multiple drug resistant tuberculosis).

How can antibiotic resistance be prevented?

- People should always complete the course of antibiotics they have been prescribed – even though they may feel better, some resistant bacteria are likely to be present and require more antibiotic to kill them.

- Hygiene in medical facilities must be strictly enforced to prevent bacteria spreading.

- Antibiotics should only be used for severe infections.

- Antibiotics should not routinely be used to *prevent* infection in farm animals.

What is HIV and how does it cause AIDS?

HIV is human immunodeficiency virus, a retrovirus that infects only the T-helper cells, a type of lymphocyte that helps cells of the immune system communicate with each other. HIV has RNA as its genetic material. It uses reverse transcriptase to convert RNA to DNA and insert its genes into helper T-cells. Even if all the free viruses in the body could be killed, infected helper T cells would continue making new ones.

AIDS is acquired immune deficiency syndrome. As the HIV virus slowly destroys helper T-cells, an infected person cannot fight off infections because they cannot produce antibodies properly. Secondary infections and certain types of cancer develop and the person is said to be suffering from AIDS. AIDS is the final stage of HIV infection and is caused by a severe failure of the immune system.

How is HIV transmitted?

The virus is passed from person to person in blood, vaginal secretions, semen and breast milk. It is most commonly passed in bodily fluids during sex and if non-sterile syringe needles are used to administer legal or illegal drugs.

In Test yourself **6.8** you are asked for differences, so make sure your answer makes the differences clear.

 List three differences between antibodies and antibiotics.

6.4 Gas exchange

Key information you should revise:

- Ventilation maintains a concentration gradient of oxygen and carbon dioxide between the air in the alveoli and blood in capillaries.

- There are two types of alveolar cells; type I are adapted to gas exchange and type II create a moist surface.

- Air travels to the lungs via trachea, bronchi and bronchioles.

- Muscle contractions allow ventilation to occur by changing pressure in the thorax.
- Different muscles are used for inspiration and expiration.
- Lung cancer and emphysema are two important diseases of the respiratory system.

Take care not to confuse respiration and ventilation. Ventilation is the physical exchange of air in the lungs; respiration is a metabolic process that takes place in cells.

hint

Practise drawing an alveolus and its blood capillary; you may be asked to do this in an exam.

What are the main structures of the human ventilation (breathing) system?

Alveoli are the site of gas exchange; they are roughly spherical in shape and made of **pneumocyte** cells less than 5 μm thick. Capillaries that surround them have very thin walls, so oxygen can easily diffuse through the alveolus into the blood.

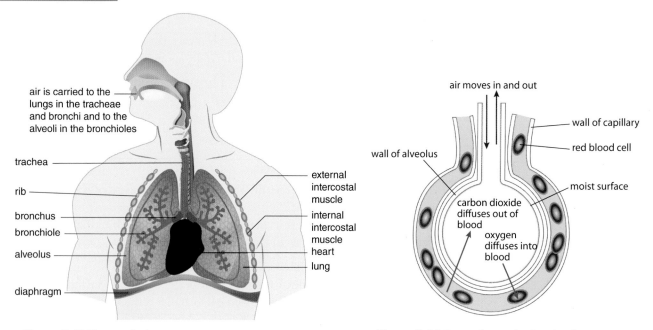

Figure 6.13 The ventilation system.

Figure 6.14 Gas exchange in the alveolus.

TEST YOURSELF 6.9

 Name two sets of antagonistic muscles that are described in Sections **6.1** and **6.4**.

What are pneumocytes and how are type 1 cells different from type II?

Pneumocytes are the cells that make up the walls of an alveolus. Type 1 pneumocytes cover most of the surface of an alveolus and are responsible for gas exchange. Type II pneumocytes are larger, rounder cells that produce and secret a liquid, containing a surfactant that reduces surface tension and prevents alveoli sticking together. Type 1 cells cannot reproduce but if they are damaged type II cells can divide to replace them. (See Option **D**.)

Table 6.4

TEST YOURSELF 6.10

Copy and complete Table **6.4** to summarise important features of alveoli that make them adapted for gas exchange.

Feature of alveoli	Why it is important for gas exchange
many small, spherical alveoli	
thin walls made of flat cells	
rich blood supply from capillaries	

How do we ventilate our lungs?

Ventilation is the process that moves air in and out of the lungs, so that fresh air is brought into the alveoli and air that has given up its oxygen and received carbon dioxide is breathed out.

Muscle contractions cause the pressure changes inside the thorax that force air in and out of the lungs to ventilate them. Different muscles are required for inspiration and expiration because muscles only do work when they contract.

Ventilation maintains the concentration gradients of oxygen and carbon dioxide between the air in alveoli and the blood flowing in adjacent capillaries.

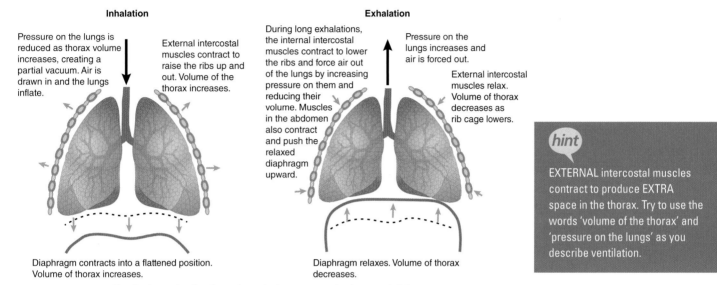

Inhalation

Pressure on the lungs is reduced as thorax volume increases, creating a partial vacuum. Air is drawn in and the lungs inflate.

External intercostal muscles contract to raise the ribs up and out. Volume of the thorax increases.

Diaphragm contracts into a flattened position. Volume of thorax increases.

Exhalation

During long exhalations, the internal intercostal muscles contract to lower the ribs and force air out of the lungs by increasing pressure on them and reducing their volume. Muscles in the abdomen also contract and push the relaxed diaphragm upward.

Pressure on the lungs increases and air is forced out.

External intercostal muscles relax. Volume of thorax decreases as rib cage lowers.

Diaphragm relaxes. Volume of thorax decreases.

The diaphragm is a flat sheet of muscle that separates the thorax and abdomen.

Figure 6.15 The mechanism of ventilation.

> **hint**
>
> EXTERNAL intercostal muscles contract to produce EXTRA space in the thorax. Try to use the words 'volume of the thorax' and 'pressure on the lungs' as you describe ventilation.

📝 Annotated exemplar answer 6.1

Describe the need for a ventilation system. **[6]**

This is part of an essay question in Section B of Paper 2. It is worth 6 marks so take care to make six clear points in your response.

Oxygen enters the blood capillaries from the alveoli by diffusion. Carbon dioxide leaves the blood and enters the alveoli by diffusion and must be exhaled and exchanged for fresh air with a higher oxygen and lower carbon dioxide concentration. Ventilation is the process of breathing in and out to exchange alveolar air with fresh air from outside.

Begin by saying that the ventilation system exchanges oxygen that the body needs for carbon dioxide it wants to get rid of for the first mark. Put the last sentence first.

Next, outline the process.

This answer would score three marks. It has not described how and why a concentration gradient is established. For full marks it should include three more points:

For gas exchange to occur a diffusion gradient must be maintained because diffusion is a passive process.

As oxygen leaves the alveoli and enters the blood the diffusion gradient reduces, so the rate of diffusion falls.

To maintain the gradient, air with low-oxygen content but high CO_2 is exchanged for fresh air.

3/6

How are lung cancer and emphysema caused?

These two diseases have similar symptoms of breathlessness, coughing and difficulty breathing but their causes are different.

Lung cancer was uncommon until smoking became popular in the early 20th century. In lung cancer the processes that control cell division (mitosis) are upset. Parts of the lung grow uncontrollably and produce tumours. Tumours take up space in the lung, prevent gases being exchanged and put strain on the heart. Most cases of lung cancer (approximately 88%) are related to smoking. Tobacco contains many mutagenic chemicals and even passive smoking causes about 3% of cancer cases.

Emphysema occurs when many small alveoli are replaced by larger air sacs with thicker, less elastic walls. The surface area for gas exchange is reduced and a person with emphysema has difficulty obtaining enough oxygen. Lower elasticity in the lungs means it is harder to ventilate the lungs. Emphysema can be linked to smoking. Smokers tend to have more phagocytes in their lungs and they produce an enzyme, elastase, which can digest lung tissue.

Why has evidence about lung cancer been hard to collect?

Nature of Science. Epidemiological studies gather data about causes and the occurrence of diseases. Most involve data collection and observations rather than experiments. It is hard to take into account many of the variables associated with human disease such as age, sex and genetic differences. The first study of lung cancer began in 1951 in the UK; but the disease develops slowly, so it was 50 years before the project was complete. Later studies have provided further strong evidence for a link between smoking and lung cancer. About 20 of the chemicals found in tobacco smoke cause tumours in laboratory animals and humans.

> **hint**
>
> To improve your answer to Test yourself **6.11** include the effect of emphysema on oxygen levels in the body.

TEST YOURSELF 6.11

 Outline two reasons why a person suffering from emphysema may feel tired. **[2]**

6.5 Neurons and synapses

Key information you should revise in this section is:

- Cells called neurons transmit electrical impulses and some of these cells have fibres which are covered with myelin.
- Sodium and potassium ions are pumped across membranes to create a resting potential.
- An action potential is a rapid depolarisation and repolarisation of the neuron membrane.
- A synapse is the junction between two neurons or between a neuron and an effector cell.
- Presynaptic neurons release neurotransmitter into a synapse when they are depolarised.

What is a neuron?

A neuron is a nerve cell, which is able to transmit electrical impulses along its length. The impulses pass from one neuron to the next or from a neuron to a muscle. Impulses are **action potentials** that consist of rapid depolarisation and repolarisation of the neuron membrane.

What are the features of a neuron?

A typical neuron has a cell body which contains the nucleus and long extensions which can be up to 1 m long. **Dendrites** carry impulses towards the nerve cell body and axons carry them away. The shape of a neuron depends on its position in the body but motor neurons, which extend out from the spinal cord to muscles in the limb, look like the one in Figure **6.16**.

Notice that the long axon is covered with a **myelin sheath**, which speeds up the transmission of impulses. Impulses can 'jump' from one gap in the myelin to the next in a process called saltatory conduction.

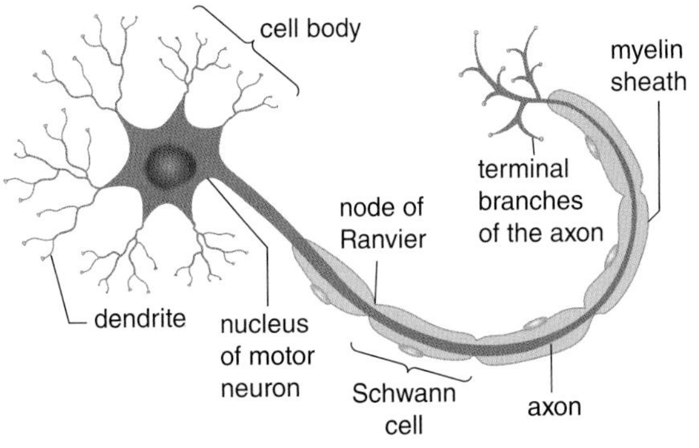

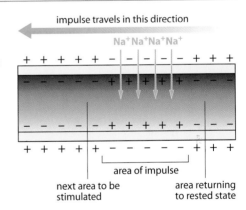

Figure 6.16 A motor neuron.

How are nerve impulses sent along a neuron?

RESTING POTENTIAL is the potential difference across the plasma membrane of a neuron when an impulse is not being transmitted. For most neurons this is 70mV.

When a neuron is not transmitting impulses, a **resting potential** is set up across its membrane. This is achieved by having an imbalance of positive and negative charges on each side of the membrane.

- Na^+ ions are pumped out of the cell and K^+ ions are pumped in by sodium-potassium pumps in the membrane.
- The sodium–potassium pump uses ATP to establish the resting potential.
- Three Na^+ ions are pumped in for every two K^+ ions pumped out.

To send a message the resting potential is changed to an action potential.

An **ACTION POTENTIAL** is a rapid change in the membrane potential. It consists of two stages: depolarisation and repolarisation.

How an action potential takes place

1 As a neuron is stimulated, gated sodium channels open and Na^+ ions from outside rush in. The neuron becomes depolarised.

2 For a short time the inside of the axon becomes positively charged with respect to the outside and the sodium channels close.

3 Gated potassium channels open and K^+ ions leave the neuron to re-establish the resting potential. This is called repolarisation.

4 The potential difference falls below the resting potential and both sodium and potassium channels are closed. The resting potential is re-established by sodium-potassium pumps during the **refractory period**. Further impulses cannot pass during this period.

Figure 6.17 When an impulse passes along the neuron, sodium ions diffuse via ion channels and the potential is reversed. This process is called an action potential.

How does the refractory period ensure that action potentials only pass in one direction? **[4]**

How is an action potential shown on a graph?

Figure **6.18** shows the membrane potential at different stages of an action potential. This process is incredibly quick, notice that the axis is measured in milliseconds. An action potential is only started if a stimulus causes the **threshold potential** to be reached.

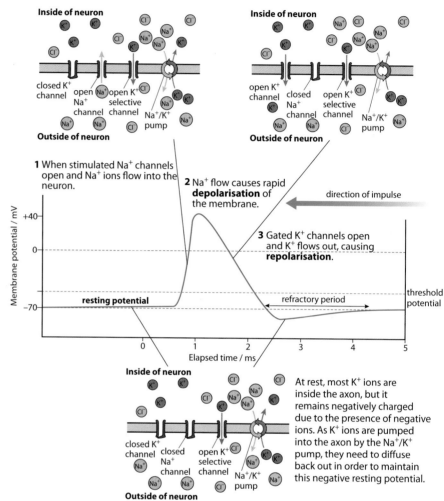

Figure 6.18 The action potential.

 Use the graph in Figure **6.18** to help you answer these multiple choice questions.

1 A typical neuron has a resting membrane potential of about:
   A +70 mV   **B** +70 V   **C** −70 mV   **D** −70 V
2 Which of the following ions are involved in action potentials?
   A Na⁺   **B** K⁺   **C** Cl⁻   **D** A and B only   **E** A, B and C
3 At what membrane potential do gated Na⁺ channels become activated?
   A −70 mV   **B** −50 mV   **C** 0 mV   **D** +50 mV

How do impulses cross a synapse?

DEFINITION

A **SYNAPSE** is a junction between two neurons or between a neuron and a receptor or effector cell.

Two neurons do not touch each other; there is a tiny gap called a **synapse** between them. Action potentials cross a synapse because neurotransmitters are released into the gap.

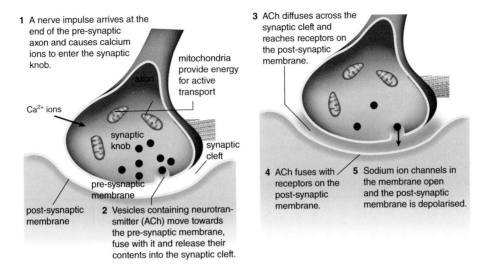

Figure 6.19 A cholinergic synapse.

The whole process is very fast and takes about 5–10 ms.

- As the nerve impulse reaches the end of the neuron, the pre-synaptic membrane is depolarised.
- Depolarisation causes Ca^{2+} ions to diffuse into the neuron.
- Vesicles containing neurotransmitter move towards the membrane and release their contents into the synaptic cleft.
- Neurotransmitter diffuses across to receptors on the post-synaptic membrane and fuses with them.
- Sodium channels open and the post-synaptic membrane is depolarised.
- Finally, acetylcholine (ACh) is broken down by an enzyme acetylcholinesterase and repackaged in vesicles in the pre-synaptic neuron.

What substances act as neurotransmitters?

Acetylcholine (ACh) is the transmitter used at many synapses. But there are more than 40 different neurotransmitters in the body. Noradrenalin and ACh are found throughout the body. Others, for example, dopamine and gamma-amino butyric acid (GABA) are found only in the brain.

How do neonicotinoids and other chemicals interfere with synapses?

Neonicotinoids are chemical pesticides used in insecticides. They are similar in structure to nicotine found in tobacco. Both substances block transmission at synapses that use acetylcholine as a neurotransmitter by binding to receptors on the post-synaptic membrane.

Many drugs affect synapses, for example cocaine and amphetamines stimulate transmission, whereas cannabis binds to receptors and prevents the transmission of impulses.

A bacterium *Clostridium botulinum* produces a very powerful toxin that also prevents messages passing across synapses to muscles so that they cannot contract. Today this neurotoxin is sold as Botox.

Table 6.5 Data about the speed of transmission of impulses in the axons of different organisms.

Organism	Speed of transmission (ms⁻¹)	Diameter of axon (μm)	Myelination
squid	30	1000	no
toad	30	10	yes
cat	50	10	yes
cat	3	1	no

Using the data shown in Table **6.5** answer the questions and outline reasons for your answer.
1 Describe the relationship between the diameter of an axon and its speed of transmission
2 Describe the relationship between myelination and speed of transmission

6.6 Hormones, homeostasis and reproduction

Key information you should revise:

- α and β cells in the pancreas secrete insulin and glucagon to control blood sugar level.
- Thyroxin is a hormone that regulates metabolic rate and temperature.
- Leptin is a hormone that acts on the hypothalamus to control appetite.
- Melatonin from the pineal gland controls daily rhythms.
- Testosterone causes the development of male genitalia before birth and sperm production and sexual development at puberty.
- A gene on the Y chromosome causes development of gonads in a male embryo so that testosterone is produced.
- Estrogen and progesterone cause development of female genitalia before birth and female characteristics at puberty.
- The menstrual cycle is controlled by hormones from the ovary and pituitary glands.
- *In vitro* fertilisation has allowed infertile couples to have children.

What is a hormone?

Hormones are chemical messengers carried in the blood. They are produced by **endocrine glands** and each hormone acts on its own specific target cells.

DEFINITION

HOMEOSTASIS is the maintenance of a constant internal environment within an organism.

How do hormones control the level of glucose in the blood?

Two hormones control blood glucose levels. Both are produced in the pancreas:

- insulin: which lowers the level is produced in β cells
- glucagon: which raises the level is produced in α cells

Glucose levels are monitored by cells in the pancreas. If the level is too high or too low, hormones are released to correct it. This response is controlled by **negative feedback**.

The pancreas is two glands in one. The Islets of Langerhans are endocrine cells, which are dotted through the pancreas and contain both α and β cells. Different exocrine cells in the pancreas produce digestive enzymes.

Table 6.6

	Response to a rise in blood glucose level above normal	Response to a fall in blood glucose level to below normal
pancreas	β cells release insulin	α cells release **glucagon**
glucose uptake or release	insulin stimulates the liver and muscles to take in glucose and convert it to stores of glycogen – blood glucose level falls	glucagon stimulates the hydrolysis of glycogen to glucose in the liver – glucose is released into the blood, blood glucose levels rise

What is negative feedback?

Negative feedback occurs when the level of glucose deviates from normal and corrective mechanisms are turned on to return the system to normal.

Many **homeostatic** mechanisms, including temperature regulation and osmotic content of the blood, work by negative feedback.

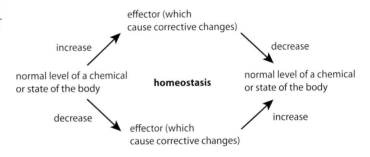

Figure 6.20 Homeostasis.

 1 State the name of the gland that is the effector for the control of blood glucose. **[1]**

2 Name the hormones that control blood glucose levels. **[2]**

What is diabetes?

Diabetes is the inability of the body to control blood glucose level. A diabetic person may have wide fluctuations in their blood glucose, well above and below normal limits.

There are two types of diabetes.

- Type I, usually begins in childhood. It occurs because the pancreas does not produce insulin and without it body cells cannot take up glucose.

- Type II is the most common form. The pancreas does produce insulin but the body fails to respond. The receptor cells which should be stimulated by it do not respond, so glucose levels remain high.

What causes diabetes?

Type I (or 'early onset') diabetes can be an autoimmune disease which means that the body's immune system destroys its own β cells.

Type II (or 'late onset') diabetes is linked to weight and diet. The main risk factors seem to be eating too much sugary or fatty food combined with a lack of exercise. This type of diabetes used to be rare in young people but is becoming more common, especially in industrialised countries. Research has also shown that genetic factors are important.

Human physiology

How is diabetes treated?

Type I diabetes must be treated with regular insulin injections to stabilise a person's glucose levels.

Type II diabetes can be treated by following a healthy diet, taking exercise and losing weight so that peaks and troughs in blood glucose are avoided. Small meals at regular intervals rather than large meals can help. Some people follow a low GI diet and eat foods which help the body to absorb carbohydrates more slowly.

TEST YOURSELF 6.16

 Figure **6.21** shows the levels of glucose and insulin in the blood of a healthy, non-diabetic person for a period of 24 hours.

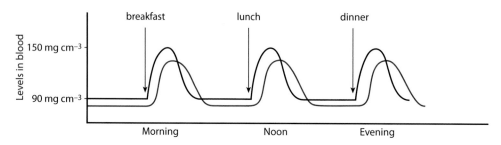

Figure 6.21 Effects of meals on blood sugar and insulin levels.

1 State which of the two lines on the graph represents insulin levels and explain your answer. **[2]**
2 Blood glucose levels fall between each meal. Outline the fate of excess glucose that is removed from the blood. **[2]**
3 Describe what would happen to the levels of blood glucose and insulin if the person did not eat lunch. **[2]**

Which hormone helps to control metabolic rate and body temperature?

Thyroxin is produced by the thyroid gland in the neck. It controls metabolic rate and can affect almost all cells in the body. Thyroxin increases the rate of metabolism and also leads to a rise in body temperature. It also stimulates growth.

Iodine in a person's diet is essential for production of thyroxin (see Option **D**).

What happens if thyroxin levels are not correct?

Lack of thyroxin can lead to	Excess of thyroxin can cause
• decreased metabolic rate • accumulation of fat as less energy is being used • reduced physical and mental activity • in childhood, it can affect mental development	• increased heart rate • increase in activity • weight loss

Which hormone helps to controls appetite?

Leptin is a protein hormone produced by adipose tissue. It acts on the hypothalamus in the brain and helps regulate appetite and energy intake.

If a person puts on weight and the amount of adipose tissue increases, the levels of leptin increase to reduce appetite and food intake.

How is leptin linked to obesity?

Experiments with leptin in mice showed that obesity could be caused by a lack of leptin. Without it mice ate uncontrollably and became very fat, but when given injections of the hormone their eating ceased.

It was hoped that leptin could be used to treat obese humans but a trial was unsuccessful because most obese people lack the receptors for leptin rather than the hormone itself.

Leptin-deficient obese mice carried mutant genes, whereas only a small proportion of humans had genetically caused leptin deficiency.

Which hormone regulates circadian rhythms?

DEFINITION

CIRCADIAN RHYTHMS are the behaviours that occur in a regular natural pattern in a period of 24 hours; they indicate times for eating, sleeping and also regulate hormone production.

Melatonin is a hormone produced by the pineal glad just above the middle of the brain. It controls our circadian rhythm and especially cycles of sleep and wakefulness. High levels of melatonin cause drowsiness and sleep at nighttime. More melatonin is produced in the evening and at night. The level falls at dawn.

What causes the secretion of melatonin?

Exposure to light stimulates a nerve pathway from the eye to the hypothalamus. Cells in the hypothalamus (the supra-chiasmatic nucleus, SCN) send signals to the parts of the brain controlling melatonin production and other hormones, as well as body temperature and other functions involved in sleeping.

In the daytime the pineal gland is inactive but at night the SCN turns it on so melatonin is produced.

What causes jet lag?

The SCN and pineal gland remain on the circadian rhythm of the departure point and it takes a short time for the body clock to be reset to the new destination.

TEST YOURSELF 6.17

 Figure **6.22** shows body temperature, heart rate and levels of the hormones melatonin and cortisol in the blood over a 24-hour period. Cortisol is a hormone released by the adrenal glands in response to stress.

  1 State the time during the 24-hour period when melatonin levels are highest.

  2 Suggest a reason for the rise in plasma cortisol at 8 am.

  3 Name two hormones, not shown in the graph, whose levels would be lower during the period 00:00–08:00. Explain your answer.

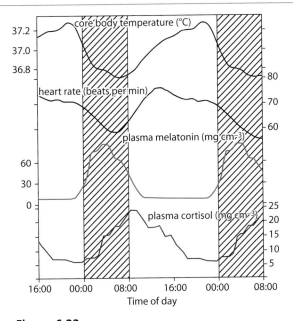

Figure 6.22

Which hormones are involved in sexual development?

Many hormones are involved in reproduction. Those discussed here are the most important and the ones you should remember.

Before birth, sex is determined by genes and **testosterone**.

The formation of male genitalia depends on the SRY gene on the Y chromosome. This causes the development of testes and the production of testosterone.

If no Y chromosome is present, there is no SRY gene. Estrogen and progesterone, first from the mother's ovaries and later from the placenta cause female reproductive organs and ovarian follicles to develop.

Can you label diagrams of the male and female reproductive systems?

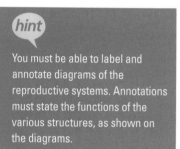

hint

You must be able to label and annotate diagrams of the reproductive systems. Annotations must state the functions of the various structures, as shown on the diagrams.

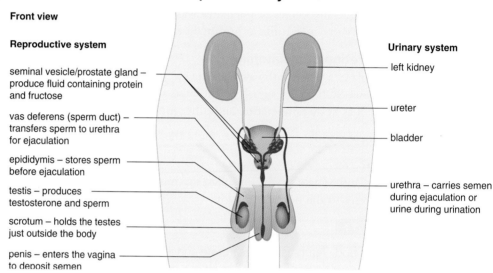

Front view

Reproductive system

seminal vesicle/prostate gland – produce fluid containing protein and fructose

vas deferens (sperm duct) – transfers sperm to urethra for ejaculation

epididymis – stores sperm before ejaculation

testis – produces testosterone and sperm

scrotum – holds the testes just outside the body

penis – enters the vagina to deposit semen

Urinary system

left kidney

ureter

bladder

urethra – carries semen during ejaculation or urine during urination

Figure 6.23 The male reproductive system. (The diagram also shows the organs of the urinary system.)

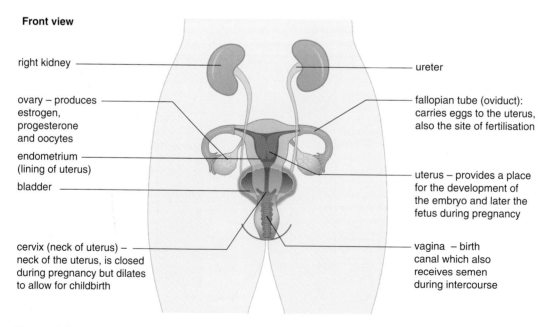

Front view

right kidney

ureter

ovary – produces estrogen, progesterone and oocytes

endometrium (lining of uterus)

bladder

fallopian tube (oviduct): carries eggs to the uterus, also the site of fertilisation

uterus – provides a place for the development of the embryo and later the fetus during pregnancy

cervix (neck of uterus) – neck of the uterus, is closed during pregnancy but dilates to allow for childbirth

vagina – birth canal which also receives semen during intercourse

Figure 6.24 The female reproductive system. (The diagram also shows the organs of the urinary system.)

Which hormones control puberty?

Table 6.7 Hormones which control puberty.

In boys	In girls
Testosterone levels rise and cause the development of secondary sexual characteristics: • growth of muscles • deepening of the voice • growth of body hair • enlargement of the penis • production of sperm • behaviour associated with the sex drive	Levels of estrogen and progesterone increase and cause development of: • breasts • growth of body hair • widening of the hips • onset of **menstrual cycle**

Which hormones control the menstrual cycle?

Four hormones are involved:

- LH (**luteinising hormone**) from the pituitary gland

- FSH (follicle stimulating hormone) from the pituitary gland

- estrogen from the ovary

- progesterone from the follicle cells in the ovary.

During the first half of the cycle, called the *follicular phase*, the egg is produced and the lining of the uterus is repaired.

During the second half of the cycle, called the *luteal phase*, the lining is maintained and thickened to prepare for implantation of an embryo.

The production of eggs is a cyclical process, which is described from the onset of menstruation in Table **6.8**.

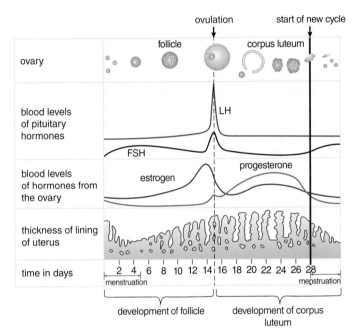

Figure 6.25 The menstrual cycle lasts an average of 28 days and involves changes in hormone levels that influence the follicles and lining of the uterus.

Table 6.8

days 1–5	• endometrium (lining) is shed and leaves via the vagina • levels of FSH from the pituitary gland rise and stimulate the development of an immature follicle • FSH also stimulate estrogen production by the ovary
days 6–14	• estrogen levels rise and promote the repair of the endometrium • as estrogen levels rise, LH levels peak at about day 14 • LH stimulates the empty follicle to produce progesterone after ovulation
day 15 (approx)	• ovulation – the follicle is fully developed and ruptures, releasing the egg
days 16–28	• the corpus luteum forms from the empty follicle and begins to release progesterone • progesterone maintains the endometrium it peaks in the luteal phase but falls again if the egg is not fertilised • progesterone inhibits FSH and LH
day 29 onward	• if the egg is not fertilised the cycle begins again

TEST YOURSELF 6.18

Name the hormone responsible for ovulation.

How are positive and negative feedback important in the menstrual cycle?

As with other hormones, the hormones of the menstrual cycle are controlled by feedback loops. But in this case both negative and **positive feedback** are important.

Over most of the cycle estrogen and progesterone have a negative feedback effect on the pituitary gland so rising levels of the two hormones cause levels of LH and FSH to fall.

But around days 12– 14 high levels of estrogen has a positive feedback effect. Rising levels of estrogen cause rising levels of LH and FSH, so ovulation is stimulated.

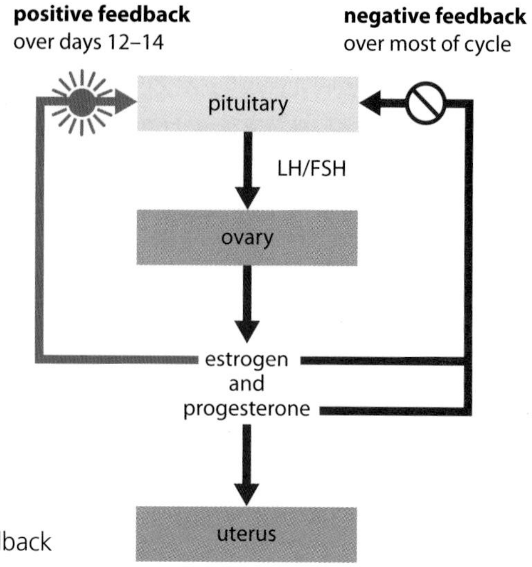

positive feedback over days 12–14   **negative feedback** over most of cycle

Figure 6.26 Negative and positive feedback in the menstrual cycle.

 When do primary oocytes develop in the primary follicles?

A during puberty

B before the birth of the woman

C from age 14–16 years

D between ages 10 and puberty

What is IVF and how are hormones used in the process?

IVF stands for *in vitro* fertilisation. It is a technique used to help infertile couples have a child. Hormones are used to interrupt a woman's menstrual cycle and then to stimulate her to produce more egg cells than normal. These can be fertilised *in vitro* (in a glass dish) and implanted in her uterus, where it is hoped they will grow and develop.

1 Hormones from the pituitary gland are suppressed so that the menstrual cycle is interrupted.

2 Synthetic FSH and LH are injected to stimulate the ovaries to produce many egg cells

3 Several eggs are removed just before the follicles rupture and mixed with sperm cells in a sterile dish.

4 If fertilisation is successful, one or more embryos will be placed back into the uterus after 48 hours.

5 The woman is given progesterone so that the lining of the uterus remains in place. If the embryos implant pregnancy will continue in the usual way.

 1 Approximately two-thirds of the male ejaculate is produced and secreted by the:

A prostate gland   **B** testes   **C** epididymis   **D** seminal vesicles

2 Why was William Harvey unable to prove that embryos were not 'preformed' in his work on reproduction?

A He studied hens' eggs, which do have preformed embryos.

B He did not have a suitable microscope to observe gametes.

C He worked in the 17th century and was not allowed to study embryos.

D He studied deer and did not have enough animals to prove his hypothesis.

🖹 Annotated exemplar answer 6.2

The graph shows the level of two ovarian hormones during the menstrual cycle of a woman.

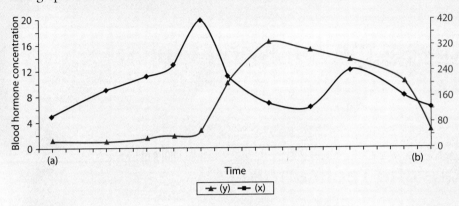

Figure 6.27

1 What would be the average time between (a) and (b)? **[1]**

2 Name the hormones (x) and (y). **[2]**

3 How many days before the onset of the next menstrual cycle does ovulation usually occur? **[1]**

4 Suggest what would happen to the level of the two hormones (a) and (b) if the woman became pregnant. Explain your answers. **[4]**

1 Approximately 28 days
— You could add 'The time will vary from woman to woman'

2 (x) = estrogen (y) progesterone
— Notice the question tells you that the hormones are ovarian hormones, so not LH or FSH.

3 Approximately 14 days
— Count the days on the graph to check your answer.

4 The level of progesterone would remain high. The level of estrogen would also rise and remain high.
— This answer only scores 2 out of 4. You are expected to make a sensible suggestion about what will happen to the hormones *and* give a reason for your suggestion so add 'to maintain the uterus lining/endometrium.' to the first sentence and 'to stimulate the development of the placenta and breast tissue.' to the second sentence to gain full marks.

6/8

7

NUCLEIC ACIDS (HL)

This chapter covers the following topics:

☐ DNA structure and replication

☐ Transcription and gene expression

☐ Translation

7.1 DNA structure and replication

Key information you should revise:

- How DNA structure relates to the way it replicates.
- Nucleosomes help DNA to supercoil and regulate transcription.
- A number of enzymes are involved in DNA replication.
- DNA polymerase only adds nucleotides to the 3' end of a primer.
- DNA replication is continuous on the leading strand but discontinuous on the lagging strand.
- Some regions of DNA do not code for proteins but have other vital jobs.

How did the discovery of the structure of DNA suggest a mechanism for replication?

Nature of Science. Watson and Crick are credited with the discovery of the double helix, but their work was made possible by X-ray diffraction analysis by Rosalind Franklin and work on molecular models and studies of bases carried out by others.

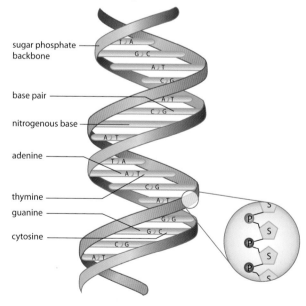

Figure 7.1 The DNA molecule

When the double helix, antiparallel strands linked by base pairs, was proposed as a model for the molecule's structure, its method of replication became easier to explain.

- Hydrogen bonding between the two strands means that they can be separated and copied during replication.
- Complementary base pairing ensures the strands are copied accurately.
- Each of the two strands acts as a template for a new strand.

What does antiparallel mean?

One of the two strands in a DNA molecule runs in the opposite direction to the other. One strand has the carbon 5 attached to a phosphate group (pointing upwards in the diagram), while the other has this linkage pointing downwards.

Review the basics of DNA structure in Section **2.7**.

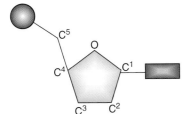

Figure 7.2 The structure of a nucleotide.

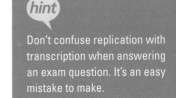

What are nucleosomes and how are they important to DNA structure?

Eukaryotic chromosomes are associated with proteins called **histones**. Histones package the DNA into structures called **nucleosomes**. These help **supercoil** the molecule, so that it can be packaged into the very small space of the nucleus. Nucleosomes also help to regulate **transcription** (see Section **7.2**)

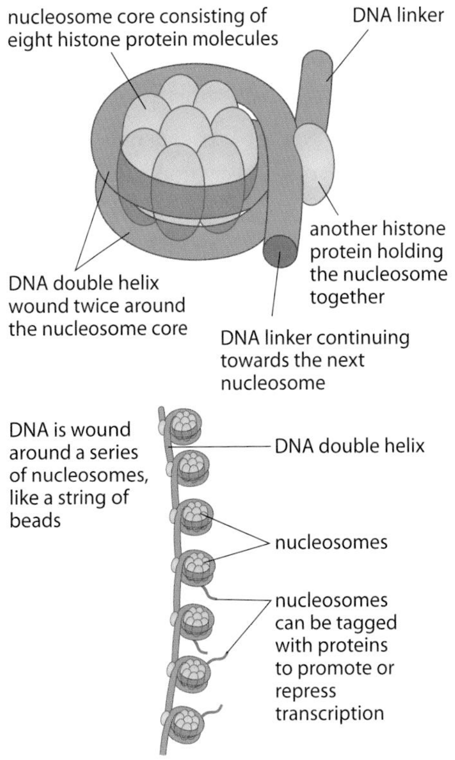

How is DNA replicated?

DNA replication ensures that exact copies of existing molecules are made before a cell divides. The process is said to be semi-conservative because each strand of DNA acts as a template for the production of a new strand.

How are new nucleotides connected to the forming strand?

Nucleotides can only be added at the 3' end of the molecule when it is forming. Replication therefore is said to occur in a 5' to 3' direction.

What are the leading and lagging strands?

DNA replication occurs differently on the two DNA strands. One strand, called the leading strand, is made continuously following the **replication fork**. This is because new nucleotides can always be added at the 3' end of the new molecule.

Figure 7.3 The structure of a nucleosome.

> **hint**
>
> Don't confuse replication with transcription when answering an exam question. It's an easy mistake to make.

The other strand, called the **lagging strand**, is copied in small fragments, called **Okazaki fragments** because the two original strands of DNA must be opened a short distance before a new strand can be made (see Figure **7.4**). The original DNA strands are called the template strands.

What enzymes are needed during replication?

For the leading strand:

- The enzyme **helicase** unwinds the DNA at the replication fork and single stranded binding proteins (SSBs) keep the strands apart and protect the single strand of DNA that is exposed.

- **DNA gyrase** relieves the tension put on the DNA molecule as it is being unwound by creating negative supercoils.

- **RNA primase** attaches to the DNA template strand.

- **DNA polymerase III** binds and adds units called deoxynucleotide triphosphates with covalent bonds. Each new nucleotide is added at the 3' end. (dNTPs have two extra phosphate groups which are later released)

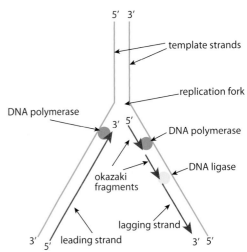

Figure 7.4

For the lagging strand:

- As for the leading strand, replication begins with the attachment of primers by **RNA primase**, but this time a short RNA primer is synthesised close to the replication fork.
- **DNA polymerase III** starts replication by attaching a nucleotide at the 3' end of the primer. As it does so it moves away from the replication fork on this strand (the opposite direction to that on the leading strand).
- **DNA polymerase I** removes the RNA primer and replaces it with DNA. There will be many primers on the lagging strand and so many Okazaki fragments are formed.
- Finally, **DNA ligase** seals up the breaks between Okazaki fragments to make a continuous strand.

 TEST YOURSELF 7.1

What is the function of DNA polymerase in DNA replication?

A separation of the DNA strands

B formation of mRNA

C unwinding the double helix

D formation of a complementary strand

Do all regions of DNA code for protein?

Some regions of DNA do not code for proteins but have other important functions:

- **Regulator genes** control the expression of one or more genes. Prokaryotic regulators often code for repressor proteins that block transcription.
- Genes for tRNA production are found on all chromosomes except 22 and Y in humans.
- Repeated sequences make up more than half of human DNA and do not code for protein.
- **Telomeres** are repeated sequences found at the ends of chromosomes. They seem to protect the ends so that vital DNA is not lost during replication.

How are repeated sequences used in DNA profiling?

Our DNA contains many short sequences of nucleotides which are repeated over and over again. These are called VNTRs or variable number tandem repeats. The number of times each individual has each sequence repeated is inherited so each person is slightly different. In DNA profiling it is easy to compare these repeated sequences and establish either genetic relationships or to match DNA to samples gathered from a crime scene.

How did Hershey and Chase's experiment prove that DNA is the genetic material?

 Nature of Science. Hershey and Chase carried out experiments in the 1950s with bacteria and viruses to prove that DNA was the genetic material. Until then, it was thought that proteins were responsible for inheritance. In their first experiment they labelled the DNA of a virus with ^{32}P. When this virus infected a bacterium they found that the genetic material of the bacterium contained ^{32}P. A virus that infects a bacterium is also called a phage or bacteriophage.

In their second experiment the protein coat of the virus was labelled with ^{35}S. Phosphorus is found in

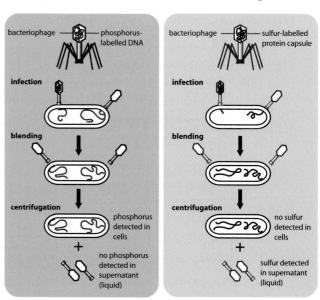

Figure 7.5 The Hershey and Chase experiment showed that the genetic material transferred to bacterial cells by infecting T2 phages is DNA, and not protein as previously believed.

DNA but sulfur is found in proteins. This time no radioactive label was found in the bacterial DNA, but the empty protein coats of the virus remained labelled.

 What observation made by Hersey and Chase led to the conclusion that DNA is the genetic material?

A viruses cannot infect bacteria if they contain ^{32}P.   **C** ^{32}P was left outside the infected bacteria.

B viruses cannot infect bacteria if they contain ^{35}S.   **D** ^{35}S was left outside the infected bacteria.

7.2 Transcription and gene expression

Key information you should revise:

- Gene expression is regulated by proteins that bind to specific sequences of bases.
- Transcription occurs in a 5' to 3' direction.
- Nucleosomes help regulate transcription in eukaryotes.
- mRNA splicing increases the number of different proteins that can be made.
- Environment of a cell and organism has an impact on gene expression.

DEFINITION

TRANSCRIPTION is the process which copies a sequence of DNA bases into mRNA that can be translated into polypeptides.

Transcription of DNA is the first stage in building a polypeptide; don't confuse it with replication of DNA.

How is DNA transcribed into mRNA?

DNA is transcribed (or copied) in the nucleus to make a length of mRNA that moves to the cytoplasm for **translation** into a polypeptide in the following process:

- DNA is separated into two strands by RNA polymerase – H bonds are broken and the strands unwind.
- Transcription begins at the promotor region, a non-coding region just before a gene.
- Only one strand, the antisense strand, is used for transcription.
- RNA polymerase uses free nucleoside triphosphates (NTPs) to build an RNA molecule that is complementary to the antisense strand.
- As the mRNA molecule lengthens, DNA is rewound into a helix once it has been transcribed.
- When the terminator region at the end of a gene is reached transcription stops.

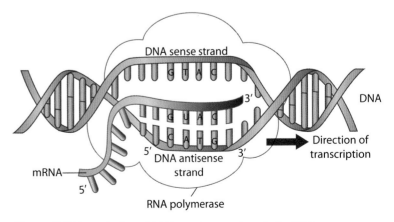

Figure 7.6 Transcription of DNA produces a strand of mRNA.

Which strand of DNA is transcribed?

What effect do nucleosomes have on the regulation of transcription?

Histone proteins found in nucleosomes may be modified to make it easier or more difficult for transcription molecules to access a gene. Histones are modified by the addition of a methyl group, a phosphate group or an acetyl group.

TEST YOURSELF 7.4

 In which direction does mRNA construction proceed?

How is mRNA modified after transcription?

Eukaryotic cells modify mRNA after it has been transcribed. The first mRNA produced is called pre-mRNA. Regions called **introns** are removed from this mRNA to leave only **exons**. These are linked together in a process called **splicing** to form mature mRNA.

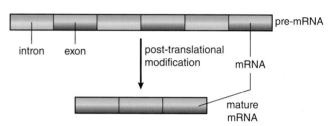

Figure 7.7 Introns and exons in mRNA.

Why is mRNA splicing important?

RNA splicing produces variation in mature mRNA, depending on which exons are included in the mature mRNA. It occurs in genes with multiple exons so that a single gene can code for more than one polypeptide. An average human gene is thought to code for three different proteins. One example is tropomyosin genes that contain 11 exons. Tropomyosin pre-mRNA can be spliced differently to give five different forms of the protein.

TEST YOURSELF 7.5

What is the difference between the sense and antisense strands of DNA?

   A Nucleotides are linked to the sense strand by hydrogen bonding during transcription, but not to the antisense strand.

   B The sense strand has the same base sequences as tRNA, but the antisense strand does not.

   C Nucleotides are linked to the antisense stand by hydrogen bonding during transcription, but not to the sense strand.

   D The antisense strand has the same base sequence as mRNA but the sense strand does not.

How do proteins affect the genes that are expressed?

In eukaryotes proteins that bind to certain base sequences in DNA affect gene expression. Activator proteins bind to a region of DNA known as the enhancer and together form an initiation complex, which allows RNA polymerase to begin transcription. Other proteins may bind to silencer regions of DNA to prevent transcription.

In prokaryotes gene expression can be modified by environmental factors. An example is the switching on of the lactose metabolising genes in the presence of lactose. In this case a repressor protein is deactivated so that transcription can begin.

What is a nucleosome?

A the protein core of a chromosome   **C** a chain of ribosomes

B histone proteins and DNA   **D** material within the nuclear membrane

What affect does the environment have on gene expression?

Environmental factors such as sunlight can 'turn on' the genes for melanin production in the skin. The coat colour of Siamese cats and Himalayan rabbits is affected by temperature as genes are switched on. Dark fur is only produced at lower temperatures, so ears, tail and paws of these animals are darker.

Drugs and chemicals can also affect genes, thalidomide is a drug that has few harmful effects on adults but severely affects limb development in the fetus.

 Determine the mRNA sequence that is coded by this strand of DNA.

Sense   A T G C T A G A C

Antisense T A C G A T C T G

7.3 Translation

Key information you should revise in this section is:

- The first stage of translation involves assembly of ribosomes.

- Synthesis of a polypeptide involves a series of events that are repeated.

- Ribosomes are disassembled after translation is terminated.

- Free ribosomes synthesise protein for use inside the cell while bound ribosomes synthesise proteins for secretion or use in lysosomes.

- In prokaryotes translation occurs immediately after transcription because there is no nuclear membrane.

- Proteins have four levels of structure – primary, secondary, tertiary and quaternary.

DEFINITION

TRANSLATION is the process which uses the information carried in mRNA to build a sequence of amino acid that eventually becomes a protein molecule.

How are the components needed for translation assembled?

Translation of mRNA takes place within ribosomes. These consist of two sub units, one large and one small. They are made of protein and ribosomal RNA (rRNA).

To begin translation a mRNA molecule binds to the small subunit at a mRNA binding site. An initiator tRNA molecule binds at the start codon and then the large subunit binds to the small one.

There are three binding sites on the ribosome. Figure **7.8** explains their functions.

What is tRNA?

tRNA is a nucleic acid made of a single strand of nucleotides folded into a 'clover leaf' shape. At one end a triplet of bases called the anticodon can bind to a codon sequence on mRNA and at the other end is a binding site for the amino acid that corresponds to the mRNA codon. Figure **2.31** shows the detailed structure of tRNA.

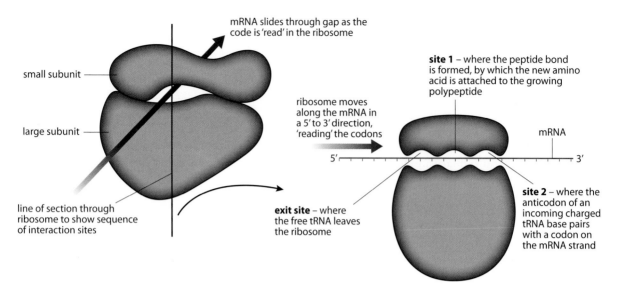

Figure 7.8 The structure of a ribosome.

How does the synthesis of a polypeptide proceed?

We can divide the process of translation into four stages:

1 Initiation involves binding the components that carry out translation as described above. The second tRNA molecule then moves into position in site 2 and a peptide bond is formed between the two amino acids that the tRNA molecules carry.

2 Elongation involves the formation of peptide bonds between amino acids that are brought into the ribosome by tRNAs in the order that is specified by the mRNA codons. The initial tRNA molecule leaves the ribosome from the 'exit' site and adjacent amino acids held by the next two tRNAs form a peptide bond. This process is repeated over and over again until a 'stop' codon is reached.

3 Translocation is simply the movement of the ribosome along the mRNA strand so that each codon is read in turn.

4 Termination occurs when the ribosome meets a stop codon that aligns in site 2. Here the polypeptide chain and the mRNA are related from the ribosome. The ribosome separates into its two parts.

Figure 7.9 The stages of translation.

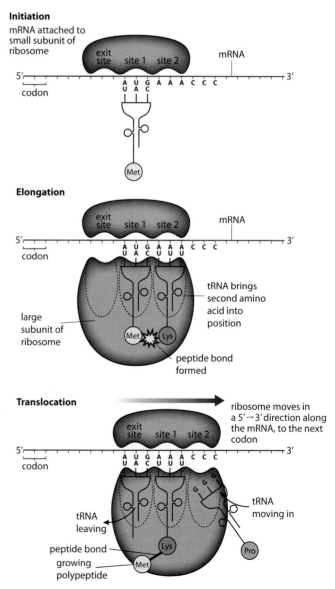

📝 Annotated exemplar answer 7.1

a Which direction is the ribosome moving during translation? **[1]**

b Name the next amino acid that will be attached to the polypeptide. **[2]**

c Explain how the correct amino acid was attached to the tRNA **[2]**

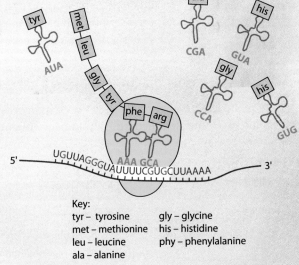

Key:
tyr – tyrosine   gly – glycine
met – methionine   his – histidine
leu – leucine   phy – phenylalanine
ala – alanine

Figure 7.10

a The ribosome moves right to left in the diagram

This is not correct; translation proceeds from 5' to 3'; that is, left to right in the diagram.

b Alanine

Correct; recall that there is complementary base pairing between mRNA and tRNA and recognise that the next codon the ribosome will cover is GCU. You must then find the correct ribosome in the diagram.

c It is attached by an activating enzyme. This process requires ATP.

(3/5)

This answer is correct but would probably score half marks. Much better to say 'The amino acid that attaches corresponds to the anticodon at the base of the tRNA molecule.' and 'The amino acid attaches at the 3' end of the tRNA at the top of the molecule.'

 TEST YOURSELF 7.8

If a polypeptide made of 25 amino acid, is being synthesised by a ribosome
  a How many mRNA bases code for the polypeptide?
  b How many bases in the coding strand of DNA would be needed to produce the mRNA molecule?

What is the difference between free and attached ribosomes?

Free ribosomes are found in the cytoplasm where they are involved in the synthesis of proteins that will be used inside the cell. Attached ribosomes are attached to the endoplasmic reticulum forming RER (see Chapter 2). These ribosomes synthesise protein that will be exported from the cell or packaged into lysosomes.

What is the difference between translation in prokaryotes and eukaryotes?

In prokaryotes there is no nuclear membrane so translation can take place immediately after transcription, whereas in eukaryotes there is a delay because mRNA must move into the cytoplasm via nuclear pores before translation can begin.

What are the four levels of protein structure?

Proteins are large complex molecules with hundreds of amino acid subunits. As each one has a specific function proteins have complex methods of folding and stabilisation (see Figure **2.19**).

Table 7.1

Level of structure	Type of bonds involved
primary	• amino acids are linked by peptide bonds
secondary	• polypeptide chain is either folded into a β-pleated sheet or coiled into an α helix
	• both are held in place by hydrogen bonds
tertiary	• protein takes up a three dimensional shape held together by bonds between the R groups of amino acids
	• bonds include: ionic bonds between R groups, disulfide bridges (covalent bonds) between sulfur atoms and hydrophilic and hydrophobic interactions between side chains
quaternary	• two or more polypeptide chains link to form a single, large protein
	• the structure is held together by the same bonds as tertiary structure, but additional molecules may also be included, e.g. the heme group in hemoglobin

TEST YOURSELF 7.9

1 Why is a three-dimensional shape important for a protein that works as an enzyme?

2 State whether these statements are true or false.

a In eukaryotic cells transcription takes place in the nucleus.

b Two types of RNA and ribosomes are essential for translation.

c During translation amino acids attach to their respective codons on mRNA.

d mRNA molecules can be used many times to synthesise a polypeptide.

e During transcription ribosomes attach to the DNA sequence being transcribed.

f Translation in eukaryotes occurs in the nucleus.

METABOLISM, CELL RESPIRATION AND PHOTOSYNTHESIS (HL)

This chapter covers the following topics:

☐ **Metabolism**   ☐ **Cell respiration**   ☐ **Photosynthesis**

8.1 Metabolism

Key information you should revise:

- Metabolic pathways are made up of chains and cycles of enzyme controlled reactions.
- Enzymes lower the activation energy of reactions.
- Enzyme inhibitors can be competitive or non-competitive.
- End product inhibition can control metabolic pathways.

What is a metabolic pathway?

DEFINITIONS

METABOLIC REACTIONS are chemical processes that occur in all cells to keep them alive. Respiration and photosynthesis are two vital metabolic reactions.

Metabolic pathways are chains or cycles of reactions that are catalysed by enzymes. Most consist of a series of steps and each step is controlled by an enzyme.

For example, in Figure **8.1** the end product D is inhibiting the first enzyme 1.

Figure 8.1

Photosynthesis and respiration are metabolic pathways, which involve cycles as well as chains of reactions.

What is activation energy?

Enzymes work by lowering the **activation energy** of a substrate or substrates (see Figure **8.2**). For a metabolic reaction to take place the substrate has to reach an unstable, high-energy transition state where the chemical bonds are destablised. This requires an input of energy known as the activation energy. When the substrate reaches this stage the reaction can occur rapidly.

Metabolic reactions in living organisms occur at body temperature, which is never high enough to bring the substrates to their transition state without a catalyst.

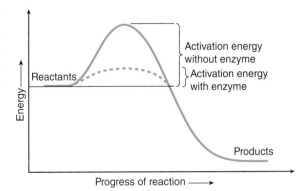

Figure 8.2 Graph to show activation energy for an exothermic reaction (such as respiration) with and without a catalyst.

TEST YOURSELF 8.1

a Draw a graph to show the energy curve for a catabolic reaction with and without an enzyme. **[2]**

b Explain how the enzyme produces this effect. **[3]**

How are competitive and non-competitive inhibitors different from one another?

DEFINITIONS

ENZYME INHIBITORS are substances that reduce or prevent an enzyme's activity.

COMPETITIVE INHIBITORS are molecules with a similar structure to the substrate which compete with the substrate to occupy the active site of the enzyme.

NON-COMPETITIVE INHIBITORS bind to enzymes but not at the active site. They bind elsewhere where they block access of the substrate or cause a change in shape of the enzyme, so that the substrate cannot enter the active site.

The effect of the two inhibitors on the rate of reaction of the enzyme at different substrate concentrations is shown in Figures **8.3** and **8.4.**

If the concentration of a **competitive inhibitor** is low, increasing the substrate concentration will reduce the inhibition. An example of a competitive inhibitor is ethanol, which is a competitive inhibitor of alcohol dehydrogenase. It is used to prevent poisoning by antifreeze (ethylene glycol), which would otherwise be converted to potentially lethal metabolites.

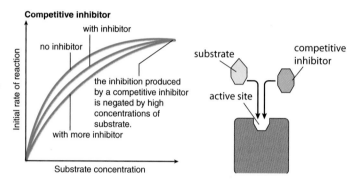

Figure 8.3 Competitive inhibition – the inhibitor stops the substrate binding to the active site.

If the inhibitor is non-competitive, increasing the concentration of substrate has no effect and inhibition stays high. An example of a **non-competitive inhibitor** is cyanide, which blocks cytochrome oxidase in the respiration chain and leads to death.

TEST YOURSELF 8.2

 What can reduce the effect of a competitive inhibitor of an enzyme?

A decrease the temperature at which the reaction occurs

B increase the temperature at which the reaction occurs

C increase the substrate concentration

D add a non-competitive inhibitor

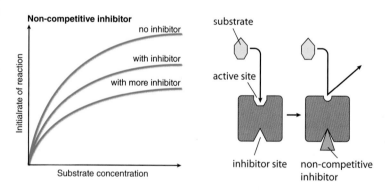

Figure 8.4 Non-competitive inhibition – the inhibitor changes the shape of the active site, thus stopping the substrate binding to it.

How does end-product inhibition control a metabolic pathway?

End-product inhibition means that an enzyme in a metabolic pathway is inhibited by the product of that pathway. This mechanism prevents a cell from over-producing a substance that it does not need. When the end-product is used up, its inhibiting effect is reduced and production can begin again.

End-product inhibition is an example of negative feedback.

An example of end-product inhibition is shown in Figure **8.5**.

TEST YOURSELF 8.3

 List three differences between competitive and non-competitive inhibitors. **[3]**

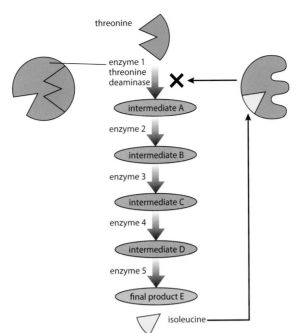

Figure 8.5 The pathway that converts threonine to isoleucine – a specific example of end-product inhibition.

As you list differences in Test yourself **8.3** make sure that you include comparisons between the two types of inhibition. You could include graphs showing rate of reaction with and without inhibitors.

8.2 Cell respiration

Key information you should revise:

- The structure of mitochondria is linked to their function.
- In cell respiration electron carriers are oxidised and reduced.
- Molecules that have been phosphorylated are less stable.
- Glucose is converted to pyruvate during glycolysis in the cytoplasm and produces a small net gain of ATP.
- In aerobic respiration pyruvate undergoes the link reaction in the mitochondrial matrix.
- During the Krebs cycle oxidation of acetyl groups is coupled with the reduction of hydrogen carriers and carbon dioxide is released.
- Energy released during oxidation is carried to the cristae of the mitochondria by reduced NAD and FAD.
- Electrons are transferred between carriers in the electron transport chain (ETC).
- During chemiosmosis protons diffuse across the cristae membrane via ATP synthase to produce ATP.
- Oxygen binds to free protons to form water.

Respiration is a series of metabolic reactions, which is summarised by the equation:

$$C_6H_{12}O_6 + 6O_2 \rightarrow 6CO_2 + 6H_2O \text{ (+ energy)}$$

It consists of series of metabolic chains and cycles involving many different enzymes. Review the basic details in Section **2.8**.

How is the structure of a mitochondrion related to its function?

The **glycolysis** reactions occur in the cytoplasm but all the other reactions of respiration take place in the **mitochondria**.

- The outer membrane keeps the mitochondrion separate from other reactions of the cell.
- The matrix contains the enzymes for the link reaction and the **Krebs cycle**.

Metabolism, cell respiration and photosynthesis (HL)

- The folded membranes of the **cristae** increase their surface area and contain **ATP synthase** and the enzymes needed for the ETC.
- The small inter-membrane space allows protons to accumulate so that **chemiosmosis** can take place.

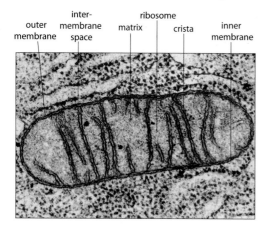

Figure 8.6 Coloured electron micrograph of a mitochondrion (×72 000).

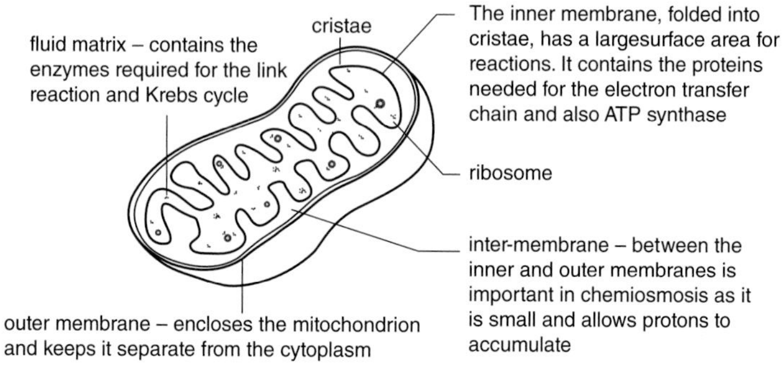

Figure 8.7 Diagram of a mitochondrion in longitudinal section.

TEST YOURSELF 8.4

 Outline how the pH of the inter-membrane space and mitochondrial matrix are different.

What are oxidation and reduction reactions and how are they important in respiration?

Oxidation and reduction are two linked chemical reactions. If one molecule is oxidised another will be reduced. Paired oxidation and reduction reactions are called redox reactions.

A molecule can be oxidised by losing electrons, losing hydrogen or gaining oxygen.

A molecule can be reduced by gaining electrons, gaining hydrogen or losing oxygen.

In respiration, glucose is oxidised as hydrogen atoms (and therefore electrons) are removed from it and added to hydrogen acceptors (oxygen atoms), which become reduced.

What are the main stages in respiration?

Respiration is usually explained in a series of steps:

1 glycolysis   3 the Krebs cycle

2 the link reaction   4 the electron transport chain.

Remind yourself exactly where these processes take place in the cell and recall the summary equation for respiration.

TEST YOURSELF 8.5

 Which of these combinations correctly shows oxidation?

	Electrons	Oxygen	Hydrogen
A	loss	gain	loss
B	loss	loss	gain
C	gain	loss	gain
D	gain	gain	loss

What happens during glycolysis?

Phosphorylation of glucose is the first stage in its breakdown. Phosphate groups from ATP are added to glucose and turn it into an unstable phosphorylated compound.

Figure **8.8** shows how the 'fuel' for respiration, which is glucose, is first destabilised by phosphorylation (the addition of phosphate groups), then split in two and oxidised to produce two molecules of pyruvate.

What is produced by glycolysis?

- Two molecules of the 2-carbon compound pyruvate, which goes forward into the link reaction.
- Two molecules of ATP – four ATPs are produced at the end of glycolysis but two are used for phosphorylation so the net production is two.
- Two molecules of NADH + H⁺ (NADH is the acceptor that carries away hydrogen to be used later in ATP formation.)

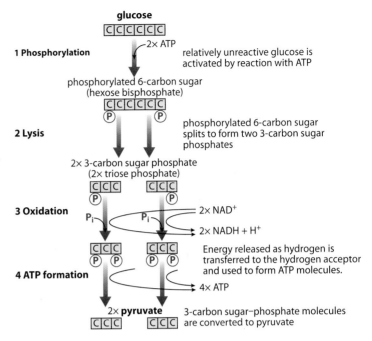

Figure 8.8 The stages of glycolysis. Note that for each molecule of glucose, two molecules of ATP are used and four are formed, so there is a net gain of two ATPs.

NAD^+ is a hydrogen carrier that accepts H atoms, removed during respiration.

TEST YOURSELF 8.6

What is the link reaction in cell respiration?

A pyruvate joining with coenzyme A to produce carbon dioxide and NADH + H⁺

B oxidation of NADH to release electrons and protons

C acetyl coenzyme A combining with a 4-carbon compound to produce a 6-carbon compound and coenzyme A

D acetyl coenzyme A passing through the mitochondrial membrane

> **hint**
>
> Use an acronym such as **P**eople **L**ove **O**utdoor **A**ctivites to help you remember the sequence outlined in Figure **8.7**.

Where do the link reaction and the Krebs cycle take place and what is produced?

The Krebs cycle is an example of a metabolic pathway that involves a cycle (see Section **8.1**).

Notice that:

- carbon dioxide is formed during the cycle
- hydrogen is removed to the hydrogen carriers NAD^+ and FAD^+.

The products of the link reaction and Krebs cycle are:

- eight molecules of NADH + H⁺
- two molecules of $FADH_2$
- two molecules of ATP
- six molecules of carbon dioxide.

These numbers are double those in the diagram because *two* molecules of pyruvate flow round the cycle for every glucose molecule used.

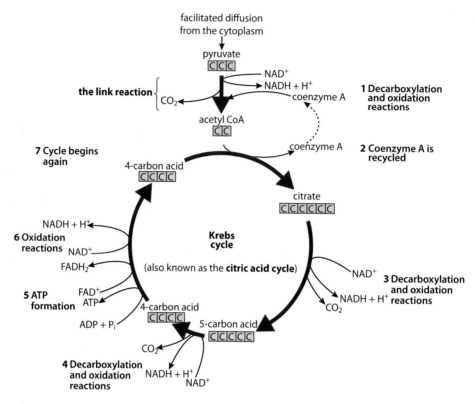

Figure 8.9 A summary of the Krebs cycle.

Table 8.1

Reaction	Location	Key steps
link reaction	matrix of mitochondria	• converts the two molecules of pyruvate to acetyl CoA using coenzyme A • a C atom is removed as CO_2 in a decarboxylation reaction • pyruvate is oxidised by the removal of hydrogen atoms which are carried by NAD^+ which becomes $NADH + H^+$
Krebs cycle (also called the citric acid cycle)	matrix of mitochondria	• acetyl CoA enters the Krebs cycle • acetyl groups are oxidised and coupled with the reduction of hydrogen carriers • coenzyme A is recycled • the remaining 2-carbon compound combines with a 4-carbon compound to form 6-carbon citrate • this 6-carbon compound passes through decarboxylation and oxidation reactions to form a 5-carbon compound, then a 4-carbon compound and finally the 4-carbon compound which can restart the cycle

Where does the electron transport chain (ETC) take place and what does it produce?

- During oxidative phosphorylation, a reaction in the ETC, inorganic phosphate is added to ADP to produce ATP.

- Reactions take place on the inner mitochondrial membrane and the inter-membrane space.

- Electron carriers in the membrane pick up electrons and pass them from one to another in a series of oxidation and reduction reactions.

- The reactions are called the **electron transport chain** because electrons from hydrogen move along it.

Electrons from $NADH + H^+$ are transferred to the first electron carrier and lose energy. Energy is used to pump a proton (H^+) from the matrix to the inter-membrane space and create an electrochemical gradient. By the end of the chain a total of nine protons have been pumped.

Electrons combine with protons and oxygen to form water. The process is called *oxidative* phosphorylation because ATP is produced using energy released by oxidation of $FADH_2$ and $NADH + H^+$.

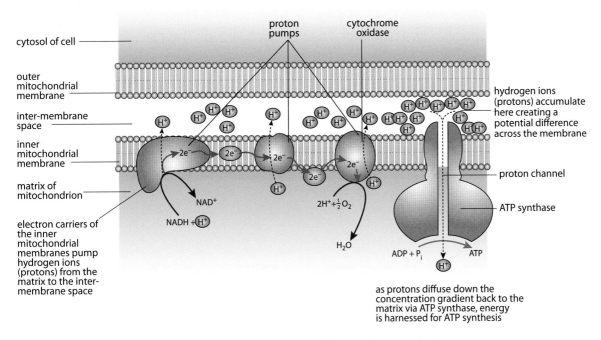

Figure 8.10 The electron transport chain showing oxidative phosphorylation and chemiosmosis.

What is chemiosmosis?

- Protons accumulate in the tiny inter-membrane space and create a concentration gradient.
- Protons flow back into the matrix through a large integral protein that contains the enzyme ATP synthase in a process known as chemiosmosis.
- ATP is produced.
- Three protons produce one molecule of ATP. Each $NADH + H^+$ results in the formation of three ATP molecules.
- $FADH_2$ also supplies electrons further along the ETC. It allows two ATP molecules to be produced.

 Nature of Science. Chemiosmosis theory was proposed by Peter Mitchell in 1961, but it took many years to be accepted because it was a radical departure from the accepted theory of the time. The chemiosmotic theory produced a paradigm shift in biochemistry.

Stage		ATP use	ATP yield
glycolysis	2 ATP used at the start	−2 ATP	
	2 NADH + H⁺		+4 ATP
	ATP formation		+4 ATP
link reaction	2 NADH + H⁺		+6 ATP
Krebs cycle	ATP formation		+2 ATP
	6 NADH + H⁺		+18 ATP
	2 FADH₂		+4 ATP
net energy yield			+36 ATP

Table 8.2 Together, glycolysis, the link reaction and the Krebs cycle yield 36 ATP molecules for each molecule of glucose. Biochemists disagree on the exact ATP yield because energy is used to move pyruvate, phosphate and ADP into the mitochondria. The figures shown in tables like these are approximate.

What is the role of oxygen in respiration?

Oxygen is the final electron acceptor in the ETC. Oxygen is reduced by accepting electrons and by forming a bond with hydrogen to produce water. Removing hydrogen maintains the gradient across the membrane of the mitochondria so that chemiosmosis can continue.

A table like Table **8.3** is a good way to check your knowledge.

TEST YOURSELF 8.7

 Table **8.3** summarises the stages of aerobic respiration. Copy out the table and fill in the gaps.

Table 8.3

Stage	Site	Oxygen needed	Processes
glycolysis			glucose is converted to………. hydrogen is removed and passed to electron carriers
	mitochondrial matrix	yes	pyruvate enters the mitochondrion is decarboxylated, dehydrogenated and combined with coenzyme A to produce acetyl coenzyme A hydrogen is removed and passed to electron carriers
			a cyclical reaction, hydrogen is passed to electron carriers, carbon dioxide is removed and a starting reactant is regenerated
electron transport chain			hydrogen from the previous reactions is split to release electrons these pass through carriers and generate……………. hydrogen is combined with oxygen to release water

☆ Model answer 8.1

Explain the reactions that occur in the matrix of the mitochondrion that are part of aerobic cell respiration. [8]

The link reaction and Krebs cycle take place in the matrix of the mitochondria. These are the second and third stages of respiration. Pyruvate, which enters from the cytoplasm, is converted to acetyl CoA in the link reaction. This is achieved by the action of coenzyme A. Acetyl CoA then enters the Krebs cycle. Oxidation of acetyl groups is coupled to the reduction of hydrogen carriers (NAD and FAD). Coenzyme A is recycled. A 2-carbon compound that is left combines with a 4- carbon compound to form 6-carbon citrate. The 6-carbon compound passes through a series of decarboxylation and oxidation reactions to form first a 5-carbon compound, then a 4-carbon compound and finally the original 4-carbon compound which can restart the cycle. The reduced carriers NADH + H+ and FADH move to the ETC.

8.3 Photosynthesis

Key information you should revise in this section is:

- The structure of a chloroplast is linked to its function.
- There are light-dependent and light-independent reactions in photosynthesis which occur in the thylakoid membranes and in the stroma, respectively.
- The light-dependent reactions result in the production of $NADP^+$ and ATP.
- As photosystems absorb light, high energy electrons are generated for use in the light-dependent reactions.
- Excited electrons are transferred between carriers in the thylakoid membranes and those from photosystem II generate a proton gradient.

- ATP synthase in thylakoids generates ATP using this proton gradient.
- Excited electrons from photosystem I reduce $NADP^+$ to $NADPH + H^+$.
- Triose phosphate is used to produce carbohydrates and regenerate RuBP.
- ATP is used to re-form RuBP.

You should review the basics of this topic in Section **2.9** before starting this section.

TEST YOURSELF 8.8

 Where in the chloroplasts do the light-dependent and light-independent reactions take place? **[2]**

How is the structure of a chloroplast related to its function?

Thylakoid membranes are stacked and folded to increase the surface area available for the **light-dependent reactions**. Each thylakoid is a flattened sac with a small space in the middle where a proton gradient can be established for chemiosmosis to occur. A stack of thylakoids is called a **granum**. The stroma is the liquid that contains the enzymes needed for the **light-independent reactions**.

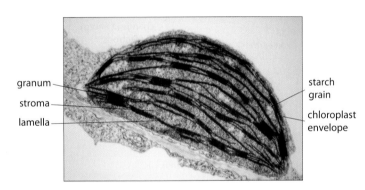

Figure 8.11 Coloured electron micrograph of a chloroplast (×20 000).

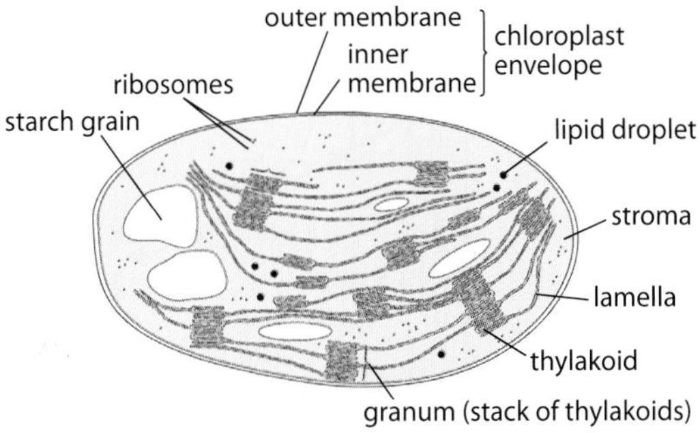

Figure 8.12 Diagram of a chloroplast.

What are the stages of photosynthesis?

The reactions of photosynthesis are summarised by the equation: $6CO_2 + 6H_2O \rightarrow C_6H_{12}O_6 + 6O_2$

Photosynthesis is a complex series of reactions that take place in the chloroplasts but we can divide them into two clear parts:

1 The light-dependent reactions only take place in the presence of light.

2 The light-independent reactions do not require light directly but do require the products of the light-dependent reactions.

TEST YOURSELF 8.9

Figure **8.13** shows a chloroplast.
1 Label the structures numbered 1–5.
2 Which reactions of photosynthesis take place in:
    a structure 2 **b** structure 3.

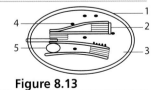

Figure 8.13

What is the light-dependent reaction and what does it produce?

Photosynthetic pigments, including chlorophyll a and b, found on the membranes of the grana, absorb light. Each pigment absorbs light at a slightly different wavelength.

Photosynthetic pigments are combined in two complex groups called photosystems I and II which absorb light energy and use it to boost electrons to a higher energy level. These electrons are called excited electrons.

The stages of the reactions are:

1 Photoactivation – light raises electrons in photosystem II to a higher energy level and electrons are accepted by a carrier protein at the start of the electron transport chain.

2 **Photolysis** – water is split into electrons, protons and oxygen. The electrons are used to replace lost electrons in photosystem II. Oxygen is released as an excretory product.

3 **Photophosphorylation** – electrons travel along the electron transport chain to photosystem I. As they do, they release energy, which pumps protons into the thylakoid interior. Protons flow out via proteins containing ATP synthase so that ATP is formed. This is called photophosphorylation.

4 Reduction of $NADP^+$ – in photosystem I, light excites more electrons which combine with protons in the hydrogen carrier $NADP^+$ to form $NADPH + H^+$. Electrons arriving from photosystem II replace those that are lost.

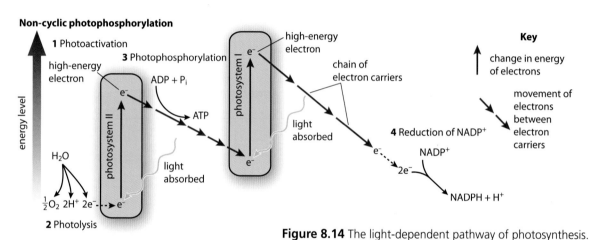

Figure 8.14 The light-dependent pathway of photosynthesis.

TEST YOURSELF 8.10

What do photosystems I and II need light for?

Figure **8.15** shows how the ATP and $NADPH + H^+$ from the light-dependent reactions drive the Calvin cycle and are recycled as $NADP^+$ and $ADP + P_i$ (inorganic phosphate).

What is the difference between cyclic and non-cyclic photophosphorylation?

Table 8.4

Non-cyclic photophosphorylation	Cyclic photophosphorylation
occurs when ATP is produced using energy from excited electrons flowing from photosystem II to photosystem I and then to $NADP^+$	• occurs when light is bright and not a limiting factor • light-independent reactions may occur more slowly than light-dependent reactions, so $NADP^+$ can run out • without an acceptor to take them, electrons from photosystem I rejoin the electron transport chain and are used to generate more ATP

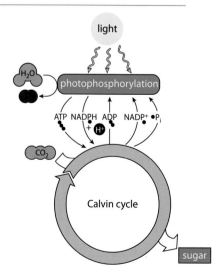

Figure 8.15 An overview of photosynthesis.

What are the two products of the light-dependent reaction?

What are the light-independent reactions and what do they produce?

Light-independent reactions take place in the stroma. They are made up of a series of reactions called the **Calvin cycle** (you may see them called the Calvin–Benson cycle in some books). The NADPH + H⁺ and ATP, formed in the light-dependent stage, supply energy and reducing power for the cycle.

The light-independent reactions fix carbon dioxide.

- Carbon dioxide is combined with a 5-carbon sugar called ribulose bisphosphate (RuBP) to produce two molecules of glycerate-3-phosphate (GP).

Rubisco, is the enzyme involved in this first step of carbon fixation. It catalyses the carboxylation of RuBP.

- GP in the presence of ATP and NADPH + H⁺ is reduced to a 3-carbon sugar triose phosphate (TP).

- Some GP molecules condense to form glucose, sucrose, starch and cellulose.

- Some GP molecules regenerate RuBP to keep the cycle going.

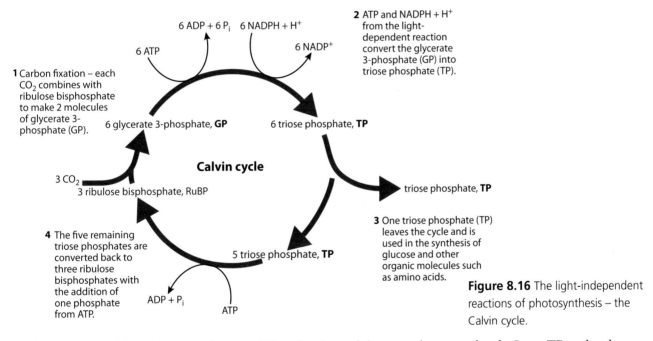

Figure 8.16 The light-independent reactions of photosynthesis – the Calvin cycle.

It takes six turns of the cycle to produce two TP molecules and thus one glucose molecule. Some TP molecules are used to make amino acids and lipids.

 ATP is produced in both chloroplasts and mitochondria. Copy and complete Table **8.5** by placing a tick in the box if the statement about ATP production is true and a cross if the statement is false.

Table 8.5

	True/False
electrons are excited by photons	
electrons pass to carriers	
oxidative photo-phosphorylation is involved	
ATP is produced from ADP and phosphate	
ATP is produced in light and dark	

9

PLANT BIOLOGY (HL)

This chapter covers the following topics:

☐ Transport in the xylem   ☐ Growth

☐ Transport in the phloem   ☐ Reproduction

9.1 Transport in the xylem

Key information you should revise is:

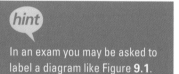

In an exam you may be asked to label a diagram like Figure **9.1**.

- Transpiration occurs as a consequence of gas exchange in the leaf.
- Water is transported from the roots to leaves to replace losses from transpiration.
- The structure of the xylem and cohesive forces allow transport of water to occur.
- Evaporation and adhesive forces lead to tension forces in plant cell walls.
- As mineral ions are taken up by active transport, water enters by osmosis.
- Plants have adaptations to prevent loss of water.

DEFINITION

TRANSPIRATION is the loss of water vapour from the leaves of plants.

XYLEM is the tissue that transports water up the stem of a plant.

Why does gas exchange in a leaf lead to transpiration?

Plant leaves are protected by a waxy cuticle, which prevents water loss, but leaves must have openings (**stomata**) so that carbon dioxide can enter for photosynthesis and the oxygen that is produced by photosynthesis can leave. When stomata open to allow gas exchange, then water vapour evaporates from the sub-stomatal air space through them. This loss of water is **transpiration**.

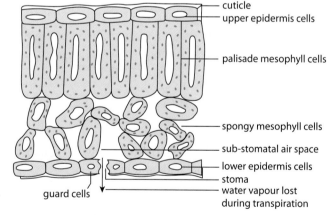

Figure 9.1 Cross section through part of a leaf.

How do plants minimise water loss?

Stomata can open and close because they have guard cells that control the size of the opening. Almost all land plants have guard cells. Some plants have structures that allow them to survive in very dry places.

How does water move from the roots to the leaves?

Water enters guard cells by osmosis so they become turgid and open the stomata. If water leaves guard cells they become flaccid and the stomata close. When stomata close, water loss is minimised.

Figure **9.2** summarises the steps needed for water to move from the roots to the leaves, where it passes out of the stomata. Loss of water vapour from the leaves results in negative pressure (or tension) in the **xylem** vessels.

Not all water leaves the plant, most passes into plant cells where it is used to maintain turgor and for metabolic processes.

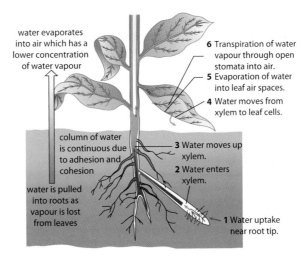

Figure 9.2 The movements of water through a plant: overall, water moves from the soil to the air (from where there is more water to where there is less water).

water evaporates into air which has a lower concentration of water vapour

6 Transpiration of water vapour through open stomata into air.
5 Evaporation of water into leaf air spaces.
4 Water moves from xylem to leaf cells.
column of water is continuous due to adhesion and cohesion
3 Water moves up xylem.
2 Water enters xylem.
water is pulled into roots as vapour is lost from leaves
1 Water uptake near root tip.

Longitudinal section of xylem vessel

walls thickened with lignin
pit
remains of end walls of adjacent xylem elements
lumen
vessel element
10 μm

Figure 9.3 Xylem vessels are not alive and have no plasma membrane, so water can easily move in and out of them.

How is the structure of the xylem important?

The structure of xylem is important for two reasons:

1 It has lignified walls help to support the plant and hold it upright.

2 The thickened walls do not collapse due to the negative pressure of transpiration.

DEFINITION

LIGNIN is a complex polymer that forms part of the xylem walls. It makes up a major part of wood.

How do cohesive forces between water molecules allow water to be transported?

Cohesive forces hold water molecules together because there is hydrogen bonding between them. This means that water is drawn up the xylem in a continuous column. You can revise the properties of water in Section **2.2**.

How do evaporation and adhesive forces lead to tension in cell walls?

The cohesion–tension theory explains how water moves in the xylem. As water evaporates, negative pressure or tension is created in the xylem. Cohesive forces between water molecules hold them together in a column. There are also adhesive forces between the column of water and the walls of the xylem. Water is drawn into the roots and up the xylem as a result of this tension. Imagine drinking through a straw. You create negative pressure as you suck the liquid. Transpiration works on a similar principle.

How are the processes of active uptake of mineral ions and osmosis in roots linked?

Roots absorb mineral ions from the soil in a number of ways including mass flow, facilitated diffusion and **active transport**. Active uptake of minerals leads to an increase in the concentration of solutes inside root cells. As this happens, water is drawn in by osmosis and enters the transpiration stream.

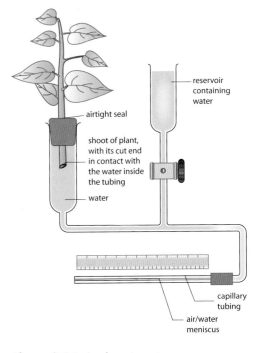

reservoir containing water
airtight seal
shoot of plant, with its cut end in contact with the water inside the tubing
water
capillary tubing
air/water meniscus

Figure 9.4 A simple potometer.

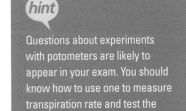

hint

Questions about experiments with potometers are likely to appear in your exam. You should know how to use one to measure transpiration rate and test the effect of temperature and humidity.

Plant biology (HL)

How is transpiration measured in the lab?

A potometer measures water loss from a leafy shoot. As water is lost from the shoot, the meniscus of the water in the capillary tubing moves along the scale and will give an estimate of water loss. The reservoir is used to reset the apparatus.

Various environmental factors can be investigated using a potometer. A fan can be used to simulate wind, temperature of the room can be varied and darkness simulated by covering the plant with a dark material.

▣ Worked example 9.1

The data in Table 9.1 was collected from a potometer.

a State three conditions, which affect transpiration.

b Calculate the rate of water movement in light, moving air at 10 °C.

c Suggest a reason for the high value in dark, still air at 20 °C.

Table 9.1

	Conditions	Time taken for meniscus to travel 100 mm min⁻¹
1	light, moving air, 10 °C	4
2	light, still air, 10 °C	12
3	light, moving air, 20 °C	2
4	light, still air, 20 °C	6
5	dark, still air, 20 °C	120

a From the data and comparing experiments 4 and 5 we can see that light affects transpiration. Comparing experiments 1 and 2 or 3 and 4 shows that wind (moving air) is important and comparing experiments 1 and 3 or 2 and 4 shows that temperature is important.

b Rate is distance/time. In this example 100/4 = 25 mm per minute.

c Transpiration occurs when stomata are open. Stomata open when a plant photosynthesises. In darkness there is no photosynthesis and stomata close, so transpiration is minimal and it takes a long time for water to move along the capillary tube in the experiment.

How are some plants adapted to prevent water loss?

DEFINITIONS

XEROPHYTES are plants that are adapted to living in very dry conditions; they include *Euphorbia spp.* cacti of North America and Africa.

HALOPHYTES are plants that live in saline soils, such as mangrove swamps, marshland and seashores where water is hard to obtain and saline water enters through roots or salt spray on shoots and leaves. Glasswort (*Salicornia* sp.) and the salt marsh grass (*Spartina alterniflora*) are examples of typical halophytes.

Table 9.2 Plants that live in deserts and other dry habitats have a range of strategies that enable them to conserve water.

For cacti these may include	Halophytes may have	Other plants found in sand dunes may have
• swollen stems that can hold water • stomata that open at night • very thick waxy cuticles • tiny leaves or leaves reduced to spines	• reduced leaves or spines • leaves that can be lost when water is unavailable • long roots • sunken stomata • methods of disposing of excess salt	• rolled leaves • stomata in small pits • hairs to trap water vapour • (e.g. marram grass)

Figure **9.5** shows the results of an experiment with two leaves. The leaves were detached from their plants and water loss from them estimated by measuring the change in mass over a period of 4 hours. One plant was a species of bean, which has leaves with thin cuticle and no hairs; the other was a geranium, which has a thicker cuticle and a hairy covering.

1 Suggest why the percentage loss in mass of both plants was high during the first 30 minutes of the experiment.

2 Suggest why the rate of loss decreases in the following 3 hours.

3 Identify which of the leaves came from the geranium and give reasons for your choice.

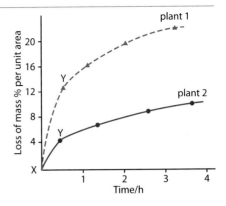

Figure 9.5

9.2 Transport in the phloem

Key information you should revise is:

- Plants transport organic compounds from a source to a sink.
- The incompressibility of water allows plants to transport substances along hydrostatic pressure gradients.
- Active transport is used to load substances into the **sieve tubes** of **phloem** at the source.
- High concentrations of solutes in the phloem at a source lead to water uptake by osmosis.
- High hydrostatic pressure causes the contents of the phloem to flow towards a sink.

DEFINITIONS

PHLOEM is the living tissue that transports food and other substances in the stem of a plant.

TRANSLOCATION is the movement of organic compounds from sources to sinks in the phloem.

hint

Learn to recognise xylem and phloem in photographs like the one in Figure **9.6** and be able to draw the structure of the xylem.

How is the structure of the phloem related to its function?

Phloem has two types of living cells; sieve tubes which are perforated at each end to allow solutes to move through them and **companion cells** which are connected to them.

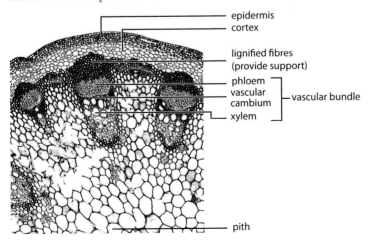

Figure 9.6 Stained micrograph of a transverse section through a stem (× 20) showing the distribution of vascular tissue.

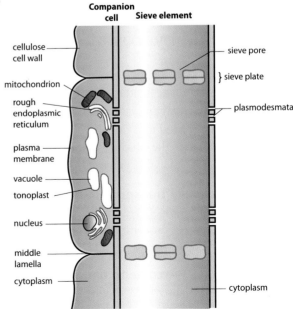

Figure 9.7 A phloem sieve tube element and its companion cell.

Plant biology (HL)

Phloem links the parts of the plant which produce sugars to areas which do not.

 List three differences between xylem and phloem.

What are sources and sinks?

A source is a part of a plant that produces sugars and supplies other substances, such as amino acids. Sinks are areas that need these substances. Plant parts that are sources can sometimes become sinks and vice versa, so the phloem can transport materials in either direction. For example, a potato tuber, when it is newly planted will be a source but later, new potato tubers will be sinks.

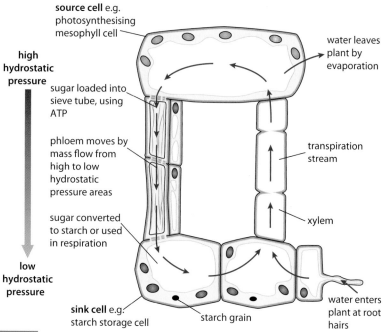

Figure 9.8 Sources, sinks and mass flow in phloem.

Table 9.3

Sources	Sinks
photosynthesising green leaves or stems	growing roots or tubers
tissues in germinating seeds	developing fruits and seeds
tubers (e.g. potato)	new, growing leaves

How are substances moved from a source to a sink?

Substances moved in the phloem are dissolved in a solution called sap. Sugar is carried in the form of sucrose and sap also contains hormones and amino acids.

 What is the most abundant source in a green plant?

How do hydrostatic pressure gradients help plant transport?

HYDROSTATIC PRESSURE is pressure exerted by a liquid.

Sucrose is loaded into the phloem at the source and unloaded at the sink. High concentrations of sucrose cause water to enter the phloem by osmosis and create a pressure gradient, which pushes the sap towards the sink. At the sink the hydrostatic pressure is lower because sugar is removed and the solute concentration is reduced.

Why is active transport important in loading the sieve tubes?

Active transport is used to load organic compounds into the sieve tubes. H^+ ions are actively transported out of the companion cell using ATP. H^+ ions and sucrose then flow through a sucrose transport protein channel into the sieve tube.

How have we come to understand how substances move in the phloem?

Aphids have provided insights into the contents of the phloem and how substances move in the phloem. Aphids 'drink' sap for food. By allowing an aphid to insert its stylet into the phloem then severing the insect from its stylet, sap can be collected and its contents analysed

Nature of Science. The development of radioactively labelled isotopes allowed scientists to trace the route substances take. $^{14}CO_2$ can be introduced into leaves, where it is used for photosynthesis. The labelled products can be traced through the phloem.

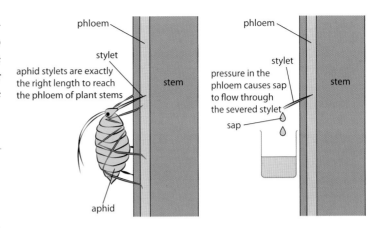

Figure 9.9 Aphid stylets can be used in the analysis of phloem.

TEST YOURSELF 9.4

In experiments with aphid stylets (see Figure **9.9**), it is found that the flow rate of phloem sap is slower closer to the sink than at the source. Suggest why this is so.

9.3 Growth

Key information you should revise is:

- Cells in the meristems are undifferentiated and allow indeterminate growth.
- Mitosis and cell division in the shoot create cells for the elongation of the stem and formation of leaves.
- Growth in the shoot apex in controlled by plant hormones.
- Plants respond to the environment with **tropisms** (growth movements).
- Concentration gradients of auxin are set up by auxin efflux pumps.
- Auxin changes the pattern of gene expression and influences cell growth.

Where are plant meristems and what is special about their cells?

Meristems are the growing regions of a plant where undifferentiated cells undergo cell division. Meristems at the tips of stems and roots are known as **apical meristems**, while lateral meristems are found in the cambium region of the **vascular bundles** (xylem and phloem tissue) of the stem.

Cells in meristems go on to form roots, leaves, buds and flowers. Small pieces of tissue from a meristem can be used to grow genetically identical whole plants. Tissue pieces are grown in sterilised growth medium (containing nutrients and plant hormones). The balance of plant hormones used will determine the range of new cells that develop.

What structures are formed as a result of mitosis in the meristems?

Mitosis and cell division in the shoot apex provide cells, which elongate the stem and develop into leaves. Shoot meristem cells also produce buds and flowers.

In the root the apical meristem cells elongate the roots down into the soil. There are always some meristem cells at shoot and root tips.

Which substances act as plant hormones?

Table 9.4 Plant hormones, also called growth-regulating substances, include auxins and cytokinins that influence the pattern of a plant's growth. Auxins influence growth of roots, development of fruits and growth of the shoot.

Hormone	Site produced	Effects
auxin (e.g. indole-3-acetic acid, IAA)	growing tips of stem and root (apical meristems)	• stimulates elongation of cells in shoots and stems • inhibits elongation of cells in roots • inhibits growth of lateral shoots (apical dominance) • stimulates development of fruits
cytokinins	actively dividing tissue in the meristem	• promotes cell division • promotes development of lateral buds

Plant biology (HL)

How do plant hormones control growth in the shoot apex?

Auxin is produced by apical meristem cells in the terminal bud, where it stimulates growth. Auxin is also transported down the plant where it inhibits growth of lateral buds, if the terminal bud is present. This is known as apical dominance. If the terminal bud is removed, lateral buds will begin to develop. The ratio of auxins and cytokinins determines whether a lateral bud will develop.

What are tropisms and how do they help plants respond to the environment?

> **DEFINITION**
>
> A TROPISM is a directional growth response to a stimulus. Phototropism is growth towards light and growth in response to gravity is a geotropism.

Phototropism turns the stem and leaves towards the light so that photosynthesis can be most efficient. Auxin affects both cell elongation and cell division of the shaded cells.

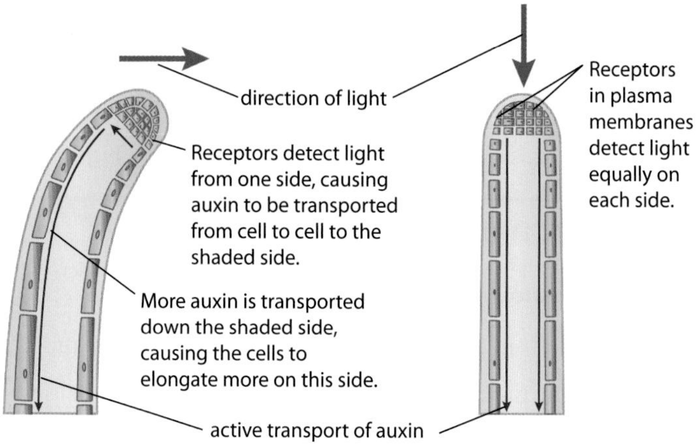

What is an efflux pump and how does it drive plant responses?

Auxin is not produced in all cells and must be moved to where it is needed. It can only move in one direction and its distribution is controlled by auxin efflux pumps. These are special protein channels in the membrane. PIN or pin-formed proteins transport the hormone and control its direction of moment. Where there is more auxin there will be more elongation and growth, so the stem will grow towards light.

direction of light

Receptors detect light from one side, causing auxin to be transported from cell to cell to the shaded side.

More auxin is transported down the shaded side, causing the cells to elongate more on this side.

active transport of auxin

Receptors in plasma membranes detect light equally on each side.

Figure 9.10 Some proteins in the plasma membranes of certain cells in plant shoots are sensitive to light. When light falls on them, they cause auxin to be transported to the shaded side of the shoot. This causes the shoot to bend towards the light.

What is the genetic effect of auxin on plant cells?

Auxin influences growth rates by changing the pattern of gene expression. Certain genes may be activated to produce a rapid response or other sets of genes may be inhibited. In a shoot, auxin promotes cell elongation possibly by stimulating factors such as elastins, which loosen bonds between cellulose fibres in cell walls. It also interacts with cyotkinins, hormones that are produced in the root and promote the development of lateral buds.

When plants are grown by micro-propagation, a growing medium to stimulate root growth must contain ten times more auxin than cytokinin. If the ratio is reduced, shoots will develop.

> **TEST YOURSELF 9.5**
>
> Aubergine plants can be grown in tissue culture. Plant scientists investigated the effects of different concentrations of auxin and cytokinin on the growth of small sections of tissue from the shoot tip of an aubergine plant. Table **9.5** shows the results of the treatment on the growth of the cells. Consider the results and answer the questions.

Table 9.5

Concentration of auxin (μM⁻¹)	Concentration of cytokinin (μM⁻¹)		
	5	25	50
0	no growth	no growth	leaves
1	no growth	leaves	leaves
5	no growth	leaves	leaves and some plantlets
10	undifferentiated cells	leaves and some plantlets	plantlets
15	undifferentiated cells	undifferentiated cells and leaves	undifferentiated cells and leaves

1 Explain how the results provide evidence that the stem tip cells are totipotent. **[2]**
2 Calculate the ratio of auxin to cytokinin that is needed to grow aubergines plants by this method. **[2]**
3 Outline two advantages for plant growers in producing plants from tissue culture rather than from seeds. **[2]**

9.4 Reproduction

Key information you should revise is:

- Flowering involves a change in gene expression in the shoot apex.

- Flowering in many plants is induced in response to the duration of light and dark periods.

- Plants depend on pollination, fertilisation and dispersal of seeds for successful reproduction.

- Most flowering plants use mutualistic relationships with pollinators to aid sexual reproduction.

What structures are found in a flower?

Table 9.6

Structure	Function
sepals	protect the flower bud
petals	usually brightly coloured to attract pollinators
stamens	male sex organs: anthers – produce pollen; filament – holds up the stamen
carpel	female sex organs: stigma – pollen lands, style down which pollen grows; where ovar – contains ovules
nectary	produces nectar

hint

You must be able to draw an animal pollinated flower like Figure **9.11** and identify the structures in slightly different flowers.

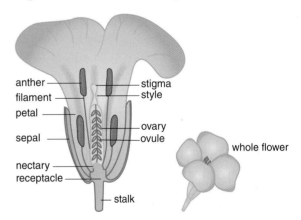

Figure 9.11 Half-flower of wallflower (*Cheiranthus cheiri*). The flower is about 2.5 cm in diameter. It is pollinated by bees and hoverflies and its petals are brightly coloured and fragrant.

What stimulates a plant to produce flowers?

Flowering occurs at specific times of year. It involves a change in the genes in cells of the shoot apex. New proteins are produced which form a reproductive shoot.

Temperature and light are the important triggers for flower production. In most plants the main factor is the length of exposure to light, or daylength. Light either inhibits or promotes activators of genes that transform leaf-producing meristem cells into flower-producing meristem cells.

Plant biology (HL)

What are long and short day plants?

DEFINITION

PHOTOPERIODISM is a plant's response to relative periods of darkness and light.

Long-day plants flower when days are longest and night are short. In the northern hemisphere this is in late spring or early summer (April–June) and in the southern hemisphere September–December. Examples of long-day plants include carnations and clover.

Short-day plants flower as nights become longer and days are shorter. In the northern hemisphere this is during late summer or autumn (fall). Examples include chrysanthemum and coffee.

The length of darkness is the key to flowering, not the time exposed to light. Plants respond to darkness with a leaf pigment called **phytochrome** that exists in two forms P_r and P_{fr}.

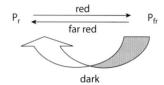

Figure 9.12 Phytochrome reaction.

Active P_{fr} is produced from inactive P_r during daylight hours using red light (600nm). In darkness the reverse reaction slowly occurs.

During long days higher levels of P_{fr} promote flowering in long day plants.

P_{fr} inhibits flowering in short day plants but when nights are long, sufficient P_{fr} is removed to allow them to flower.

P_{fr} is the active form of phytochrome and receptor proteins in the cytoplasm binds to it. This promotes transcription of the genes needed for flowering.

TEST YOURSELF 9.6

 Two plants A and B are used to investigate the control of flowering. Plant A is a long-day plant that flowers only if daylength is greater than 14 hours. Plant B is a short-day plant that flowers only if daylength is less than 15.5 hours. Both plants will flower in a regime of 15 hours light and 9 hours darkness.

1 Which plant would flower if the two plants were exposed to 8 hours of light and 16 hours of darkness? **[1]**

When plant B is grown in 8 hours of light and16 hours of darkness but with a flash of white light half way through the dark period, different results are obtained.

2 Name the form of phytochrome present in the light period. **[1]**

3 State what happens to this form of phytochrome in darkness. **[1]**

How are pollination, fertilisation and seed dispersal essential for plant reproduction?

DEFINITIONS

POLLINATION is the transfer of pollen from the anthers to the stigma of another flower.

FERTILISATION is the fusion of the nuclei of a pollen grain (male gamete) and ovule (female gamete).

SEED DISPERSAL is the transport of seeds to a place away from the parent plant to reduce competition between them.

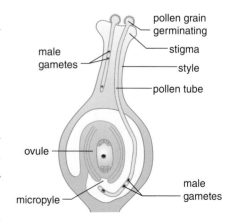

Figure 9.13 Fertilisation of an ovule in the ovary of a plant.

All three processes are essential for successful reproduction. **Pollen** is transferred from one flower to another by insects, birds, bats and other animals. Some plants such as grasses are wind pollinated.

Once pollen has arrived on the stigma of the correct species of plant, a pollen tube grows down the style to the ovule. The male nucleus passes down the tube to reach the female nucleus. Fertilised ovules develop into seeds.

Seeds are dispersed in many different ways including:

- being eaten by birds or animals, passing through their digestive systems, and then being deposited some distance away

- collected by animals e.g. nuts which are buried by squirrels

- explosion of dry seeds, such as those in the pea family

- feathery or winged structures that can be carried in the wind.

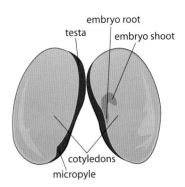

Figure 9.14 Two halves of a broad bean seed showing the main parts of a dicotyledonous plant seed.

Table 9.7

Part	Function
testa (seed coat)	protects dormant seed
micropyle	small hole in testa where water enters for germination
cotyledons	embryo leaves (in some plants) and food store (endoderm)
embryo root	emerges to form first root
embryo shoot	emerges to become first shoot

TEST YOURSELF 9.7

In flowering plants, which of the following helps seed dispersal?

   A bees   **B** pollen   **C** germination   **D** mammals

> **hint**
>
> You must be able to draw the structure of a typical seed, such as the broad bean and annotate it with the functions of the parts.

What is a mutualistic relationship and is one established between a plant and its pollinator?

DEFINITION

A **MUTUALISTIC RELATIONSHIP** is a close association between a pollinator and plant that benefits them both.

When a bee visits a flower, it gains the benefit of food in the form of nectar. The flower benefits as it receives pollen to fertilise its ovules. Pollen may be carried on the hairy back or sides of a pollinator. Different plants have different adaptations to establish relationships with pollinators. These may be colours, shape of flowers or scents that attract specific insects or animals. For example, elongated flowers of some tropical trees match perfectly with the long beaks of the hummingbirds that extract nectar from them.

📑 Annotated exemplar answer 9.1

Explain the difference between pollination and fertilisation. **[3]**

This is a commonly asked question, don't confuse the two terms.

Pollination is the transfer of pollen from one flower to another. If pollen is transferred to a flower of the same plant the process is called self-pollination, if it falls on the flower of a different plant of the same species it is cross-pollination.

You will lose marks if you don't mention the anthers (of one flower) and stigma (of another). The question doesn't ask about cross-pollination so this could be left out.

Fertilisation, on the other hand, is meeting of male and female gametes. It takes place in the ovary after a male nucleus has moved down the pollen tube to fuse with the female gamete. (2/3)

This is too vague. To gain all the marks you must say 'Fertilisation is the fusion of the nuclei of...'.

It is good to say where fertilisation happens, and to include a comparative phrase to highlight the difference.

GENETICS AND EVOLUTION (HL)

This chapter covers the following topics:

☐ **Meiosis**   ☐ **Inheritance**   ☐ **Gene pools and speciation**

10.1 Meiosis

Key information you should revise is:

- Chromosomes are replicated in interphase before meiosis.
- Crossing over is the exchange of genetic material between non-sister homologous chromatids.
- Crossing over produces new combinations of alleles in the cells produced after meiosis.
- Formation of chiasmata can result in exchange of alleles.
- Homologous chromosomes separate in meiosis I.
- Sister chromatids separate in meiosis II.
- Independent assortment of genes is due to random orientation of homologous pairs of chromosomes during meiosis I.

DEFINITION

MEIOSIS is a division of the nucleus which produces cells containing half the number of chromosomes of the parent cell. It is essential for the formation of haploid gametes and it produces genetic variety.

When do chromosomes replicate for meiosis?

DNA is replicated during interphase in a part of the cell cycle called the S phase. Each chromosome then consists of two chromatids.

DEFINITION

A **CHROMATID** is one of the two copies of a chromosome after it has replicated and before the centromeres have separated.

How do chromosomes behave during meiosis?

Before you begin to revise this section, review meiosis in Section **3.3**.

- During prophase I chromosomes shorten and coil.
- Homologous pairs come together to form a bivalent – maternal and paternal chromosomes are next to each other. (In some books you may see bivalents referred to as tetrads because they are composed of four chromatids).
- At this point non-sister chromatids may touch and break at a region called a **chiasma**.
- During metaphase I bivalents line up on the equator and are separated.
- During meiosis II chromatids are separated.

TEST YOURSELF 10.1

Which processes always occur in meiosis but not in mitosis?

I formation of chiasmata

II recombination of genes

III separation of homologous chromosomes

A I and II only   **C** I and III only

B II and III only   **D** I, II and III

What is crossing over?

DEFINITION

CROSSING OVER is the exchange of genetic material between homologous chromosomes during meiosis.

Homologous pairs of chromosomes (one maternal and one paternal) contain the same genes but may have different alleles. As they line up together during prophase I each chromosome is made up of two chromatids. Non-sister chromatids may touch and break and the two segments re-join at the corresponding position on the other chromatid.

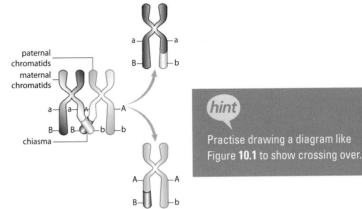

Figure 10.1

hint

Practise drawing a diagram like Figure **10.1** to show crossing over.

What is a chiasma and how does crossing over produce new combination of alleles?

DEFINITION

A **CHIASMA** (plural chiasmata) is the point where chromatids break and then rejoin at the point of crossing over in prophase 1.

Figure **10.1** shows how genetic material is exchanged and because the maternal and paternal chromatids contained different alleles, a new combination of alleles is now present in each of the two chromatids.

When do homologous chromosomes separate?

During metaphase I the bivalents (pairs of homologous chromosomes) line up together on the equator and are pulled apart by the spindle apparatus.

When do sister chromatids separate?

Sister chromatids are separated during meiosis II (see Section **3.3**). Gametes that are formed will contain either a paternal or maternal chromatid. Sister chromatids are separated but it is unlikely they will be identical because of crossing over.

How do alleles and genes become assorted during meiosis I?

Meiosis produces an assortment of the parent's alleles and genes in the gametes that form. This is a result of several factors. If we consider two pairs of chromosomes:

hint

Test yourself **10.2.2** could form part of a short-answer question in an exam.

- During metaphase I paternal chromosomes could both line up on one side of the equator with the maternal ones on the other side. In this case two of the gametes formed would contain only paternal chromosomes and two only maternal chromosomes.

- Paternal chromosomes could line up with maternal and paternal chromosomes on both sides of the equator. Then all four gametes would contain a mixture of maternal and paternal chromosomes.

With just two chromosomes several different combinations are produced. In humans that have 23 pairs of chromosomes, the total number of possible combinations is over 8 million.

What does independent assortment mean?

This term is used in connection with Gregor Mendel's work on inheritance of unlinked genes. Mendel's law of independent assortment says that 'When gametes are formed the separation of one pair of alleles into the new cells is independent of the separation of any other pair of alleles.' Independent assortment of genes is due to random orientation of homologous pairs of chromosomes during meiosis I. Independent assortment does not take place if genes are linked (see Section **10.2**).

Imagine body cells containing one pair of alleles for red hair / not red hair and another for blue color blindness / normal blue vision.

Chromosomes from the father are shown in blue and from the mother in red.

At metaphase I, bivalents for chromosomes 4 and 7 could align like this ...

chromosome 4

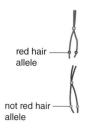

red hair allele

not red hair allele

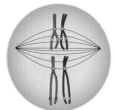

The result of this is that red hair and blue color blindness genes would be inherited together

or they could align like this ...

chromosome 7

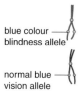

blue colour blindness allele

normal blue vision allele

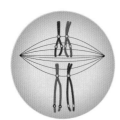

The result of this is that red hair and normal blue vision genes would be inherited together.

Figure 10.2 How independent assortment produces variation, diagram shows just two chromosome combinations.

TEST YOURSELF 10.2

1 The seven characteristics of pea plants studied by Mendel displayed independent assortment. What does this show?

  A all seven pairs of alleles were on a single set of homologous chromosomes

  B the seven different pairs of alleles were on the same chromosomes

  C the seven different pairs of alleles behaved as if they were on different chromosomes

  D each parent plant had two alleles for each characteristic, but only one passed to the offspring

2 Explain what is meant by the statement 'chiasmata disrupt linkage groups' **[3]**

3 Outline how meiosis compensates for fertilisation **[2]**

10.2 Inheritance

Key information you should revise is:

- That unlinked genes segregate independently as a result of meiosis.

- How to predict the outcomes of dihybrid crosses using Punnett grids.

- That gene loci on the same chromosome are said to be linked.

- **Variation** in a species may be **continuous** or **discrete**.

- Phenotypes of polygenic characteristics tend to show continuous variation.
- How the chi-squared test is used to determine if the differences between observed and expected frequency distributions are significant.

How are unlinked genes defined and how do they segregate as a result of meiosis?

Unlinked genes are genes found on different chromosomes. They segregate independently at meiosis. Segregation is the separation of the two alleles of every gene that occurs during meiosis. Independent assortment means that the alleles of one gene segregate independently of the alleles of other unlinked genes.

What is a dihybrid cross?

A dihybrid cross is one involving two different genes. We can investigate how the two genes are inherited. Mendel carried out dihybrid crosses with the garden pea using pure breeding peas (homozygous for a chosen characteristic). In one trial he crossed peas with round, yellow seeds with peas that had wrinkled, green seeds.

Round is dominant to wrinkled and yellow is dominant to green, and Mendel observed that all the plants in the F_1 generation had wrinkled, yellow seeds.

He allowed these plants to self-pollinate and observed four phenotypes of seeds in the F_2 generation: round, yellow seeds; wrinkled green; round green; and wrinkled yellow. Worked example **10.1** shows how this cross is drawn in a Punnett grid.

⚙ Worked example 10.1

1 Name the two alleles: R= round, r = wrinkled and Y = yellow, y = green.

2 The round yellow seeds are homozygous (pure-breeding) so their genotype is RRYY. The wrinkled, green seeds are also homozygous and their genotype is rryy.

3 Draw a Punnett grid to show the cross.

4 Now consider the cross between the round, yellow seeded plants from the F_1 generation with the genotype RrYy. The possible combinations of alleles are:

  a RY, Ry, rY and ry

  b This time the Punnett grid must have 16 possible combinations:

Check the grid and remember that any plant with a R allele will have round seeds and any plant with a Y will have yellow seeds. We can see that the ratio of phenotypes Mendel observed was: 9 yellow round; 3 green wrinkled; 3 yellow wrinkled; 1 green wrinkled.

		Gametes from round yellow seeds (RY)	
Gametes from wrinkled green seeds (ry)			RY
	ry		RrYy Round, yellow seeds

Gametes	RY	Ry	rY	ry
RY	RRYY	RRYy	RrYY	RrYy
Ry	RRYy	RRyy	RrYy	Rryy
rY	RrYY	RrYy	rrYY	rrYy
ry	RrYy	Rryy	rrYy	rryy

What are linked genes?

Genes are said to be linked if they are found on the same chromosome. In dihybrid crosses, linked genes do not produce Mendelian ratios.

In dihybrid crosses genotypes are written in the form AABB but for linked genes a different notation is used. The genotype is always written with horizontal lines to signify that the two genes are on the same chromosome.

hint

You may be asked to construct or interpret Punnett grids like the ones shown here.

Here in Figure **10.3** E is linked to t and e is linked to t.

Autosomal gene linkage refers to genes on the same autosome (non-sex chromosome) and sex-linked genes are found on the X chromosome.

How do linked genes segregate at meiosis?

Since linked genes are on the same chromosome, it follows that they will be inherited together because they move together to the same pole when the cell divides during meiosis. Linked genes are not inherited independently and can give a variety of different ratios.

Figure 10.3

Worked example 10.2

In *Drosophila*, red eyes (R) are dominant to purple (r) and long wings (N) are dominant to short wings (n). A fly that had red eyes and long wings was crossed with a fly that had purple eyes and short wings. The two genes are linked on the same chromosome.

1 The genotypes of the two flies are:

$\dfrac{R\ N}{R\ N}$ and $\dfrac{r\ n}{r\ n}$

2 The gametes produced by the two flies are all RN, and all rn, respectively.

3 A cross between them produces flies with the genotype in the F₁

$\dfrac{R\ N}{r\ n}$

These F₁ flies all have the phenotype red eyes and long wings.

4 If two flies with heterozygous genotype are then crossed, the results can be shown in the following Punnett grid.

Gametes from parent 1 = RN and rn

Gametes from parent 2 = RN and rn

		Gametes from parent 1	
		RN	**rn**
Gametes from parent 2	RN	$\dfrac{R\ N}{R\ N}$	$\dfrac{R\ N}{r\ n}$
	rn	$\dfrac{R\ N}{r\ n}$	$\dfrac{r\ n}{r\ n}$

In the F₂ generation the ratio of phenotypes is 3 red eye long wing: 1 purple eye, short wing.

Notice that the 3:1 ratio is what we see in a monohybrid cross and because only one chromosome is involved here, it appears in this type of cross too.

How can recombinants in crosses, involving linked genes be identified?

DEFINITION

RECOMBINANTS are offspring in which the genetic information has been rearranged by crossing over so that · phenotypes that are different from the parents are produced.

Crossing over can occur between chromatids that carry linked genes in the same way as for unlinked genes. It will also lead to new combinations of alleles in gametes produced. In the diagram four types of gamete MN, mn, Mn and mN are possible but the chances of a chiasma forming between the two loci is very small.

Crossing over will only occur in some of the chromatids so only small numbers of offspring will carry the new, non-parental combination of alleles.

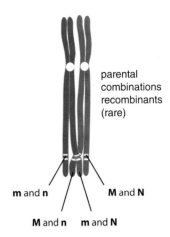

parental combinations
recombinants (rare)

m and **n**   **M** and **N**
M and **n**   **m** and **N**

Figure 10.4 Single chiasma, demonstrating the recombinant genotypes that can be formed.

🖾 Worked example 10.3

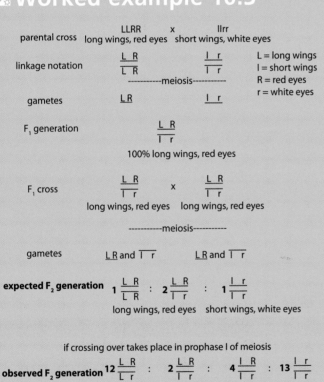

Nature of Science. This example is similar to the one that T. H. Morgan used when he bred the fruit fly drosophila as he studied the inheritance of mutations. Morgan's observations that there were some crosses that did not follow Mendel's rules led to his hypothesis that genes could be linked.

If crossing over takes place in some of the chromatids, only small numbers of offspring will carry the new, non-parental combination of alleles. The proportion of non-parental genotypes increases with the physical distance between alleles.

hint

Chi-squared tests are used to work out whether expected and observed frequencies are significant in genetics.

Figure 10.5

What is a polygenic characteristic?

DEFINITIONS

DISCRETE VARIATION involves characteristics that cannot be measured, for which there are clear distinguishable categories of variation. Examples include blood groups and left or right-handedness.

CONTINUOUS VARIATION is not categorical and is a product of many genes. It is possible to make a range of measurements of continuous variation from one extreme to another.

A **polygenic** characteristic is controlled by two or more genes that produce a number of different phenotypes. Examples include human height and skin colour or the mass of seeds produced by a broad bean plant. If many genes are involved the distribution of the characteristic follows a normal distribution with a range from one extreme to the other with the greatest number of individuals being found at the median value. A normal distribution produces a bell-shaped curve.

Polygenic characteristics can also be influenced by environmental factors, such as diet.

TEST YOURSELF 10.3

 Why is it often difficult to identify how some characteristics are inherited in humans?

    A the environment varies very little   **C** mutation rates are high in humans

    B inheritance may be polygenic   **D** most human genes are linked

---

How is the chi-squared test used in genetic problems?

The chi-squared (χ^2) test is used to test whether the differences between observed results are significantly different from the expected results. Slight differences can be attributed to sampling counting errors but if the differences are statistically significant characteristics may be due to a lack of independent assortment or another reason. The greater the calculated value of chi-squared, the greater the difference between observed and expected results.

DEFINITION

A **NULL HYPOTHESIS** proposes that there is no statistically significant difference between two measured sets of observations.

Step 1 is to state a null hypothesis that there is no significant difference between the observed and expected results

Step 2 is to place your results in a table, Table **10.1**

Step 3 is to calculate the expected frequencies (*E*) using observed values and the actual total.

Imagine you are expecting a 3:1 ratio between green and yellow seeds and a total of 7324 seeds are produced, you would expect ¼ of these to be yellow and ¾ to be green so you can calculate the expected result.

Table 10.1

Phenotype	Observation (*O*)	Expected (*E*)
green	5474	¾ × 7324 = 5493
yellow	1850	¼ × 7324 = 1831
TOTAL	7324	7324

Step 4 is to work out the degrees of freedom – the number of categories being considered minus 1. We use this to select the correct line of the chi-squared values table.

Step 5 is to calculate the value of χ^2 (chi-squared) using the formula in Worked example **10.4**.

Step 6 is to look up the result in the chi-squared table at the 0.05 (or 5%) probability level. This level is used for biological investigations.

🔲 Worked example 10.4

If we want to test the results of a cross where the parental genotypes are AABB and aabb. We know that the offspring of this dihybrid cross will all have the genotype AaBb in the F_1 generation. (Let A = tall, a = short and B = blue, b = white)

This F_1 generation produces a 9:3:3:1 ratio in the F_2 generation. This is our *expected* number. When an experiment is carried out we must record our *observed* result. We must use the test to check whether our observations are consistent with our expectations. We can use these data we calculate the chi-squared value using the formula:

$$\chi^2 = \sum \frac{(O-E)^2}{E}$$

Where O = observation and E = expectation

A Punnett Grid like this one is drawn to work out the genotypes and phenotypes of the offspring.

Gametes	AB	Ab	aB	ab
AB	AABB	AABb	AaBB	AaBb
Ab	AABb	AAbb	AaBb	Aabb
aB	AaBB	AaBb	aaBB	aaBb
ab	AaBb	Aabb	aaBb	aabb

Then we can calculate the χ^2 values as in Table **10.2** to set out the results.

Table 10.2

Phenotype	Tall and blue	Tall and white	Short and blue	Short and white	Total
Observed numbers (O)	40	20	16	4	80
Expected numbers (E)	45	15	15	5	80
$O - E$	−5	5	1	−1	0
$(O - E)^2$	25	25	1	1	
$\dfrac{(O - E)^2}{E}$	0.56	1.67	0.07	0.20	$\chi^2 = 2.50$

The chi-squared value is 2.50

The degrees of freedom are $(n - 1) = (4 - 1) = 3$

Using Table **10.2**, we find that a χ^2 value of 7.82 or greater is necessary to reject the null hypothesis. So we reject our null hypothesis and accept that our results are consistent with the expected ratio.

◫Worked example 10.5

In the Peruvian sunflower, yellow petals (g) are recessive to the normal colour (G). When a yellow plant was crossed with a normal colour plant, 55 normal offspring were produced and the other 45 plants had yellow petals.

A hypothesis to explain these results is that the normal parent was heterozygous. The chi-squared value calculated is 1.0. The table shows the probability values.

What is the correct response to the hypothesis?

A Reject the hypothesis because the probability is less than 0.05

B Accept the hypothesis because the chi-squared value is less than 5.99

C Reject the hypothesis because there is not enough information

D Accept the hypothesis because the chi-squared value is less than 3.84

Table 10.3 Example of a chi-squared table.

	χ^2 values			
Probablility	0.99	0.950	0.05	0.01
Degrees of freedom				
1	0.000	0.004	3.84	6.64
2	0.020	0.103	5.99	9.21
3	0.115	0.352	7.82	11.35

The first step is to check the degrees of freedom. As the offspring are either normal colour or yellow there are two classes so the degrees of freedom is (number of classes – 1) = (2 – 1) = 1 and we use the top line of Table **10.3** for our answer.

Now examine each answer in turn.

- We can reject answer A because the chi-squared test uses a specific degree of freedom not simply a probability level.

- We can reject answer B because this value appears in the incorrect row for degrees of freedom, the examiner has included it to check we understand this.

- Answer C is incorrect because we have all the information needed, we know there are two characteristics, and we know the number of offspring.

- Answer D is correct. 3.84 appears in Table **10.3** on the correct row for the degrees of freedom and at the 0.05 probability level – the one used for biological tests.

TEST YOURSELF 10.4

 In Drosophila grey body is dominant to black body and normal wings are dominant to vestigial wings. A researcher expects the characteristics to appear in a Mendelian ratio of 9:3:3:1 but obtained the results shown in Table **10.4** (O = number of flies) when heterozygous flies were crossed.

Carry out a chi-squared test to see whether the results are different from the expected ratio.

1 State a null hypothesis. **[1]**
2 Calculate the values of (O – E) and (O – E)² and insert them into Table **10.4**. **[2]**

Table 10.4

Phenotype	Observed (O)	Expected (E)	(O – E)	(O – E)²
grey/normal wing	180			
black/vestigial wing	52			
grey/vestigial wing	14			
black/ normal wing	11			

3 Calculate the value of chi-squared. **[2]**

4 State the number of degrees of freedom. **[1]**

5 The critical value of chi-squared with this number of degrees of freedom is 11.35. Should you accept or reject the null hypothesis? Explain your answer. **[3]**

6 Suggest an explanation for the observed results. **[1]**

10.3 Gene pools and speciation

Key information you should revise is:

- A gene pool is defined as all the genes and their different alleles that are present in an interbreeding population.
- As species evolve, allele frequencies in a population changes.
- Reproductive isolation of populations may be temporal, spatial or behavioural.
- Speciation due to the divergence of isolated populations can be gradual.
- Speciation may occur abruptly.

Check you understand the definition of a **species** in Chapter **4** and the ideas about evolution in Chapter **5**.

DEFINITIONS

EVOLUTION is defined as the cumulative change in heritable characteristics of a population.

A **SPECIES** is a group of potentially interbreeding individuals.

A **GENE POOL** consists of all the alleles that make up the heritable characteristics of a population of the same species.

How do allele frequencies change as a species evolves?

DEFINITION

ALLELE FREQUENCY is the frequency of a particular allele as a proportion of all the alleles of that gene in a population.

Allele frequencies change because they depend on the reproductive success of the individuals. If a single allele changes in frequency over a long period of time we can say that the population has evolved. Any process that allows favourable alleles to be passed on or prevents the transmission of unfavourable alleles can contribute to evolution.

Evolution can happen if:

- mutations produce new alleles
- selection pressure favours one allele over another
- there are barriers to the flow of genes between two populations.

What is reproductive isolation and what causes it?

A population can become isolated from other populations of the same species so that they no longer interbreed. This can happen when:

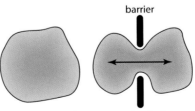

single gene pool

gene pool splits into two regions but gene flow between them means they remain a single species

gene pool separated into two regions and gene flow between them prevented – differences in selection pressure may result in different allele frequencies in each new gene pool so they become genetically different

Figure 10.6

- Physical barriers such as mountains or water separate them.
- Temporal barriers mean that two populations breed at different times.
- Behavioural isolation that occurs when the mating behaviour of one population is no longer recognised or compatible with the other.

The result of reproductive isolation is that the **gene pool** is divided and this may lead to the development of new species if the two groups evolve separately.

Notice that in Test yourself **10.5** the command word is 'outline', so you need to make two points clearly and concisely for each of your answers.

TEST YOURSELF 10.5

 Outline why these statements are not correct.
1 Cross-pollination enlarges the gene pool of a species. **[2]**
2 Different phenotypes are always the result of different genotypes. **[2]**

What is the difference between sympatric and allopatric speciation?

Sympatric **speciation** occurs within the same geographic area (i.e. without geographic separation).

Allopatric speciation occurs in different geographic areas (i.e. with geographic separation).

How quickly does speciation occur?

Speciation due to the divergence of two separated populations can be gradual with changes slowly accumulating over many generations and eventually leading to new species. This view, known as gradualism, was proposed by Charles Darwin but the lack of intermediate forms of organisms in the fossil record has led to an alternative explanation known as punctuated equilibrium.

Punctuated equilibrium proposes that long periods of stability can be punctuated by periods of rapid change. Since the driving force for evolution is selection pressure, changes may not occur at all in a stable environment; the population will remain in equilibrium. A sudden dramatic change in the environment can lead to rapid speciation.

Rapid change is most common in short-lived species, such as prokaryotes and invertebrates, which have short generation times.

How can we identify examples of directional, stabilising and disruptive selection?

As the environment influences a species, some individuals will have characteristics that are favourable and their numbers will tend to increase. We can observe three types of selection occurring in different situations, as shown in Figure **10.7**.

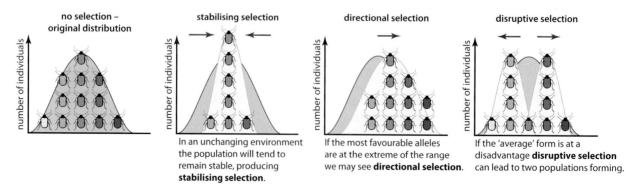

Figure 10.7 Three types of selection occurring in different situations, stabilising, directional and disruptive.

What is polyploidy and how has speciation in the genus *Allium* occurred by polyploidy?

A **POLYPLOIDY** organism has more than two sets of homologous chromosomes.

Polyploidy occurs when sets of chromosomes are not completely separated during cell division so that one cell receives extra sets of chromosomes.

Polyploid organisms with three sets of chromosomes are known as triploid (3n), with four sets tetraploid (4n) and so on.

Polyploidy can occur if:

- species hybridise
- chromosomes duplicate ready for meiosis but the division of the cell doesn't happen
- during mitosis, a cell fails to divide after telophase; it will become tetraploid and will be able to undergo meiosis to form fertile gametes.

Polyploidy occurs most commonly in plants. A polyploid plant can reproduce by self pollination or by crossing with other polyploids, but will be reproductively isolated from the original population.

Allium oleraceum is field garlic, a plant that is present throughout Europe, and has four different levels of polyploidy. Today the original diploid species only exists in a small part of southern Europe but tetraploid (4n) and pentaploids (5n) are far more common. Different ploidy levels occur in different areas and the new characteristics each group of plants have seem to allow them to survive in slightly different habitats.

The genus *Allium* also includes leeks, onions and chives. Many reproduce asexually.

TEST YOURSELF 10.6

 Figure **10.8** shows three types of natural selection. The shaded areas show the individuals in the population that are being selected against.

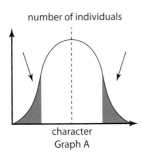 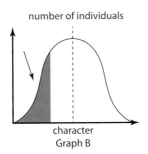 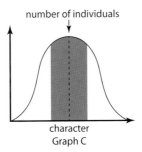

character
Graph A

character
Graph B

character
Graph C

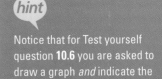
hint

Notice that for Test yourself question **10.6** you are asked to draw a graph *and* indicate the mean; do not forget this second requirement.

Figure 10.8

1 Name the three types of selection shown in graphs A, B and C. **[3]**
2 Draw new graphs on these axes to show the distribution of phenotypes after selection has occurred for several generations.
3 Show the mean in each case. **[3]**

📝 Annotated exemplar answer 10.1

Two closely related species of palm *Howea belmoreana* and *Howea fosteriana* are found together on a very small island about 500 km off the coast of Australia. Both species are diploid ($2n = 32$) and both are wind pollinated. Hybrids are seldom found. Male and female flowers are produced on different trees and mature at different times. Figure **10.9** shows the flowering patterns for each species (left) and the distribution of the plants in relation to soil pH and altitude (right).

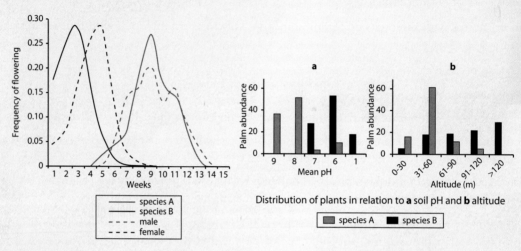

Distribution of plants in relation to **a** soil pH and **b** altitude

Figure 10.9

a Explain how the two species of palm have become reproductively isolated. **[3]**

b Outline the evidence that suggests sympatric speciation has taken place without the separation of the two species by a physical barrier (allopatric speciation). **[2]**

a Isolating mechanisms have prevented gene flow between the two species as they do not hybridise. The two species show temporal isolation in their reproduction. Male plants of each species release pollen at different times and female parts of the other species are not ready to receive pollen at those times. This timing of reproduction separates the two species and prevents hybridisation.

(2/3)

This answer is good but does not mention the data on pH and altitude. When a question contains two graphs make sure you use them both.

Adding the following would gain full marks:

'The species are found in slightly different habitats which also makes gene flow less likely.

Soil pH – *H. fosteriana* is more abundant in soil of pH 8–9 and *H. belmoreana* is more abundant at pH 5–7.

Altitude – *H. fosteriana* occurs mostly at altitudes between 30 and 60 m. *H. belmoreana* is found at all altitudes but is more common above 90 m.'

b Sympatric speciation occurs without geographic isolation. These two species live on the same small island so this is likely to be an example of sympatric speciation because of the limited space for geographic separation by a barrier.

(1/2)

The answer could be enhanced by adding:

'The differences in the habitats and the different times of reproduction of the two species could have separated them and prevented gene flow between them. Different reproduction times could have arisen by mutation.'

ANIMAL PHYSIOLOGY (HL)

This chapter covers the following topics:

☐ Antibody production and vaccination   ☐ The kidney and osmoregulation

☐ Movement   ☐ Sexual reproduction

11.1 Antibody production and vaccination

Key information you should revise is:

- Every organism has unique molecules on its cell surfaces.
- Some pathogens can cross the species barrier, others cannot.
- In mammals, B lymphocytes are activated by T lymphocytes and multiply to form a clone of memory cells.
- Antibodies are secreted by **plasma cells** and help to destroy pathogens.
- White blood cells secrete histamine in response to allergens.
- Histamines cause allergic reactions.
- Immunity depends on the persistence of memory cells in the body.
- Vaccines contain antigens that trigger immunity but do not cause disease.
- Hybridoma cells are created by fusing a tumour cell and an antibody-producing plasma cell.
- Hybridoma cells are used to produce monoclonal antibodies.

Check Section **6.3** and review your knowledge of antibodies, antigens and antibiotics.

> **DEFINITION**
>
> **IMMUNITY** is resistance of the body to invasion by pathogens or any cell which is not recognised as being part of the body.

Immunity is possible because an animal's body can recognise cells that are its own 'self' and distinguish them from those which are not 'non-self'.

How does the body recognise cells which are not its own?

> **DEFINITION**
>
> An **ANTIGEN** is a 'foreign' molecule that can cause an immune response.

Each organism has its own unique molecules on the surfaces of its cells. Proteins on the plasma membrane, and other large polysaccharides, are called antigens and can be recognised by certain leucocytes (a type of white blood cell) found circulating in our blood. These white blood cells can recognise the body's own cells by antigens present on the cell surfaces and distinguish them from cancer cells, transplanted tissues or organs, pathogens such as bacteria and parasites, and pollen grains. Antigens may also be present in the secretions or toxins of a pathogen.

11

Animal physiology (HL)

Why do some pathogens cause disease in only one species?

Measles, gonorrhoea and polio are diseases that only affect humans. But *Shigella* bacteria cause dysentery in both humans and baboons, but not chimpanzees.

A species may not be susceptible to a disease because:

- It does not have the correct receptors on its cells for the pathogen to bind.
- There is a body temperature difference e.g. frogs are resistant to anthrax and tuberculosis because their temperature is lower than mammals.

In a few rare cases, a pathogen can cross a species barrier and cause serious health concerns. Most newly emerging diseases are caused by viruses, which have passed from other animals to humans. Genetic adaptations occur within the virus so that it can infect a new host. An example is avian (bird) flu which has arisen because of the interaction between humans and birds in farming communities.

How do mammalian lymphocytes co-ordinate the body's response to pathogens?

When the body is invaded by a pathogen the immune system is activated to produce large amounts of antibody to fight the infection. The reaction is known as 'challenge and response'. Antigens challenge the immune system, which responds as follows:

1 Pathogens are consumed by macrophages (phagocytes), which display antigen proteins on the surface of their own membrane (antigen presentation).
2 Lymphocytes called helper T cells, with receptors that match these antigens, bind to the macrophages and are activated.
3 Activated **helper T cells** then bind to other lymphocytes called **B cells** with the correct matching protein.
4 The selected B cells divide into two clones, the first group are able to produce and secrete antibodies as they divide, while the second group produce **memory cells**.
5 Antibodies help to destroy the pathogen and memory cells remain in the circulation in case of a future infection.

What are antibodies?
Review the structure of an antibody shown in Figure **6.12**.

> **DEFINITION**
>
> **ANTIBODIES** are protein molecules produced by lymphocytes in response to antigens. There are many different antibodies and each one works to destroy a specific pathogen.

What is histamine, how is it produced and how does it cause allergies?

Histamine is a nitrogen-containing molecule that is released by mast cells (found in connective tissue) and basophils (a type of white blood cell) in response to infection.

It causes dilation of blood vessels that become leaky so plasma escapes into the surrounding tissue and causes swelling. Plasma carries lymphocytes and antibodies to the area and the local temperature may rise. Histamine also causes itching or pain.

Sometimes histamine leads to an excessive **immune response** to substances such as fur, pollen or dust, causing sneezing, secretion of mucus and inflammation. Asthma, hay fever and eczema are common allergic reactions.

Histamine causes blood capillaries to become more permeable. Suggest how this helps with phagocytosis. **[2]**

How do vaccines prevent infections?

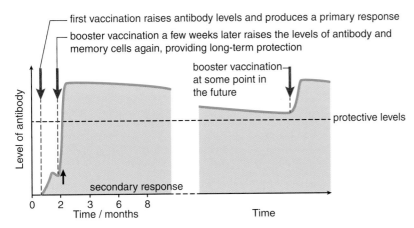

Figure 11.1 Antibody levels after vaccination. The persistence of antibodies varies and depends on the vaccine used.

Immunity develops after the body is exposed to a pathogen. Immunity is often due to the presence of antibodies and memory cells from previous infections that remain after an infection. Memory cells enable large amounts of antibody to be produced very quickly if the pathogen should enter the body again.

For serious conditions vaccines are used to raise the level of antibodies and memory cells so that a person develops immunity and is protected from disease without having to suffer from it.

Vaccines contain antigens such as dead or weakened pathogens, or their toxins.

 State why the action of B and T cells is limited to just one antigen. **[1]**

How are hybridomas produced and how are they used to manufacture monoclonal antibodies?

The fusion of a tumour cell with an antibody-producing cell forms a **hybridoma** cell, see Figure **11.2**.

Selected hybridoma cells have the immortality of tumour cells but produce useful antibodies for therapy and diagnosis. Cloned hybridoma cells are grown in a fermenter and release large quantities of one selected type of monoclonal antibody.

What are monoclonal antibodies used for?

Monoclonal antibodies are used in the diagnosis of diseases such as: HIV (the ELISA test), herpes, malaria and streptococcal infection.

In pregnancy testing kits, monoclonal antibodies bind to human chorionic gonadotrophin (HCG), which is only produced during pregnancy.

They may also be useful in new cancer treatments. Cancer cells have specific antigens on their surfaces. Monoclonal antibodies that can bind to them may be able to carry cytotoxic drugs directly to the cancer cells.

Explain why organs donated for transplant will be rejected by the recipient's body unless immunosuppressant drugs are given. **[3]**

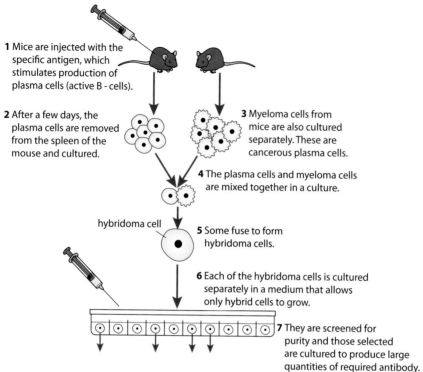

1 Mice are injected with the specific antigen, which stimulates production of plasma cells (active B - cells).

2 After a few days, the plasma cells are removed from the spleen of the mouse and cultured.

3 Myeloma cells from mice are also cultured separately. These are cancerous plasma cells.

4 The plasma cells and myeloma cells are mixed together in a culture.

hybridoma cell

5 Some fuse to form hybridoma cells.

6 Each of the hybridoma cells is cultured separately in a medium that allows only hybrid cells to grow.

7 They are screened for purity and those selected are cultured to produce large quantities of required antibody.

Figure 11.2 Formation of monoclonal antibodies.

11.2 Movement

Key information you should revise:

- Bones and exoskeletons provide anchorage for muscles and act as levers.
- Synovial joints allow a certain range of movements.
- Muscles work in antagonistic pairs to cause movement.
- Skeletal muscle fibres contain specialised endoplasmic reticulum and are multinucleate.
- Muscle fibres contain many myofibrils, each composed of contractile sarcomeres.
- ATP hydrolysis and formation of cross-bridges are essential for filaments to slide.
- Calcium ions and the proteins troponin and tropomyosin control muscle contraction.

How do skeletons and exoskeletons provide anchorage for muscles and enable movement?

DEFINITION

An **EXOSKELETON** is a firm outer skeleton that protects and encloses the bodies of arthropods, such as lobsters and insects.

Bones of vertebrates and exoskeletons of invertebrates provide places for muscles to attach and also act as levers so that animals can move. Levers change the direction and size of a force. When a muscle contracts it provides a force and joints provide a pivot.

Muscles are attached to the inside of an exoskeleton but to the outside of bones. Muscles are attached to bones by tendons made of collagen which are able to withstand tension as a muscle contracts.

What are antagonistic muscles?

Muscles can only cause movement when they contract and pull a bone or exoskeleton. Joints allow various parts of the body to bend, but to move a limb from its original position and back again two muscles are needed. One muscle flexes or bend a limb and a second extends or straighten it. Muscles like this form an antagonistic pair.

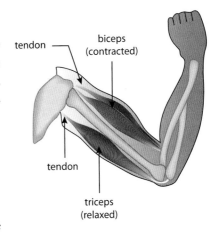

Figure 11.3 Muscles and tendons in the arm.

What is the structure of a synovial joint and what type of movement can these joints allow?

Synovial joints, containing synovial fluid are found in the elbow, knee and hip joints. Each allows a different type of movement which depends on the ligaments that hold them in place:

- Elbow and knee – hinge joints; movement is in one plane like a door hinge.
- Hip and shoulder – ball and socket joints, movement is in a circle.

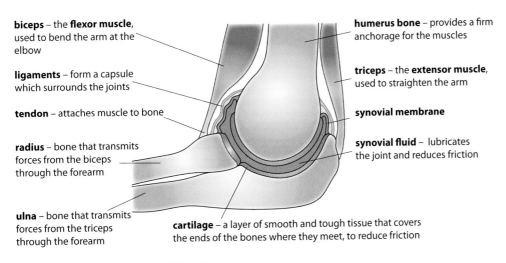

biceps – the **flexor muscle**, used to bend the arm at the elbow

ligaments – form a capsule which surrounds the joints

tendon – attaches muscle to bone

radius – bone that transmits forces from the biceps through the forearm

ulna – bone that transmits forces from the triceps through the forearm

humerus bone – provides a firm anchorage for the muscles

triceps – the **extensor muscle**, used to straighten the arm

synovial membrane

synovial fluid – lubricates the joint and reduces friction

cartilage – a layer of smooth and tough tissue that covers the ends of the bones where they meet, to reduce friction

Figure 11.4 The hinge joint of the elbow.

hint

For your exams you must be able to label and annotate a diagram of the elbow joint.

TEST YOURSELF 11.4

 What is the function of ligaments at the elbow joint?
- **A** attach radius to biceps
- **B** reduce friction between the bones
- **C** hold the humerus, ulna and radius in proper alignment
- **D** secrete synovial fluid

What is the structure of skeletal muscle?

Muscle structure is complex. Study Figure **11.5** carefully.

Skeletal muscle is used to move the body. It consists of multi-nucleate fibres which have specialised endoplasmic reticulum.

Important structures in a **muscle fibre** are:

- **sarcolemma** – the plasma membrane that encloses the fibres
- myofibrils – many of these make up a fibre
- **sarcoplasmic reticulum** – similar to smooth endoplasmic reticulum.

Important structures to remember in a myofibril are:

- actin and myosin – contractile proteins, myosin is thicker than actin
- **sarcomere** – repeating subunits within a myofibril
- Z lines – the end of each sarcomere.

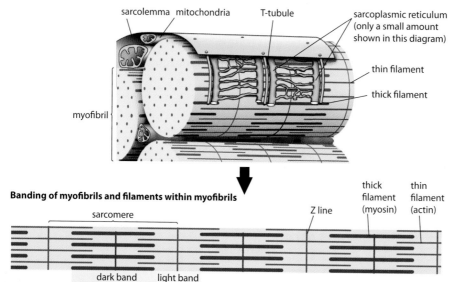

Figure 11.5 The structure of skeletal muscle.

How does muscle contraction occur?

Muscle contraction is explained by the sliding filament theory. Contraction begins when a nerve impulse arrives from a motor neuron. **Myosin** filaments pull the **actin** filaments inward towards the centre of the sarcomere. As each sarcomere is shortened, the whole muscle contracts.

1 Nerve impulses travel along the sarcolemma and pass inside the fibre to the sarcoplasmic reticulum. Ca^{2+} ions are released.

2 Before contraction myosin binding sites on actin molecules are covered by troponin and tropomyosin and myosin heads are upright as ATP binds to them.

3 Ca^{2+} binds to troponin. Troponin and tropomyosin change shape and expose binding sites. Myosin heads bind to actin and form cross bridges.

4 Inorganic phosphate (P^i) and ADP are released at each cross bridge and the myosin heads bend, pulling the actin inward towards the centre of the sarcomere.

5 New ATP molecules bind to the myosin heads, cross bridges are broken and detached so that myosin is ready to repeat the process.

Actin and myosin do not change in length when a muscle contracts.

How does the appearance of light and dark bands change as muscle contracts?

As muscle contracts, the interleaved fibres slide past one another so light bands appear narrower and dark bands remain the same length.

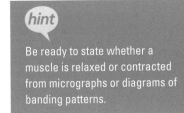

Be ready to state whether a muscle is relaxed or contracted from micrographs or diagrams of banding patterns.

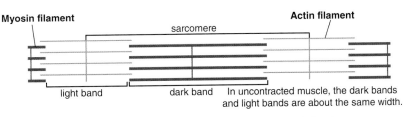

light band   dark band   In uncontracted muscle, the dark bands and light bands are about the same width.

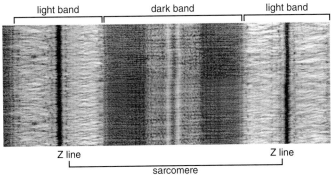

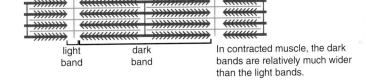

In contracted muscle, the dark bands are relatively much wider than the light bands.

Figure 11.6 When muscle contracts, the interleaved fibres slide inward, past each other. This makes the light bands appear narrower, but the dark bands remain the same width.

TEST YOURSELF 11.5

 Figure **11.7** show a sarcomere in different stages of contraction.

1 Name the parts labelled P, Q and R.
2 Outline why no cross bridges are shown in diagram **a**.
3 State which diagram shows contraction with the greatest force.
4 Explain how the muscle in **d** could be changed to the state shown in **a**.

5 Describe what happens when calcium ions enter the sarcoplasmic reticulum. **[3]**

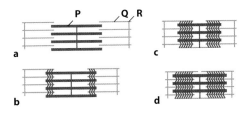

Figure 11.7

11.3 The kidney and osmoregulation

Key information you should revise is:

- Animals are either osmoregulators or osmoconformers.
- The kidney and the Malpighian tubule system in insects remove nitrogenous waste and carry out osmoregulation.

- The composition of blood in the renal artery is different from that in the renal vein.
- The structure of the Bowmans's capsule and glomerulus allow ultra filtration to occur.
- Selective reabsorption of useful substances occurs by active transport in the proximal convoluted tubule.
- The loop of Henlé maintains **hypertonic** conditions in the medulla of the kidney.
- ADH controls the reabsorption of water in the collecting duct.
- There is a positive correlation between the length of the loop of Henlé and the need for water conservation.
- The type of nitrogenous waste an organism produces depends on its habitat and evolutionary history.
- Dehydration and overhydration can have serious consequences.
- Hemodialysis can treat kidney failure.
- Urine tests can detect blood cells, glucose, protein and drugs.

DEFINITIONS

OSMOREGULATORS are animals which can maintain a constant internal solute concentration even if their environment has very different conditions. Terrestrial animals, freshwater animals and some marine organisms are osmoregulators. Many animals have kidneys for osmoregulation; insects use a system of Malpighian tubules.

OSMOCONFORMERS are animals whose internal solute concentration is about the same as the concentration in their environment. Examples are jellyfish and echinoderms.

How is osmoregulation achieved in insects?

An insect's body cavity is filled with a fluid called hemolymph. Its solute concentration is maintained by the Malpighian tubules, which are branches from the posterior region of the hindgut. When animals break down excess amino acids, nitrogenous waste is produced and must be excreted. Insects excrete uric acid.

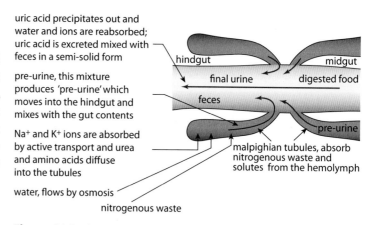

uric acid precipitates out and water and ions are reabsorbed; uric acid is excreted mixed with feces in a semi-solid form

pre-urine, this mixture produces 'pre-urine' which moves into the hindgut and mixes with the gut contents

Na+ and K+ ions are absorbed by active transport and urea and amino acids diffuse into the tubules

water, flows by osmosis

nitrogenous waste

hindgut   midgut
final urine   digested food
feces
pre-urine
malpighian tubules, absorb nitrogenous waste and solutes from the hemolymph

Figure 11.8 Diagram to show the Malpighian tubules of a typical insect.

What is the structure of a mammalian kidney?

Substances in the renal artery are regulated and removed by the kidney so blood in the renal vein will contain lower levels than the renal artery.

TEST YOURSELF 11.6

 Compare the composition of the blood in the renal artery and renal vein. **[2]**

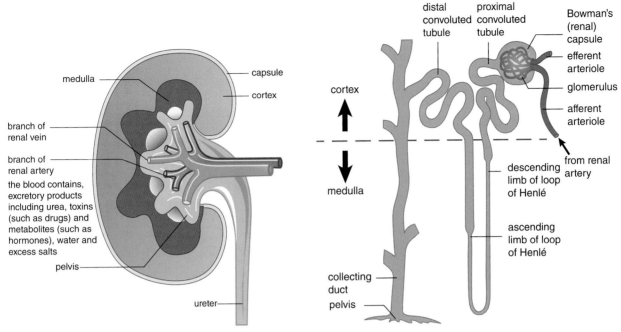

Figure 11.9 Longitudinal section of a human kidney.

Figure 11.10 The location, structure and blood supply of a nephron.

11.4 Which processes occur in the sections of a kidney tubule?

The **glomerulus** and Bowman's capsule:

1 The structure of the glomerulus relates to its job of **ultrafiltration** of blood. Key points to remember:

- Blood is at high pressure in the capillaries because the efferent and afferent arteries are different diameters.

- Plasma is forced out of the capillaries into the **Bowman's capsule**.

- Ultrafiltration occurs through fenestrations in the capillaries. Fluid but not blood cells, passes through the basement membrane. Almost all large proteins remain in the blood. Podocytes support the capillaries.

Particles, which are small enough, can pass into the Bowman's capsule and become glomerular filtrate.

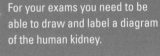

hint

For your exams you need to be able to draw and label a diagram of the human kidney.

hint

You should be able to name and describe the different sections of a nephron and identify where they are found in the kidney.

Table 11.1 The mean content of blood plasma and glomerular filtrate.

Molecule or ion	Concentration plasma (g dm⁻³)	
	In blood plasma	In filtrate
glucose	1	1
urea	0.3	0.3
protein	80	0.6
inorganic ions	7.5	7.5

The arrows show how the net effect of higher pressure in the capillary and lower solute concentration in the renal capsule is the movement of fluid out of the capillary and into the lumen of the capsule.

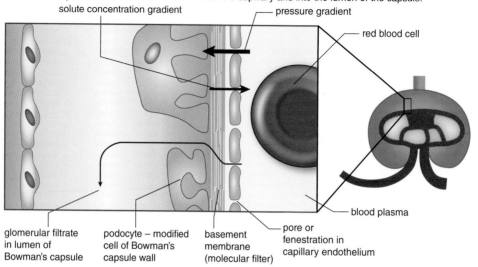

solute concentration gradient — pressure gradient

red blood cell

blood plasma

glomerular filtrate in lumen of Bowman's capsule

podocyte – modified cell of Bowman's capsule wall

basement membrane (molecular filter)

pore or fenestration in capillary endothelium

Figure 11.11 Detail of the Bowman's capsule showing the basement membrane, fenestrated capillary and podocytes. Podocytes are supportive cells of the capsule wall that form a network of slits. Filtrate passes through these slits, and into the capsule.

2 Proximal convoluted tubule:

- Here useful substances are reabsorbed by active transport.

- Sodium ions move by active transport. Chloride ions follow. Glucose is moved by transport proteins and water follows by osmosis as the concentration gradient of solutes is changed.

- By the end of the tubule, all glucose and amino acids as well as 80% of the water will have been reabsorbed.

- The cells of the proximal convoluted tubule have many mitochondria to provide energy for active transport; in electron micrographs, many vesicles are visible.

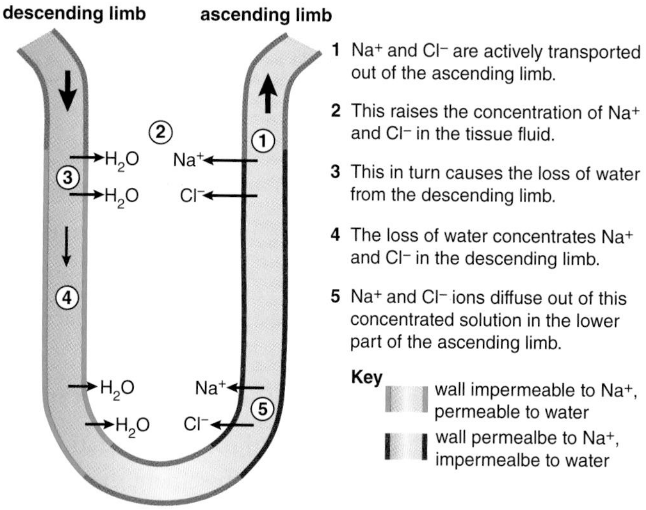

3 Loop of Henlé:

- This U shaped section of the tubule maintains a solute gradient in the medulla of the kidney.

descending limb   ascending limb

1 Na^+ and Cl^- are actively transported out of the ascending limb.

2 This raises the concentration of Na^+ and Cl^- in the tissue fluid.

3 This in turn causes the loss of water from the descending limb.

4 The loss of water concentrates Na^+ and Cl^- in the descending limb.

5 Na^+ and Cl^- ions diffuse out of this concentrated solution in the lower part of the ascending limb.

Key

wall impermeable to Na^+, permeable to water

wall permealbe to Na^+, impermealbe to water

Figure 11.12 The counter-current mechanism in the loop of Henlé builds up a high Na^+ ion and Cl^- ion concentration in the tissue fluid of the medulla.

- A counter current mechanism ensures that the concentration of Na^+ ions is greatest at the lowest part of the 'U' so that water is drawn out of the descending limb along its entire length.

4 Distal convoluted tubule:

- Ions are exchanged between the filtrate and blood, Na^+, Cl^- and Ca^{2+} ions are reabsorbed. H^+ and K^+ may be actively pumped into the tubule.

- Collecting duct:

- ADH (antidiuretic hormone) is secreted by the pituitary gland in response to stimuli from the hypothalamus.

- If the solute concentration of the blood is too high (more water is needed in the body), ADH is released and increases the permeability of the duct to water. Water is reabsorbed and a small volume of concentrated urine is produced.

- If the solute concentration of the blood is low (water must be lost from the body) ADH is not secreted and dilute urine is produced.

How is the structure of the kidney related to the need for water conservation?

The length of the loop of Henlé is correlated with the need that animals have to conserve water in their bodies.

Animals that live in very dry habitats such as camels and jerboas have long loops of Henlé. Animals in wetter environments, such as beavers and otters, will have shorter loops of Henlé.

If loops of Henlé are longer, the medulla will also be larger.

What types of nitrogenous waste do animals from different habitats produce?

Breaking down amino acids produces ammonia, which is very toxic and reactive. Fish and aquatic invertebrates can release it into the water but other organisms use energy and convert it into less toxic alternatives; either uric acid or **urea**.

Table 11.2 Nitrogenous waste animals produce.

Animal	Habitat	Type of waste	Reasons
aquatic invertebrates and most fish	water	ammonia	ammonia is very toxic but easily diluted in water
birds, insects land snails, some reptiles	terrestrial	uric acid	low solubility, non-toxic. Uric acid is released inside eggs because it crystallises birds do not have to carry water for excretion which would make flying difficult
mammals, amphibians and some fish	terrestrial and aquatic	urea	low toxicity, soluble, can be concentrated for excretion

What problems occur if a person becomes overhydrated?

Overhydration is caused when a person drinks too much water without replacing lost salts, for example after endurance exercise. Their blood becomes too dilute and cells may swell as water enters by osmosis. Symptoms are headache and disorientation as nerve and brain function are disrupted. Overhydration can cause death in severe cases.

How is kidney failure treated?

Hemodialysis can keep a person alive for a limited period, but if kidneys fail completely, a kidney transplant from a carefully matched donor will be needed.

Hemodialysis machines take the place of a kidney.

- Blood from the patient's arm is passed through the machine, inside dialysis tubing.

- The tubing is surrounded by dialysis fluid, containing measured levels of sodium ions, glucose and water.

- Urea and excess salts diffuse through the dialysis tube into the fluid.

- Excess water will leave the blood by osmosis.

- Blood is returned to the patient's vein, after its temperature has been checked and bubbles of gas removed.

- Dialysis fluid is renewed regularly to ensure the correct concentrations of substances are present in it.

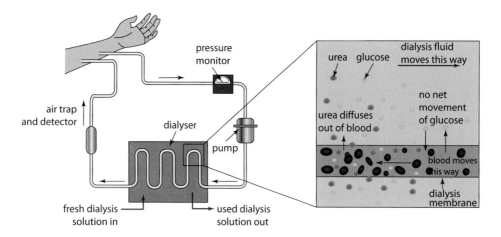

Figure 11.13 Dialysis treatment. Patients may be connected to the machine for 8 hours at a time, three times a week.

 What are the excretory products of birds, mammals and freshwater fish?

	Freshwater fish	Birds	Mammals
A	urea	ammonia	uric acid
B	ammonia	urea	uric acid
C	uric acid	ammonia	urea
D	ammonia	uric acid	urea

What substances are urine tests used to detect?

Illness, drug taking or other events can disrupt processes that control water levels, excretion and metabolism. Tests can detect abnormal levels of substances in urine.

Table 11.3 Substances found in urine.

Substances present in urine	Indications
glucose or ketones	uncontrolled diabetes
amino acids or protein	inflammation of the kidneys
red blood cells	kidney stones or blockage in the urinary tract
HCG residues	pregnancy
traces of steroids, banned or controlled drugs or alcohol	illegal drug use in sport or when driving

☆ Model answer 11.1

Explain the function of the loop of Henlé in the human kidney. [3]

The loop of Henlé: makes the medulla have higher solute concentration; by releasing sodium ions into medulla (out of the ascending limb); so it allows concentrated urine to be produced; and helps maintain the correct water balance in the body by drawing water from the filtrate in the loop.

11.5 Sexual reproduction

Key information you should revise is:

- Spermatogenesis and oogenesis involve mitosis, cell growth, two divisions of meiosis and differentiation.
- Spermatogenesis and oogenesis result in the production of different numbers of gametes with different amounts of cytoplasm.
- Fertilisation in animals may be external or internal.
- Mechanisms in fertilisation prevent polyspermy.
- The blastocyst must implant in the endometrium for pregnancy to occur.
- HCG stimulates the ovary to secrete progesterone in the early stages of pregnancy.
- The placenta enables mother and fetus to exchange materials and it secretes estrogen and progesterone.
- Birth is mediated by positive feedback mechanisms involving estrogen and oxytocin.

What are the similarities and differences between spermatogenesis and oogenesis?

DEFINITIONS

SPERMATOGENESIS is the production of sperm in the testes.

OOGENESIS is the production of oocytes in the ovaries.

Both processes produce gametes for sexual reproduction.

Table 11.4 Oogenesis and spermatogenesis compared.

	Oogenesis	Spermatogenesis
Similarities	• both begin with production of cells by mitosis • in both, cells grow before meiosis • in both, two divisions of meiosis produce the haploid gamete	
Differences	• usually only one secondary oocyte is produced per menstrual cycle • only one large gamete is produced per meiosis • occurs in ovaries, which tend to alternate oocyte production • early stages occur during fetal development • ova released at ovulation during the menstrual cycle • ceases at menopause	• millions of sperm cells are produced continuously • four small gametes are produced per meiosis • occurs in testes, which both produce sperm cells • process begins at puberty • sperm cells released at ejaculation • continues throughout an adult male's life

How are sperm cells formed in the testes?

Spermatogenesis occurs in the seminiferous tubules.

- Outer layers of germinal epithelium divide by mitosis to produce more diploid cells.
- Diploid cells grow to form primary spermatocytes.
- These divide by meiosis to produce two secondary spermatocytes.
- The two secondary spermatocytes divide by meiosis to produce four spermatids.
- Spermatids attach to Sertoli cells and differentiate to form sperm cells, which will detach and pass along the tubule.

hint

You should be able to annotate a diagram like Figure **11.14** with information about spermatogenesis and Figure **11.15** about oogenesis.

Enlarged portion of the wall of a seminiferous tubule showing stages in sperm development.

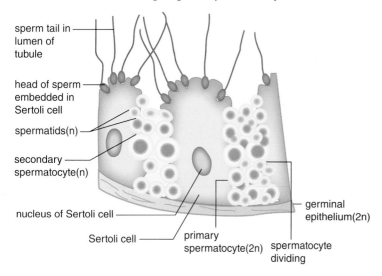

sperm tail in lumen of tubule

head of sperm embedded in Sertoli cell

spermatids(n)

secondary spermatocyte(n)

nucleus of Sertoli cell

Sertoli cell

primary spermatocyte(2n)

spermatocyte dividing

germinal epithelium(2n)

Figure 11.14 Structure of the testis. Enlarged portion of the wall of a seminiferous tubule showing stages in sperm development.

How do oocytes develop in the ovaries?

- **Oogenesis** begins in the ovaries of the female fetus.

- Germ cells divide by mitosis.

- At about 5 months of fetal development the cells grow and undergo the first division of meiosis. They are surrounded by follicle cells in the ovary. This is called a primary follicle.

- No further development occurs until puberty.

- FSH stimulates follicle development at puberty

- The first meiotic division produces one large and one small haploid cell.

The larger cell is the secondary oocyte, the smaller is a **polar body**.

- At ovulation a secondary oocyte is released into the oviduct.

- At fertilisation the secondary oocyte completes meiosis II to become a mature ovum and expels a polar body

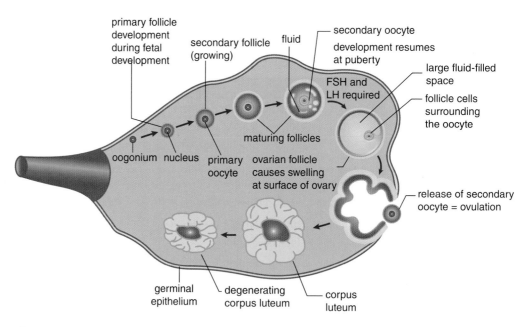

primary follicle development during fetal development

secondary follicle (growing)

fluid

secondary oocyte development resumes at puberty

FSH and LH required

large fluid-filled space

follicle cells surrounding the oocyte

maturing follicles

oogonium   nucleus   primary oocyte

ovarian follicle causes swelling at surface of ovary

release of secondary oocyte = ovulation

germinal epithelium

degenerating corpus luteum

corpus luteum

Figure 11.15 Stages in the development of one follicle in a human ovary. The arrows show the sequence of events.

hint

In an exam you may be asked to recall or draw the structures found in sperm cells and a secondary oocyte at ovulation.

TEST YOURSELF 11.8

 Which stage of spermatogenesis occurs when spermatids are attached to Sertoli cells?

A Differentiation

B 1st meiotic division

C Testosterone production

D 2nd meiotic division

What are the structures found in a mature sperm and secondary oocyte?

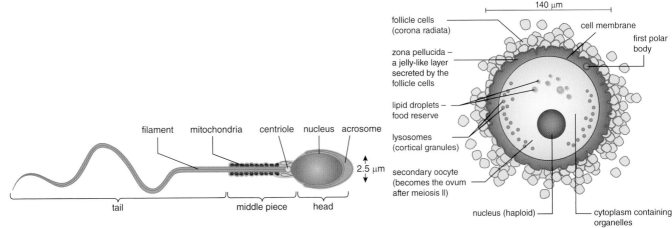

Figure 11.16 Structure of a human sperm cell. Total length is 50 μm.

Figure 11.17 Structure of the secondary oocyte and surrounding structures at ovulation.

Where does fertilisation take place?

Some aquatic animals such as fish, amphibians and invertebrates fertilise their eggs outside their bodies in water. This is known as external fertilisation. Behaviour patterns and courting rituals ensure that eggs and sperm are released close together and at the same time. Large numbers of gametes are produced because many will fail to meet and be wasted.

Internal fertilisation usually takes place in one of the oviducts (fallopian tubes) of birds, reptiles and mammals. It increases the chance that gametes will meet. Fewer gametes are produced by these animals and fertilised eggs either develop in a protective shell or inside the female's body.

How does the process of fertilisation prevent more than one sperm entering the ovum?

The **cortical reaction** occurs as vesicles near the membrane of the oocyte release their contents. Binding proteins on the oocyte surface are digested away so it is impossible for another sperm to bind to the membrane and polypermy is prevented.

The stages of fertilisation

The fusion of one sperm cell with the secondary oocyte to form a zygote. In mammals we can recognise several stages in the process.

1 Many sperm cells arrive at the secondary oocyte.

2 Sperm pass through the follicle cells.

3 Sperm reach the zona pellucidaand bind to it.

4 The **acrosome reaction** occurs. Enzymes from inside the acrosome are released and proteases digest a pathway through the zona pellucida.

5 The membranes of the sperm and oocyte fuse, triggering the cortical reaction and the sperm nucleus enters.

6 Cortical granules fuse with the plasma membrane and release their contents. Enzymes cause the zona pellucida to harden so that no further sperm can enter.

7 The secondary oocyte completes meiosis II and a second polar body is expelled.

8 When the sperm and ovum nuclei have merged, the ovum is fertilised and known as a zygote.

What are the first stages of pregnancy?

After fertilisation in humans:

- The zygote travels slowly down the oviduct to the uterus. The single cell divides by mitosis.

- After about 7 days, the zygote has become a **blastocyst**, a hollow ball of about 100 cells.

- The blastocyst settles in the endometrium (uterus lining). It continues to divide and becomes an embryo.

- Extensions of the outer layer of the blastocyst develop into villi which penetrate the lining. Here they receive nutrients that diffuse from the mother's blood.

How does HCG control the early stages of pregnancy?

HCG is human chorionic gonadotropin, a hormone produced by the developing embryo. HCG stimulates the **corpus luteum** (the cells of the empty ovarian follicle) to continue releasing the hormones progesterone and estrogen. These two hormones keep the endometrium in place and stimulate it to thicken.

After the first 3 months of pregnancy the **placenta** is fully formed and produces its own progesterone and estrogen.

What is the structure and role of the placenta?

The placenta is the structure that supplies the developing fetus with the nutrients it requires and removes waste products from it.

Table 11.5 Passage of substances through the placenta.

Substances that pass from mother to fetus	Substances that pass from fetus to mother
• oxygen, glucose, amino acids, vitamins, minerals, water • hormones • antibodies, some drugs e.g nicotine and alcohol • some viruses e.g rubella	• carbon dioxide • urea • water • some hormones (HCG)

The placenta is made up of fetal villi and maternal endometrium.

Villi that develop from the chorion (the outer layers of cells which surround the embryo) penetrate into the endometrium to produce a very large surface area for exchange of materials. Fetal blood remains inside the capillaries of the villi but the maternal blood capillaries break down so that the mother's blood is brought as close as possible to the fetal blood without them ever mixing.

A baby may have a different blood group from its mother so their bloods must not mix.

TEST YOURSELF 11.9

Outline the role of human chorionic gonadotropin (HCG) in early pregnancy. **[2]**

How do hormones mediate the process of birth?

- During pregnancy high levels of progesterone and estrogen inhibit contractions of the uterus, supress the menstrual cycle and promote the growth of breast tissue.

- At the end of pregnancy, the baby is ready to be born and the levels of progesterone and estrogen fall. The endometrium secretes hormones known as prostaglandins, which initiate contractions of the uterus wall.

- The hormone **oxytocin** from the posterior pituitary gland stimulates continued contractions of the uterus in a positive feedback process. This causes a gradual increase in the strength of contractions.

- The amniotic sac breaks, the cervix opens and the baby is eased out of the mother's body through the vagina. The **umbilical cord** is cut and the baby begins its independent life.

- Gentle contractions continue until the placenta is expelled.

- After birth, levels of the hormone prolactin from the anterior pituitary increase. Prolactin and oxytocin stimulate milk production and release from the mammary glands.

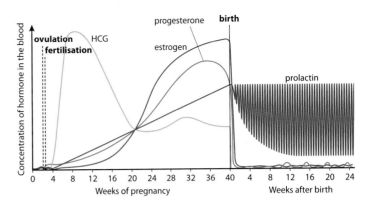

Figure 11.18 Changes in the levels of hormones during pregnancy and after the birth.

TEST YOURSELF 11.10

 State the levels of the four hormones which control the menstrual cycle at day 14, immediately before ovulation. **[3]**

📑 Annotated exemplar answer 11.1

Explain how a larger number of sperm than egg cells are produced in human reproduction. **[4]**

This would form part of an essay style-question.

Testes produce many cells all the time but ovaries only produce one egg cell per month. Men produce sperm all their lives but women do not.

This is too vague. In an essay-style question you must include detail if the command term is explain. To improve make the statements clearer, for example:

- *Sperm production is continuous throughout a man's life but egg production is monthly.*

- *No eggs are produced after menopause/ or during pregnancy.*

(1/4)

More marks can be gained from adding:

- *In spermatogenesis all four cells produced after meiosis become sperm but in oogenesis only one becomes an egg.*

- *The number of eggs that can be produced is limited because the early stages of oogenesis only take place during fetal development.*

You could also mention:

- *FSH inhibits oocyte production at certain times.*

A

NEUROBIOLOGY AND BEHAVIOUR

This chapter covers the following topics:

☐ Neural development

☐ The human brain

☐ Perception of stimuli

☐ Innate and learned behaviour

☐ Neuropharmacology (HL)

☐ Ethology (HL)

A1 Neural development

Key information you should revise:

- How the neural tube of embryonic chordates forms.
- How differentiation of the neural tube produces neurons.
- That immature neurons migrate to a final location.
- That chemical stimuli influence growth of axons to other parts of the body.
- Multiple synapses form with developing neurons.
- Unused synapses are lost.
- That neural pruning removes unused neurons.
- How plasticity allows the nervous system to change.

How does the neural tube develop in an embryo?

Embryonic chordates produce the nerve cord along their dorsal side at an early stage of development. In humans this happens during the first month after conception.

How are neurons produced from the neural tube?

Cells of the neural plate form the neural tube, and some of them differentiate and go on to become neurons, which make up the nervous system. Neurons continue to develop in both the brain and spinal cord but most cell division stops before birth.

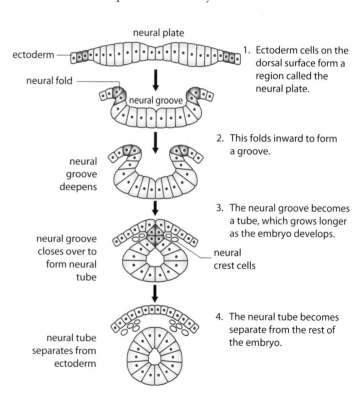

Figure A.1 Neural tube development. Only the ectoderm is shown here – the mesoderm, from which the notochord forms, and the endoderm lie beneath the ectoderm and the neural tube.

State when neural tube development begins in a human embryo.

How do immature neurons reach their final location?

Neural migration is a process which neurons use to move to new locations. Cytoplasm and organelles move to one side of the cell and the whole cell is then drawn in that direction. It is important in brain development. Neurons may move from one side of the developing brain to the other. Mature neurons do not usually move.

Axons extend from the neuron body in response to chemical stimuli which determine the length and direction of axon growth.

Some axons are short but others are very long and can reach from the neural tube to the tip of the foot. Only one axon develops per cell but it may have several branches.

How do synapses develop and what happens to those that are not used?

As axons and dendrites grow from developing neurons they make many connections with other neurons. Axons of **motor neurons** also develop synapses with muscle or gland cells.

Synapses that are not used will disappear. Neural transmission at a synapse causes the synapse to become 'stronger' and so these will be retained.

What is the consequence of plasticity in the nervous system?

Plasticity in the nervous system describes its ability to change as a person has new experiences. Neurons that are not used are removed in a process known as neural pruning, which may remove a whole cell or part of one. Neural pruning allows the nervous system to 'rewire' itself. New experiences cause new connections to form and old ones may be lost. Plasticity is also important in the repair of the system. In some cases, if part of the nervous system is damaged, new connections can be made to enable the body to function again.

 What is meant by the term 'neural migration'?

A2 The human brain

Key information you should revise:

- The anterior part of the neural tube forms the brain.
- That different parts of the brain have specific functions.
- The autonomic nervous system controls involuntary processes.
- The cerebral cortex forms a large part of the human brain and is folded so that it will fit within the cranium.
- That cerebral hemispheres are responsible for higher order functions.
- That the left hemisphere receives input from the right side of the body and right side of the visual field in both eyes and vice versa.
- The left hemisphere controls the right side of the body and vice versa.
- Large amounts of energy are needed for brain activity.

How does the brain develop from the neural tube?

The anterior (front) part of the embryonic neural tube develops to become the brain, and by the end of the embryonic phase of development, at 3 months after fertilisation, the basic structure of the complete brain is in place. From then onward, the brain of the fetus grows rapidly and fibres of the nervous system form. After birth, the brain continues to enlarge and will be four times bigger by the time the child is 6 years old.

What are the functions of the different parts of the brain?

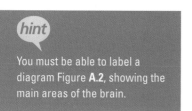

You must be able to label a diagram Figure **A.2**, showing the main areas of the brain.

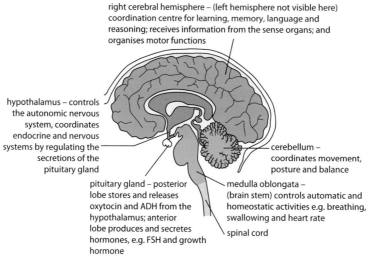

Figure A.2 The human brain.

Which aspects of the body are controlled by the ANS?

The autonomic nervous system controls involuntary processes in the body such as swallowing, breathing, regulation of heart rate.

The autonomic nervous system is subdivided into two parts that receive impulses from the medulla oblongata:

- the sympathetic nervous system causes responses that are important in an emergency – the so-called 'fight or flight' responses and is excitatory in its effects
- the parasympathetic nervous system controls events in non-urgent, relaxed situations and is inhibitory in its effects.

Table A.1

Organ	Effect of parasympathetic system	Effect of sympathetic system
eye	causes contraction of circular muscles of the iris, which constricts the pupil	causes contraction of radial muscles of the iris, dilating the pupil
heart	heart rate is slowed down and stroke volume is reduced as the body is relaxed	heart rate is increased and stroke volume increased so that more blood can be pumped to muscles
digestive system	blood vessels are dilated, increasing blood flow to the digestive system	blood flow to the digestive system is restricted as blood vessels constrict

How has the cerebral cortex evolved in humans?

The **cerebral cortex** of a human brain is the outer layer of the two **cerebral hemispheres** known as 'grey matter'. It controls functions, such as speech and decision making. Only mammals have a cerebral cortex. It is folded so that its large surface area can fit into the skull.

Which area of the brain is responsible for higher order functions?

DEFINITION

HIGHER ORDER FUNCTIONS are learning, memory, recall, speech and emotions.

The cerebral hemispheres control higher order functions. The two cerebral hemispheres contain different types of cells and different **neurotransmitters**. Different areas of the cerebral cortex also have different functions. Sensory areas receive impulses from sense organs, association areas process the information received and motor areas send impulses to effectors in the body.

You may be asked to examine the correlation between brain and body size in mammals. The two are related but not directly proportional.

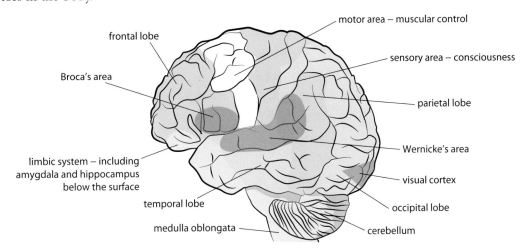

Figure A.3 Approximate locations of important areas of the cerebral hemispheres.

What are the different roles of the left and right sides of the brain?

The right hemisphere receives information from the left side of the body and the left hemisphere receives information from the right side of the body. Likewise, motor signals are sent to each side of the body from the opposite hemisphere. Both hemispheres process information, but there is some division between the functions of each one. For example, association areas of the left hemisphere are important in our use and understanding of language – Broca's area is responsible for speaking and writing and Wernicke's area is responsible for understanding of language.

Make sure you don't confuse cerebellum, cerebral cortex and cerebral hemispheres. All are part of the brain but have their own specific jobs.

TEST YOURSELF A.3

Figure **A.4** shows the relationship between brain and body weight for some mammal species.
1 Which mammals have the smallest brain mass. **[1]**
2 State the relationship shown by the graph. **[1]**
3 Evaluate whether it true to say that humans have the largest relative brain mass. **[3]**

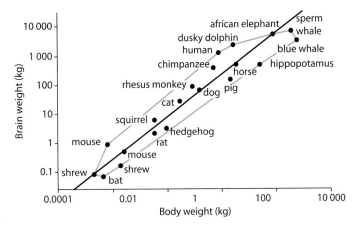

Figure A.4

How is the activity of the brain powered?

The brain needs a great deal of energy to fuel its neurons and maintain the membrane potential of brain cells. It uses up to 25% of the energy needed for basic metabolism. The majority of the energy comes from the aerobic respiration of glucose. Active regions of the brain use more energy than non-active regions, and fMRI scanning can be used to identify those regions that are active during different activities.

TEST YOURSELF A.4

 Name two 'higher order' functions and the area of the brain which controls these functions. **[2]**

What techniques are used to investigate the activity of the brain?

Studies of brains that were damaged by injury to certain regions were used in the 19th century. Examples include Phineas Gage who was injured by a metal rod that penetrated his skull. Damage caused by tumours or strokes can help link the area of damage with the function of that area. MRI scanning can locate abnormalities and fMRI scans monitor brain activity from the blood flow to different areas.

TEST YOURSELF A.5

 If a person suffered an injury to the Broca's area of his brain, what functions might be affected? **[1]**

A3 Perception of stimuli

Key information you should revise:

- That receptors detect changes in the environment.
- Rods and cones are photoreceptors that differ in sensitivity to light intensity and wavelength.
- The retina contains bipolar cells that send impulses from rods and cones to ganglion cells and these send message to the brain.
- Information from the right visual field from both eyes travels to the left part of the visual cortex and vice versa.
- The structure of the ear and how the middle ear transmits and amplifies sound.
- How the cochlea detects sounds of different wavelengths.
- That impulses from the ear are transmitted to the brain via the auditory nerve.
- That the semi-circular canals detect movements of the head.

What is meant by the term receptor?

DEFINITION

A **RECEPTOR** is a nerve ending of a sensory neuron that can detect a change in the environment.

Different types of receptor include:

- photoreceptors – respond to light
- thermoreceptors – respond to heat
- chemoreceptors – respond to chemicals and pH changes in the blood
- mechanoreceptors – respond to movement or forces such as pressure.

How is the structure of the eye related to its function?

Photoreceptors in the human eye make it a very efficient light-sensitive organ. Light rays entering the eye are bent by the cornea and lens and focused onto the retina.

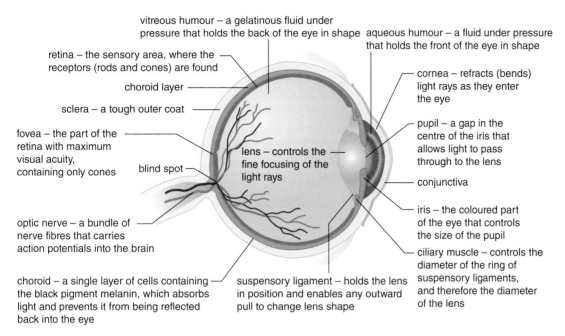

Figure A.5 The structure of the human eye, in transverse section (the eyelids are not shown).

What is the detailed structure of the cells of the retina?

The retina contains two types of photoreceptor cells; these are the rods and cones. They are arranged in a single layer in the retina.

Rays of light that fall on the retina first pass through the layers of nerve fibres and neurons before reaching the light-sensitive rods and cones.

Rods are connected in groups to a single bipolar cell whereas each cone cell has its own bipolar cell. Rods are very sensitive to light and respond even in very dim light.

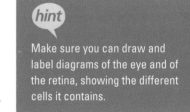

hint

Make sure you can draw and label diagrams of the eye and of the retina, showing the different cells it contains.

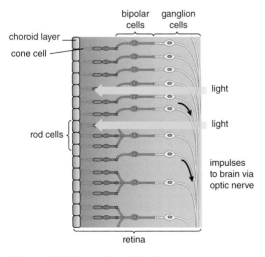

Figure A.6 The retina of the human eye.

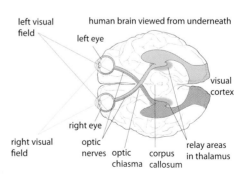

Figure A.7 Both sides of the brain work together to enable us to recognise objects. Contralateral processing of information allows us to work out the size of an object and its distance from us.

How are messages conveyed to the brain?

Bipolar cells send impulses from rods and cones to ganglion cells. Ganglion cells then send message to the brain via the optic nerve. Axons of ganglion cells pass across the front of the retina. The optic nerve leaves the retina at the blind spot where there are no rods or cones. Light passes through the bipolar cells before it hits the rods and cones. Information from the right field of vision from both eyes passes to the left part of the visual cortex and vice versa.

Table A.2

Rods	Cones
highly sensitive to light, work in dim light, produce a view of the world in shades of grey	less sensitive to light, work in bright light, enable us to see in colour
one type of rod can respond to all wavelengths of light	three different cones respond to red, blue and green light so we can detect colour
groups of rods are connected to a single bipolar cell	each cone is connected to its own bipolar cell
not present in the fovea	not present at the very edge of the retina

How is the structure of the ear related to its function?

We can study the ear in three parts, the outer, inner and middle ear (Figure **A.8**).

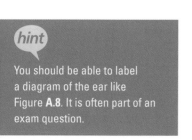

hint

You should be able to label a diagram of the ear like Figure **A.8**. It is often part of an exam question.

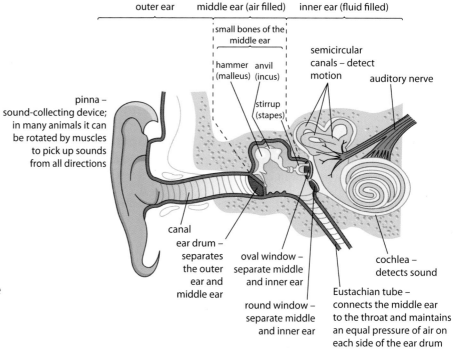

Figure A.8 Section through the human ear. Note that the pinna is not drawn to scale with the internal structures of the ear.

What are the roles of the cochlea, auditory nerve and semi-circular canals?

The cochlea converts vibrations into nerve signals. Inside it sensory hair cells, attached to membranes, move as fluid moves and initiate nerve impulses that are passed via the auditory nerve to the brain.

Different regions of the cochlea respond to different frequencies of sound. High frequencies (short wavelengths) are detected nearest to the oval window and the lowest frequencies (longest wavelengths) further away. Quiet sounds stimulate only a few hair cells so few nerve impulses are sent; louder sounds produce more nerve impulses to the brain.

The semicircular canals give us a sense of position and balance by enabling us to detect movements of the head. The three fluid-filled canals are arranged so that each one is aligned at right angles to the others

Sensory hairs inside the canals are embedded in a jelly-like cap, which is deflected by movements. The inertia of the fluid inside each canal means that the cap is deflected in the opposite direction to the movement of the head. This pulls on the hair cells, which send impulses to the brain.

TEST YOURSELF A.6

 Compare rods and cones. **[3]**

Notice that Test yourself **A.6** asks you to 'compare'. Include three comparisons to get the three marks and use words such as 'but' or 'on the other hand'.

☆ Model answer A.1

Explain how sound is received and transmitted to the auditory nerve in humans. [5]

Eardrums vibrate as sound waves hit them. Then earbones vibrate and pass sounds to the oval window. Here sounds are amplified because the oval window is smaller than the eardrum. Sound waves pass to the cochlea via the oval window and different areas of hair cells move with different frequencies of sound. Hair cells transmit nerve impulses to the auditory nerve.

A4 Innate and learned behaviour

Key information you should revise:

- Innate behaviour is inherited and not influenced by the environment.
- Reflexes are autonomic and involuntary actions.
- A reflex arc consists of neurons which cause reflexes.
- Learned behaviour is influenced by the environment.
- Reflex conditioning involves new associations between neurons.
- Imprinting is learning that occurs at a particular stage of life and is independent of the outcome of the behaviour.
- Operant conditioning is learning which consists of trial and error.
- Learning is defined as acquisition of knowledge or skill.
- Memory is the process of encoding, storing and retrieving information.

What is the definition of innate behaviour?

DEFINITION

INNATE BEHAVIOUR is inherited and genetically programmed. It develops independently of the environment.

There are two types of behaviour innate and learned. Innate behaviour is unaffected by the external environment of an organism. It is often called 'instinct'. It can change through evolution but this takes much longer than changes to learned behaviour.

What is a reflex action?

DEFINITIONS

A **REFLEX** is a rapid, specific reaction that is always produced in response to a particular stimulus, and which does not require prior learning.

A **STIMULUS** is a change in the environment (either internal or external) that is detected by a receptor and elicits a response.

A **RESPONSE** is a reaction or change in an organism as a result of a stimulus.

A   Neurobiology and behaviour

Sometimes a rapid response to a stimulus is vital for an animal's survival and **reflex actions** all take place quickly and automatically. Human reflexes include the pupil reflex, which reduces the diameter of the pupil in very bright light to prevent damage to the retina, and the choking reflex, which occurs when a piece of food enters the trachea.

Which neurons are involved in reflex actions?

The neural pathway involved in a reflex action is known as a **reflex arc**.

All reflex arcs involve this sequence:

Receptor → sensory neuron → relay neuron(s) → motor neuron → effector

Receptors perceive a stimulus; examples include the pain receptors in the skin or light receptors in the retina. Effectors may be muscles or glands which carry out the response.

> **hint**
>
> Ensure that you can draw and label a simple reflex arc like the one in Figure **A.9**.

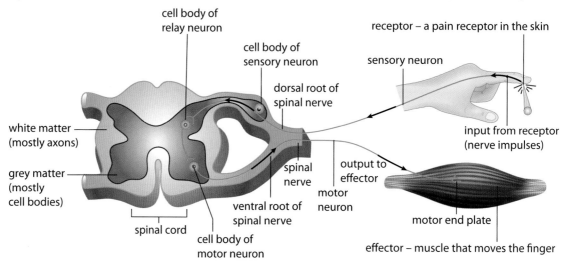

Figure A.9 The spinal reflex arc for the pain withdrawal reflex. The pain withdrawal reflex is an innate response to pain. Impulses travel to the spinal cord.

📝 Annotated exemplar answer A.1

Explain the role of receptors, sensory neurons, relay neurons, motor neurons, synapses and effectors in the response of animals to stimuli. **[5]**

This is a longer answer question so use sentences.

Receptor cells detect change in the environment and send messages to the CNS.

It's always better to include an example so mention mechanoreceptors or photoreceptors here.

Sensory neurons connect receptors to the CNS and carry the impulse along their axons.

In an essay, say that the CNS consists of the brain and spinal cord to be sure of the mark.

Relay neurons found in the brain and spinal cord coordinate a response to the stimulus. Synapses are junctions between two nerve cells or between a nerve cell and an effector. Chemicals called neurotransmitters pass impulses across them.

This is good. You are not asked about the role of neurotransmitters so no detail is needed, but it's important to mention them.

A motor neuron carries the nerve impulse from the CNS to the effector which may be a muscle or a gland. When an impulse reaches the effector it causes a response.

It's good to cover the roles of the structures in the question in the order they are given. In this case it follows the path from stimulus to response.

(4/5)

168

How is learned behaviour defined and what influences it?

LEARNED BEHAVIOUR is behaviour which develops as a result of experience. It may be learned from parents or experience individuals have of their environment. Examples are bird song and human language.

Primates, big cats, wolves and many other mammals spend a long time with their parents learning social and hunting skills from them. For example, the matriarch elephant in a herd remembers where water supplies are and younger members of the herd learn from her. Primates show the ability to acquire new skills that help them to survive. For example chimpanzees may learn to use sticks to extract termites from mounds.

TEST YOURSELF A.7

 Define the terms stimulus, response and reflex in the context of animal behaviour. **[3]**

What are three types of learned behavior?

DEFINITION

REFLEX CONDITIONING involves the formation of new neural pathways.

IMPRINTING is a type of learning that occurs at a particular stage in an animal's life and is independent of the outcome of the behaviour.

OPERANT CONDITIONING is behaviour that develops as a result of the association of reinforcement with a particular response. It is a type of trial and error learning.

Table A.3

Reflex conditioning	Imprinting	Operant conditioning
• learning investigated by Pavlov in experiments with salivation in dogs • 'conditioned' dogs salivated in anticipation of food if they were given a pre-feeding stimulus such as a ringing bell	• investigated in the 1930s by Konrad Lorenz who studied geese • imprinted young geese followed Lorenz	• investigated by Skinner using pigeons and a Skinner box • animals learned by trial and error
• before training, the normal behaviour involved an unconditioned stimulus (the food) producing an unconditioned response (the release of saliva) • after training, the dogs responded to the conditioned stimulus (the sound of a bell) and produced the conditioned response (the release of saliva without the appearance of food)	• in a natural situation newly hatched goslings follow their mother, but if eggs are removed from a nest and hatched in an incubator, the chicks will 'imprint' on the first moving object they see and follow it • isolated, newly hatched goslings would follow Lorenz instead of the mother bird • this effect only occurred within 13 to 16 hours after hatching – the critical period	• the box contains a lever that an animal, such as a pigeon, can press to obtain a reward of food • a hungry animal learns by trial and error that pressing the lever causes food to be released • the animal learns to associate the lever with the food reward • the reward is known as reinforcement
• this type of reflex conditioning also enables birds to avoid bad tasting food as they come to associate certain colours of insect with a bad taste and will avoid all species with those colours		• this type of learning is different from conditioning because the animal discovers the effect of their behaviour • if the consequences are good, the behaviour is repeated. If not the animal will learn not to repeat it

What are learning and memory and how do they develop?

LEARNING is the acquisition of skill or knowledge.

There are many examples of learning that enable animals to survive and reproduce. For example, birds sing to defend their territories and to attract mates. A male bird's song is crucial to both its survival and reproductive success. A bird's song is a complex series of notes, which can be analysed using spectroscopy. Within a species the basic song is the same for all members of the species but variations do develop. Young birds are born with an innate ability to sing a basic song but learn details of their species' song from their fathers.

MEMORY is the process of encoding, storing and accessing information.

Wild male white-crowned sparrow

Adult male white-crowned sparrow song.

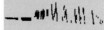

The young bird uses the adult song to modify its basic template. At around 150 days old, the juvenile bird starts to sing and gradually matches what he hears to the modified template.

At about 200 days, the bird's song matches what he heard as a youngster.

Hand-reared male white-crowned sparrow

At around 150 days, the juvenile bird reared in isolation begins to sing and matches what it hears to its basic, unmodified template.

At about 200 days, the full song has developed but is not as mature and complex as the song of a wild bird.

Data from Peter Marler, Animal Communication Laboratory, Section of Neurobiology, Physiology and Behavior, University of California, Davis, CA 95616, USA

Figure A.10 Sonograms of North American white-crowned sparrows.

Memory is a higher order function of the brain. It involves converting information to a form that can be stored. Changes take place in an animal's neurons and neural pathways and can be influenced by neurotransmitters. (Section **A.5**).

 Outline the role of inheritance and learning in the development of birdsong in young birds. **[2]**

A5 Neuropharmacology (HL)

Key information you should revise in this section is:

- Neurotransmitters may excite or inhibit post-synaptic membranes.
- Impulses may be initiated or inhibited as a result of all excitatory and inhibitory neurotransmitters from the pre-synaptic membrane.
- Slow-acting neurotransmitters affect fast synaptic transmission in the brain and memory and learning involve changes in neurons caused by these transmitters.
- Anesthetics interfere with transmission between sensory neurons and the CNS.
- Stimulant drugs speed up the action of the sympathetic nervous system.
- Genetic predisposition, the environment and other factors can influence addiction to drugs.

How are post-synaptic membranes influenced by neurotransmitters?

Review your work on synapses in Section **6.5** before you begin this section.

NEUROTRANSMITTERS are the chemical substances that are released from the pre-synaptic neuron at a synapse, diffuse across the synaptic cleft, and activate receptors on the post-synaptic membrane.

There are many different types of synapses and many different neurotransmitters. Some neurotransmitters excite post-synaptic neurons and others inhibit them.

When a neurotransmitter is released from the pre-synaptic membrane, the post-synaptic membrane is depolarised as positive ions enter the cell and stimulate an action potential.

Some pre-synaptic neurons release neurotransmitters that inhibit the post-synaptic neuron by increasing the polarisation of its membrane (hyperpolarisation) making it harder to depolarise the membrane so post-synaptic transmission is therefore inhibited at these synapses.

Receptors on the post-synaptic membrane determine whether the neurotransmitter will cause depolarisation of the post-synaptic membrane or not – that is, whether the stimulus is excitatory or inhibitory.

Effects of neurotransmitters are shown Table **A.4**.

Table A.4

Effect	How received	Example
• causing depolarisation of post synaptic membrane	• received by excitatory receptors that increase the probability of an action potential in the post-synaptic membrane	glutamate
• inhibiting of depolarisation of post synaptic membrane	• received by inhibitory receptors that decrease the probability of an action potential	GABA
• both stimulatory and inhibitory effects	• received by both excitatory and inhibitory receptors	acetylcholine (ACh)

SUMMATION is when nerve impulses are initiated or inhibited in the post-synaptic cell as a result of the total excitatory and inhibitory stimuli they receive from pre-synaptic neurons.

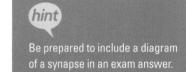

hint

Be prepared to include a diagram of a synapse in an exam answer.

What effect do slow-acting neurotransmitters have on synaptic transmission, memory and learning?

Slow-acting neurotransmitters include noradrenalin, dopamine and serotonin. They do not affect the ion channels in the post synaptic membrane directly but cause the release of secondary substances, which regulate fast synaptic transmission. Slow-acting neurotransmitters may take up to 100 times longer than fast neurotransmitters such as acetylcholine, to have their effect.

Memory and learning involve changes in neurons caused by slow acting neurotransmitters. Secondary substances released in post synaptic cells can promote transmission, for example by increasing the receptors in the membrane.

SYNAPTIC PLASTICITY is the ability of synapses to change the way a pre-synaptic depolarisation causes an action potential to be stimulated in the post-synaptic membrane.

Glutamate is thought to play an important role in learning and memory and has a key role in synaptic plasticity. The plasticity associated with glutamate is long-term potentiation (LTP) and occurs at synapses in several parts of the brain. LTP is a long-lasting enhancement in signal transmission between two neurons and is thought to be an important process in learning and memory. Memories are probably encoded by modifications like this.

What effect does an anesthetic have on the nervous system?

An anesthetic works by interfering with the transmission of impulses between sensory inputs and the **central nervous system**. They cause a reversible loss of sensation.

- Local anesthetics, such as dental novocaine, are used to block the transmission of impulses to pain centres in the CNS during minor surgical procedures. They work by binding to and inhibiting sodium channels in the cell membranes. The patient will still be awake and will not have any change in perception in other parts of the body.

- General anesthetics cause a reversible loss of consciousness. They induce a state of general insensibility to pain. During medical procedures an anesthetised patient loses consciousness but their vital functions, such as breathing and heartbeat, continue.

What effects do stimulant and inhibitory psychoactive drugs have on the nervous system?

Table A.5

Stimulant (excitatory) drugs	Inhibitory (sedative) drugs
• promote the transmission of impulses at **excitatory synapses** • inhibit transmission at **inhibitory synapses** • mimic the stimulation provided by the sympathetic nervous system • make a person more alert and confident • cause increases in heart rate, blood pressure and body temperature	• increase transmission at inhibitory synapses • suppress transmission at excitatory synapses • includes anesthetics used in medicine • make a person relaxed and drowsy
Examples include: • cocaine • amphetamines • nicotine	Examples include: • alcohol • benzodiazepines • THC (tetrahydrocannabinol) found in cannabis

---

TEST YOURSELF A.9

 1 Outline the effects of alcohol on synapses in the brain. **[2]**

2 What effect does this have on the behaviour of a person who has drunk alcohol? **[1]**

Which factors influence drug addiction?

DEFINITION

ADDICTION is a chemical dependence on a psychoactive drug.

Many different factors are involved in addiction as the body becomes tolerant of a drug, needing more and more of it to produce the same effects.

Three factors seem to be common to all addictions, whether drugs have been taken for therapeutic reasons or recreation.

- Social factors – peer pressure to use a drug, social acceptability of a drug habit such as smoking and factors such as deprivation can be important.

- Genetic predisposition – the tendency to become addicted has been shown to be more common in some families and groups than others. Studies of identical twins support this view.

- Dopamine secretion – drug users find it hard to give up because of the feelings of well-being that are induced by dopamine.

TEST YOURSELF A.10

 Levels of two neurotransmitters, dopamine and serotonin, were measured in the brains of mice given doses of MDMA (ecstasy). During an experiment dopamine levels rose to a peak four times above the normal level 1 hour after treatment but had not returned to normal levels after 3 hours.

1 State the effect of dopamine on the brain in normal conditions. **[1]**

The drug also caused levels of serotonin in the brain, to rise to 2000 times above normal, but the levels fell after a few hours. Low serotonin levels can cause depression and memory loss.

2 Suggest two reasons why MDMA can cause anxiety, restlessness and feelings of sadness some time after it has been taken. **[2]**

A6 Ethology (HL)

Key information you should revise:

- Ethology is defined as the study of animal behaviour in natural conditions.

- The frequency of animal behaviour is influenced by natural selection.

- Behaviour that increases the chance of survival and reproduction will become more prevalent in a population.

- Learned behaviour can spread through or be lost from a population more rapidly than innate behaviour.

DEFINITION

BEHAVIOUR is the pattern of responses of an animal to one or more stimuli, and the study of animal behaviour in natural conditions is called ethology.

How does natural selection influence behaviour?

Natural selection acts on the behavioural responses of animals in just the same way as it does on other characteristics. Behaviour that increases the chances of survival and reproduction will tend to become more prevalent in a population.

One well-documented example is the migratory behaviour of a small European songbird called the blackcap (*Sylvia atricapilla*) (Figure **A.11**). Some of these birds have modified their migration pattern so that many now over winter in the UK instead of their former sites in Spain, so that they can quickly return to their summer breeding grounds in Germany and occupy the best nest locations.

 Nature of Science. Experiments with eggs from the birds in Spain and the UK have shown that the differences are inherited.

Figure A.11 Changes in migration patterns of the blackcap. Blackcaps tended to breed in Germany in the summer and migrate in winter to feed in Spain. In recent decades, increasing numbers have instead travelled north-west from Germany, to overwinter in the UK.

hint

Blackcap migration is one example of behaviour that you should be able to recall. You could include an annotated map in an exam answer if there is sufficient space available in your answer booklet.

Which types of behaviour are likely to become prevalent in a population?

There are many examples of innate and learned behaviours which enhance the survival and reproductive success of a population. These tend to become established in the population and are likely to be retained unless the environmental conditions change. Some examples you should be familiar with are summarised in Table **A.6**.

Table A.6

Example	Consequence
synchronised oestrous in lions	• within a pride, females lions come into oestrus and are ready to mate at the same time • synchronised oestrus produces cubs that are born at the same time and so can be suckled and protected by more than one female in the pride
breeding strategies in coho salmon	• males adopt one of two strategies in their mating behaviour; either they mature early at a smaller body size (jacks) or delay maturation until they are larger, when they are known as hooknoses • hooknoses fight for access to females but jacks avoid fighting and sneak up on females to mate
mate selection in birds of paradise	• males of many species of the bird of paradise have elaborate plumage and complex mating displays • females watch the displays and select a mate from the quality of the display
vampire bats – the evolution of altruistic behaviour	• altruistic behaviour is 'unselfish' behaviour that does not benefit the individual itself but benefits another • female bats that have fed and return to their colony will regurgitate food into the mouth of a bat that has been unable to feed and might otherwise die
foraging in shore crabs (*Carcinus maenas*) – optimising prey size.	• hunting and foraging has an energy cost in finding, catching and consuming food, which has to be balanced with the energy the animal gains • crabs are able to change their behaviour to ensure the overall benefit is greater than the cost as they feed on mussels
blue tits and cream – behaviour learned and lost	• blue tits learned a new behaviour feeding on cream from milk bottles and also passed on the skill to other members of their species • this behaviour has largely been lost today as milk is not sold in bottles, people now buy milk in cartons from a supermarket

TEST YOURSELF A.11

 Table **A.7** shows the foraging behaviour of the Bluegill sunfish is related to the density of its prey *Daphnia* (water fleas) in a pond.

1 Suggest why the sunfish select only large *Daphnia* when the density is high. **[1]**

2 Outline the feeding strategy of the fish when prey density is low. **[1]**

Table A.7

Density of *Daphnia*	Sizes of *Daphnia* selected by sunfish
low	all
medium	middle-sized or large
high	largest

Why does learned behaviour spread through a population more quickly than innate behaviour?

Innate behaviour can only be modified by natural selection. It occurs slowly because there must be new variations in the allele frequencies that affect behaviour. Learned behaviour may take time to be learned but it can spread rapidly in a population as individuals learn from one another. Learned behaviour is much more adaptable and produces a greater range of behavioural patterns than innate behaviour.

TEST YOURSELF A.12

1 Explain how animal responses can be affected by natural selection, using one named example.
2 Explain why blood sharing in vampire bats is an example of altruistic behaviour. **[3]**

hint

Notice that both questions in Test yourself **A.12** ask you to 'explain', so be sure to include some detail in your answer.

B BIOTECHNOLOGY AND BIOINFORMATICS

This chapter covers the following topics:

☐ Microbiology: organisms in industry   ☐ Medicine (HL)

☐ Biotechnology in agriculture   ☐ Bioinformatics (HL)

☐ Environmental protection

B1 Microbiology: organisms in industry

Key information you should revise:

- Different microorganisms have different metabolisms.
- Microorganisms are used in industry because they are small and grow quickly.
- Pathway engineering is a technique that optimises genetic and regulatory processes.
- Pathway engineering is used to produce useful metabolites in industry.
- Fermenters are used for large-scale production of microorganisms and their products.
- Fermentation is carried out by batch or continuous culture.
- Microorganisms are limited by their own waste products.
- Fermenters are monitored by probes so that optimal growth conditions are maintained.

What metabolic diversity can be seen amongst microorganisms?

Microorganisms have a varied range of metabolic processes that enable them to use different sources of energy and carbon. As Table **B.1** shows, microbes are divided into four groups based on their methods of metabolism.

Table B.1

Method of metabolism	Energy source to generate ATP	Carbon source used	Example organisms
photoheterotrophic	light	organic compounds	• *Heliobacter* is able to fix nitrogen so it is probably important in soil fertility
chemoheterotrophic	chemical reactions	organic compounds	• yeast (*Saccharomyes* sp.) cannot photosynthesise, so must use organic material as an energy source, respiring or fermenting sugars to make ATP • most bacteria are also chemoheterotrophs
photoautotrophic	light	inorganic carbon dioxide	• *Anabaena*, a cyanobacterium (filamentous blue–green bacterium) found among freshwater plankton and on grass • it fixes nitrogen and forms symbiotic relationships with some plants
chemoautotrophic	chemical reactions	inorganic carbon dioxide	• *Nitrobacter* and *Nitrosomas* are nitrifying bacterium found in the soil • others include the sulfur-oxidising *Archaea* that live in deep sea vents

How are Gram-positive and Gram-negative bacteria identified?

Gram staining is a practical technique used to distinguish two important groups of bacteria. It uses properties of their cell walls which are differently stained by crystal violet (Figure **B.1**).

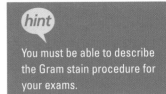

hint

You must be able to describe the Gram stain procedure for your exams.

What are the advantages of using microorganisms in biotechnology?

Microorganisms are used in commercial processes that produce foodstuffs, medicines and industrial products, such as enzymes. Their fast growth rate and small size means that suitable amounts of product can be produced relatively quickly and efficiently. Different organisms are used in the production of yoghurt, cheese, wine, bread and cheese.

What is pathway engineering?

Pathway engineering is a way of manipulating metabolic pathways in microorganisms so that particular metabolites of interest are produced in useful quantities. The technique uses knowledge analysis of metabolic reactions to extend the range of substrates produced or eliminate unwanted by-products that may slow reactions down.

Study of genomics, proteomics, fluxomics and physiomics are all used in pathway engineering, and can significantly increase the amount of product produced per cell.

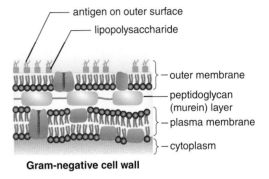

Gram-negative cell wall

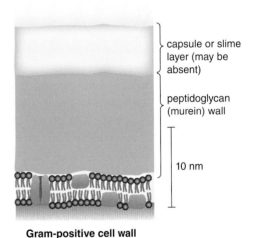

Gram-positive cell wall

Figure B.1 Peptidoglycan consists of sugar molecules joined to polypeptides, which surround and protect the cell.

DEFINITIONS

GENOMICS is the study of the genome of an organism.

PROTEOMICS is the study of the structure and functions of proteins.

FLUXOMICS is the study of the flow of fluids and molecules within cells.

PHYSIOMICS is the study of an organism's physiome, the interconnections of aspects of physiology that result from genes and proteins in the organism.

How is pathway engineering used in biotechnology?

Metabolic pathway engineers use four key strategies to achieve their results:

1 Optimisation of the primary metabolic pathway by removal of factors that limit the rate of the reaction or transcription, as well as removing allosteric regulation, so that more product is produced.

2 Genetic blocking of any competing pathways.

3 Maximising the amount of carbon substrate that is directed to the metabolic pathway of interest and away from other pathways.

4 Modification of secondary metabolic pathways to direct maximum energy for metabolism as well as enzymes and cofactors to the pathway of interest.

Two examples of successful pathway engineering have been in the production of penicillin from *Penicillium* sp. bacteria and of citric acid from the fungus *Aspergillus niger*.

Aspergillus was modified by genetic engineering to increase citric acid yields by increasing the 'metabolic flux' or flow through the pathway forming citric acid (Figure **B.2**).

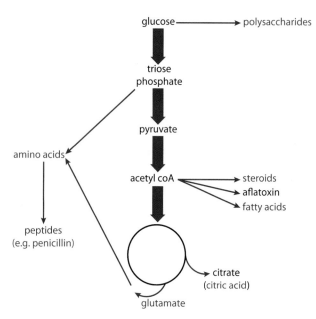

Figure B.2 Diagram to show some useful products of the metabolism of glucose by fungi. Useful substances are shown in red. Pathway engineers optimise genetic or regulatory processes in microorganisms to maximise production of these substances.

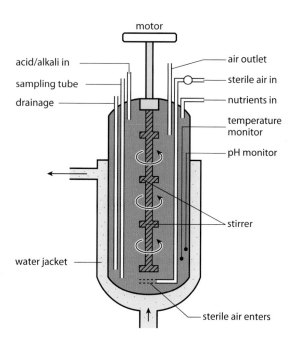

Figure B.3 The inputs and outputs of a typical fermenter.

How are fermenters used in large-scale industrial production?

- Fermenters can hold up to 200 000 litres.
- Most organisms are cultured in aqueous culture, involving a substrate with high water content.
- Cells receive nutrients and environmental conditions to grow at their maximum rate.
- Aerobic microorganisms receive air and the culture is stirred to ensure even mixing of nutrients.

hint

Be prepared to discuss the production of penicillin and citric acid for your exams.

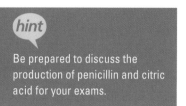

Fermenters used in biotechnology are not only used to produce alcohol. The term is used for any large-scale culture of microorganisms. Fermenters allow production and harvesting of useful metabolites of microorganisms. Growth in a fermenter can be limited by accumulation of waste products (Figure **B.3**).

Nutrients enter fermenters through valve-operated pipes so that exact quantities can be controlled to maximise growth. All fermenters must be sterile before the process begins and this is usually achieved by passing steam through the pipes and tanks. People who work in the biotechnology industry must also take precautions and wear protective clothing to avoid contamination.

What are the two different ways of producing products in fermenters?

Two different processes, batch culture and continuous culture, can be used depending on the organism being grown (Table **B.2**).

Table B.2

Batch culture	Continuous culture
• used in the production of penicillin, carried out in closed fermenters. *Penicillium* and sterilised nutrients are added and the fermenter is left for the process to take place	• used to manufacture citric acid using *Aspergillus*; nutrients and products are added or removed from the fermenter as the reaction proceeds
• only waste gases leave the fermenter. This process is used to manufacture secondary metabolites of the microorganism, which are not essential for normal cellular functions	• continuous culture matches supply and demand so that the organisms can be kept in an exponential phase of growth
• product is separated from the mixture at the end	• product is harvested continuously
• conditions inside the fermenter change (although temperature is monitored)	• all environmental factors are monitored and kept as constant as possible (sometimes this is difficult and production can be disrupted)
• cells have a relatively short time in the exponential growth phase	• cells are kept in the exponential growth phase
• larger 'deep tank' fermenters are needed	• smaller fermenters can be used – process is more productive
• usually less cost effective, but if a batch is contaminated only one batch is lost	• continuous process is more economical, but if a fermenter is contaminated losses are greater

What limits industrial fermentation?

Several factors limit the growth of microorganisms in fermenters (Figure **B.4**). These include accumulation of waste products or shortage of a required nutrient. In **continuous culture** supply and demand for nutrients are matched and waste products removed so that the organisms can be kept in an exponential phase of growth. Other factors limiting growth include:

- heat – produced by metabolism
- oxygen level – if this falls too low aerobes cannot respire
- accumulation of alcohol – eventually kills the organisms producing it
- carbon dioxide – produced by metabolism, can affect the pH.

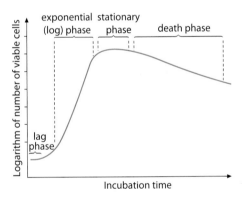

Figure B.4 Growth curve of microorganism in batch culture.

TEST YOURSELF B.1

 In your notebook copy and complete Table **B.3** to show how conditions are regulated in a fermenter.

Table B.3

Condition	Leads to	Controlled by
	enzyme inefficiency	cooling jackets
low oxygen levels		
	changes in pH	

How are optimum conditions maintained in fermenters?

Probes are used to monitor the levels of nutrients, oxygen, waste products, temperature, pH, carbon dioxide and cell density. The conditions each microorganism needs are different. For example, the yeast *Saccharomyces* is tolerant of low oxygen levels, whereas *Penicillium* is not.

What is biogas and how is it produced?

Biogas is methane produced from animal manure and agricultural waste. A simple, small-scale fermenter can be used to produce biogas for domestic use. Manure and straw are fed into the bioreactor, where they decompose anaerobically as different groups of bacteria present in the manure break down the organic material. The slurry that remains is a useful fertiliser (Figure **B.5**).

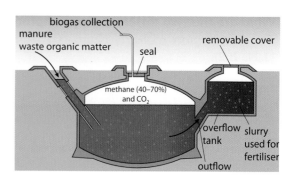

Figure B.5 Cross section of a biogas reactor.

 1 State the type of fermentation process used to produce penicillin. **[1]**

2 Using the information in the diagram Figure **B.6** and your own knowledge, state three factors that affect the quantity of penicillin produced. **[3]**

3 Outline the meaning of the term 'secondary metabolite'. **[2]**

4 Identify the time on the graph when the *Penicillium* fungus had reached the plateau phase of growth. **[1]**

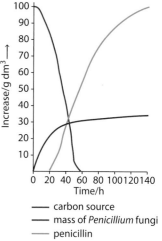

carbon source
mass of *Penicillium* fungi
penicillin

Figure B.6

B2 Biotechnology in agriculture

Key information you should revise:

- Transgenic organisms produce proteins that were not previously part of their proteome.

- Genetic modification can be used to increase crop yield or produce new products.

- Bioinformatics helps to identify useful target genes.

- Target genes are linked to others that control gene expression.

- An open reading frame is a significant length of DNA from a start to a stop codon.

- Marker genes identify successful uptake.

- **Recombinant DNA** must be inserted into a plant cell chromosome or chloroplast DNA. It can be introduced into whole plants, leaf discs or protoplasts.

- Recombinant DNA can be introduced by physical or chemical methods or indirectly via a vector.

What is a transgenic organism?

Recall some examples of transgenic organisms, such as bacterial genes transferred to plants and human genes transferred to bacteria, for your exam.

DEFINITION

TRANSGENIC describes an organism that contains genes from another organism.

Gene technology enables scientists to transfer genes from one species to another different species and create a transgenic organism in just one generation. Gene transfer is possible because the genetic code is universal. The genetic code produces an amino acid sequence in one species that is exactly the same in any other species.

Why is it useful to genetically modify crop plants and domestic animals?

Most genetic engineering has involved commercial crops, such as soybeans, maize, potatoes, tomatoes and cotton. Plants have been modified to make them:

- resistant to pests and disease, e.g. maize resistant to rootworm pests
- tolerant to herbicides, e.g. glyphosate resistant soybeans
- be able to produce novel products, e.g. vaccine production in tobacco
- extend their ranges, so they can tolerate drier or more saline conditions, e.g. maize that can retain water in drought conditions
- increase crop yields.

There are very few examples of genetically modified animal species. But animals have been farmed for the production of proteins for therapeutic use. One example is Factor XI, a clotting factor used in the treatment of hemophilia, which can be produced in the milk of genetically modified sheep and another is alpha-1 anti-trypsin. Humans who cannot produce this protein suffer breakdown of their lung tissue.

What are target genes? What are marker genes?

In gene technology, manipulated DNA that contains genes for the protein or proteins of interest is called recombinant DNA (Section **3.5**). The first stage in any gene technology process is to find and isolate the target genes for the protein to be produced. These genes are also linked to other genes, which may control the way they are expressed, for example if a protein is to be produced in milk, genes to ensure that it is produced on the endoplasmic reticulum and secreted from mammary gland cells are added. In some cases additional sequences must be added later to regulate the target gene.

Marker genes are often added to a selected gene to show that it has been taken up into a new organism Screening markers identify cells that have taken up new genes by their appearance. The most common screening markers are:

- a green fluorescent protein (GFP), which makes cells glow under UV light
- the blue–white method, used as both a plant and bacterial marker, which uses a bacterial gene coding for beta galactosidase enzyme. If galactosides are added to a culture medium, cells containing the gene convert it to a blue substance, which can be seen easily.

How is recombinant DNA introduced into plants?

In order to modify plants, new DNA sequences must be introduced into their cells and taken up either by the plant's chromosomes or by the chloroplast DNA (Figure **B.7**). Recombinant DNA can be introduced into:

- whole plants
- leaf discs kept in tissue culture
- protoplasts (cells that have had their cell walls removed).

When plants, leaf discs or protoplasts have taken up DNA, they can be grown to make new transgenic plants.

Recombinant DNA can be introduced to organisms by direct physical processes, chemical methods or by using **vectors**:

- Electroporation – applying an electric field, which forms temporary pores in cell membranes so that DNA can enter the cell.

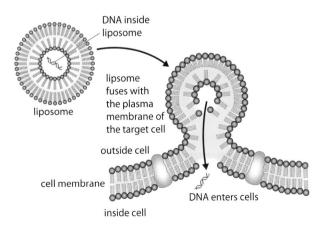

Figure B.7 Liposome structure and transinfection.

- Biolistic methods (ballistic incorporation) – using a gene gun which shoots DNA attached to a nanoparticle of material directly into the nucleus.

- Microinjection – using a micropipette to inject DNA into a living cell under a microscope.

- Liposomes – sequences of DNA or bacterial plasmids are enclosed in liposomes, which fuse with cell membranes and release DNA into the target cell.

- Infection – a virus is used as a vector that transfers DNA into cells.

TEST YOURSELF B.3

 Name two types of sequences that must be inserted together with the target gene into the host genome in order to produce a transgenic organism. **[2]**

How has gene technology been used in industry?

In paper production using potatoes

Potato starch consists of approximately 80% amylopectin and 20% amylose (Section **2.3**) but most of the useful properties for industry come from amylopectin. The Amflora® potato with deactivated amylose genes produces only amylopectin and so it is ideal for use in the paper-making and the adhesive industries.

In herbicide-resistant soybeans

Glyphosate is a commonly used herbicide that is broken down by soil bacteria. Genes from soil bacteria transferred into plants make them resistant to the herbicide, which will kill weeds and leave crop plants unaffected.

Glyphosate-resistance genes are introduced into soybeans or maize using a vector, the bacterium *Agrobacterium tumefaciens*. Recombinant plasmids are placed in *A. tumefaciens* cells, which then infect plant cells susceptible to glyphosate. Plant cells with included resistance are grown in tissue culture (Figure **B.8**).

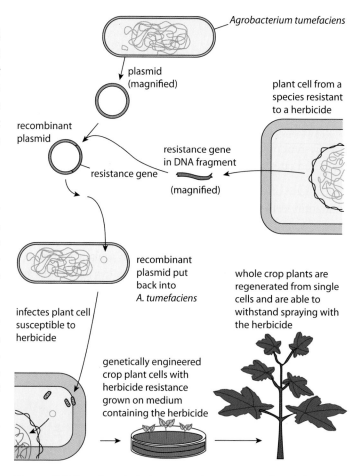

Figure B.8 Transfer of glyphosate-resistance genes by Ti plasmid.

Table B.3 Risks and benefits of using genetically modified (GM) glyphosate-resistant plants

Risks	Benefits
• transfer of glyphosate resistance to wild species	• less spraying with herbicide – 40% less on glyphosate-resistant crop between 1995 and 1998
• increase in weeds which are resistant to glyphosate	• reduction in environmental degradation due to less digging and turning

What is an open reading frame?

An open reading frame (ORF) is a sequence of nucleotides in a DNA molecule that starts with a 'start' codon (ATG) and has no stop codons within it. The site that terminates transcription is found after the ORF and beyond the translation stop codon. This means that, once transcribed and translated, the ORF has the potential to produce a complete polypeptide chain.

ORFs are very useful in helping to predict which sections of a DNA molecule are likely to be genes. Long ORFs can be used to identify regions of DNA likely to code for proteins. Researchers search for a start codon followed by an ORF that is long enough to code for a typical protein in the particular organism they are investigating.

Worked example B.1

The start codon is ATG and stop codons are TGA, TAA and TAG

a Identify an open reading frame in this base sequence:

GTG/ATC/ATG/TAC/GTC/CGA/ACG/TAT/TTT/CAA/GTA/AGA/CAA/TTT/CGT/CAC/CAA/CTT/GAG/TCC/ GAT/TTT/ACA/TGA/TAA/TTA/GAT/CAT/GCC/GAA

To do this you must look carefully through the codons at the start of the sequence and find a start codon. Remember that a codon is made up of three bases so you must divide the sequence into 'threes' from the first base. You should spot the start codon as the third triplet in the sequence.

b State how many codons are in the open reading frame.

Now you must continue to examine the codons in the sequence and check for one of the three stop codons. If it occurs soon after the start codon, this is unlikely to be an open reading frame, which must be long enough to code for about 100 or so amino acids. You should find the codon TGA seven codons from the end. In this example the sequence is shorter than a normal ORF and we have separated the codons for you.

TEST YOURSELF B.4

 Genetically modified potatoes known as Amflora® have been produced by BASF. State one difference and one advantage of these potatoes over non-modified potatoes? **[2]**

B3 Environmental protection

Key information you should revise:

- Bioremediation together with physical and chemical procedures can be used in response to pollution incidents.
- Microorganisms are used in bioremediation and can metabolise some pollutants.
- Biofilms are formed of cooperative aggregates of microorganisms and possess emergent properties.
- Organisms in biofilms cooperate through quorum sensing.
- Water systems can be disinfected using bacteriophages.

What methods are used to clean up after pollutants have entered the environment?

If chemicals such as oil, heavy metals or sewage are accidentally released into the environment, they must be removed as quickly as possible so that organisms and food chains are not harmed. Both physical and **bioremediation** methods are used:

- physical methods include using detergents and scrubbing
- soil can be removed and burned
- soil can be removed and chemical contaminants 'washed' out
- chemicals that speed up the destruction of toxins can be added to soil
- bioremediation using microbes to break down the pollutants can be used.

How are microorganisms used in bioremediation?

Bioremediation involves microorganisms which use the pollutant as a source of carbon or energy. Many bacteria have metabolic pathways which enable them to do this. For example:

- *Marinobacter* species can degrade hydrocarbons in the sea. The bacteria tolerate marine conditions well.
- *Pseudomonas aeruginosa* uses crude oil as its sole source of carbon. If surfactants are also used, oil can be removed more quickly.
- Two species of bacteria, *Pseudomonas* sp. and *Azospirillum* sp. are capable of breaking down organophosphate pesticides.
- *Pseudomonas balearica* carry mercury-resistance genes and can decompose methyl mercury to produce inorganic mercury, which can be precipitated and collected.

If contaminated soil is mixed with bulking agents such as hay and kept moist, conditions will favour chosen microorganisms that can feed on pollutants.

TEST YOURSELF B.5

 State two reasons why bioremediation can help in clearing up after incidents of environmental pollution. **[2]**

What is a biofilm?

DEFINITION

A **BIOFILM** is an aggregate of microorganisms that form a cooperative colony.

Most bacteria live as single cells but some, such as *Streptococcus mutans* which occurs widely in the mouth, form groups of cells that are connected together. *S. mutans* forms a **biofilm** on teeth, at the junction with the gums. The bacteria convert sucrose to a glue-like extracellular polysaccharide substance (EPS), which allows the bacteria to stick to each other and form plaque.

Other biofilms include the persistent slime that forms in a bathroom drain and the coating on the surface of submerged rock, which may include bacteria, algae and fungi and make rocks slippery and dangerous. Biofilms can cause major problems and can be a health hazard if they form on food-production surfaces; cause clogging and corrosion in pipes; form in catheters, nasal tubes or on heart valves in hospitals.

Some biofilms are useful. One example is their use in bioremediation in sewage treatment. Secondary treatment uses trickle filter beds containing biofilms of bacteria and fungi on the surface of a porous material (clinker). As water trickles through the biofilm, microorganisms break down the organic matter it contains. Oxygen levels are kept high by the trickling water and small invertebrates, such as worms and protozoans, feed on the biofilm, so that it does not grow too thick and impede the filtering process.

What are the properties of biofilms that make them difficult to remove?

1 Biofilms are very flexible and are described as being viscoelastic, which means they can stretch and change their shape as a flow of liquid pulls or pushes them.

2 Biofilms cannot be removed by rinsing them away.

3 A flow of liquid over a biofilm may cause clumps to disconnect and fall away to settle elsewhere.

4 Biofilms protect the organisms within them from the human immune system and make them highly resistant to treatment with antibiotics and other antimicrobial agents.

5 The organisms communicate with one another and there may be channels which allow water to pass through the colony.

6 Cells may also use the EPS matrix to move the biofilm and it provides a physical barrier to antibiotics used to attach the colony.

What is quorum sensing?

Microorganisms living close to one another within a biofilm communicate using quorum sensing; they release signalling molecules into the environment. The accumulation of signalling molecules enables a single cell to detect the density of other cells in the area, and allows cells to coordinate their behaviour. If an environmental factor, such as the availability of nutrients changes, they can respond quickly in order to survive. They are able to defend themselves against competitors that share the same food source.

> **hint**
>
> Be ready to answer questions about emergent properties – the features of biofilms that single organism do not have.

How are bacteriophages used to kill bacteria in water systems?

DEFINITION

BACTERIOPHAGES are viruses that infect and kill bacteria but which have no effect on plant or animal cells.

Today, as antibiotic resistance is on the increase (Section **6.3**) and it is becoming more and more difficult to kill bacteria, there are roles for bacteriophages as antibacterial agents.

Bacteriophages have been used to remove biofilms of *Pseudomonas aeruginosa* bacteria, which can clog filters at water purification plants. Usually these bacteria must be cleaned away with chlorine and expensive flushing treatments. Bacteriophages can kill almost 90% of these biofilms and treatment is almost 100% effective if the bacteriophages are followed by a single treatment with chlorine.

Bacteriophages have also been used to kill the filamentous bacteria (*Sphaerotilus natans*) that grow in long threads during the settlement stage of sewage treatment. The bacteria interfere with the process by preventing sludge settling in the settlement tanks.

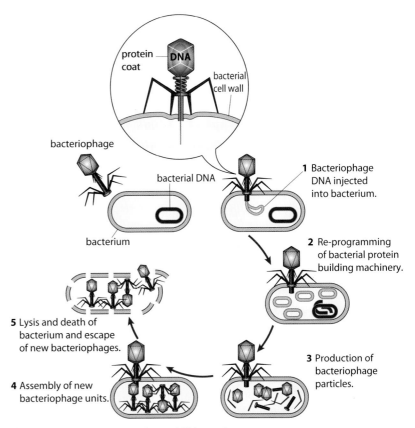

Figure B.9 How bacteriophages kill bacteria.

TEST YOURSELF B.6

 Define quorum sensing.

📑 Annotated exemplar answer B.1

Give an example of a biofilm and list two reasons why biofilms are difficult to remove. **[3]**

> An example of a biofilm is plaque on teeth.
>
> They are difficult to remove because they are often found in difficult places such as catheters.

(2/3)

You could also use the example of biofilms in catheters or slime in pipes or biofilms at sewage treatment plants.

This is correct but a better answer would be to mention the EPS (matrix) that protects biofilms from antimicrobial agents. You should also mention that rinsing may cause them to move as a colony.

B4 Medicine (HL)

Key information you should revise:

- Infection by a pathogen can be detected by its genetic material or antigens.
- Predisposition to a genetic disease can be detected from markers.
- DNA microarrays are used to test for genetic predisposition or to diagnose disease.
- Metabolites detected in blood and urine can indicate disease.
- Tracking experiments provide information about the location and interaction of desired proteins.
- Biopharming uses genetically modified (GM) animals and plants to produces therapeutic proteins.
- Viral vectors can be used in gene therapy.

How can an infection by a pathogen by detected?

Infections can be detected by the presence of a pathogen's genetic material or antigens in the body. Early diagnosis can then lead to faster treatment.

The three most important techniques used are:

- detection of pathogen-specific antibodies in the blood
- detection of the pathogen's antigens
- detection of genetic material from the pathogen.

How are antigens detected?

One of the mostly commonly used tests is the ELISA (Enzyme Linked Immuno Sorbent Assay). The test uses an antibody that is specific to a particular antigen from a known pathogen and a colour change shows whether or not antigens are present in a sample. The antigens chosen for use in the test are those that appear in blood or urine during an infection – for example, polysaccharides from viral capsules or proteins produced by bacteria.

In a negative test the free antibody is washed away so there is no colour change. In a positive test the antibodies bind to the target molecules so a colour change is seen. Quantitative results can be obtained by measuring the degree of colour change.

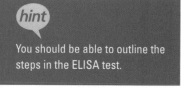

hint

You should be able to outline the steps in the ELISA test.

How is genetic material detected in an infection?

Genetic material from pathogens, such as influenza viruses can be detected using the reverse transcriptase polymerase chain reaction (RT-PCR). It uses genetic material from retroviruses, such as influenza (which contain only RNA), as a template for reverse transcription. Complementary DNA is produced from the virus RNA. Alternatively, for other pathogens, DNA samples can be used directly. The DNA is amplified using the **polymerase chain reaction (PCR)** (Section **3.5**) and detected either by gel electrophoresis or by using hybridisation with known sequences of DNA to assess the degree of matching to identify the pathogen.

What can medical staff find out from metabolites in blood and urine?

Metabolites that indicate disease can be found in blood and urine samples.

DEFINITION

A **BIOMARKER** is a substance that can be measured and which can indicate the presence or severity of a disease.

Biomarkers used in medicine include LDL (low density lipoprotein), which can be measured to indicate blood cholesterol levels, and genetic biomarkers for specific cancers or a predisposition to them.

DEFINITION

METABOLOMICS is a name given to the analysis of metabolites in a blood or urine sample.

In many cases diseases cause disruption of metabolic pathways and the accumulation of, or lack of, metabolites can be biological indicators of certain diseases.

Conditions that are diagnosed in this way include:

- diabetes – from the presence of ketones in urine
- PKU – from phenylalanine in blood samples
- porphyria – accumulation of precursors for the synthesis of porphyrins and heme in blood or urine.

How can predisposition to a genetic disease be detected?

DEFINITION

GENETIC PREDISPOSITION means that a person may not be born with a disease or condition but has a high risk of acquiring it.

Markers present in the person's body can indicate the likelihood they will be susceptible to disease. Markers may be coding or non-coding sequences of DNA (they may contribute to the disease or occur close to the defective gene) and they can be located using PCR or DNA profiling.

Important diseases that can be detected in this way include:

- breast cancer – BRCA genes on chromosomes 13 and 17
- prostate and other cancers – tumour markers found in blood, urine or tissue samples may be elevated.

What is a DNA microarray and how is it used?

DNA microarrays are used to test for genetic predisposition or for diagnosing disease. A microarray is a small tray with a range of DNA probes fixed to its surface. Each probe contains a specific DNA sequence that is used to hybridise samples of target DNA.

Hybridisation occurs when complementary nucleotide sequences in probe and target DNA molecules pair up by forming hydrogen bonds.

The more complementary sequences present, the greater and stronger the bonding between the two strands.

Hybridisation is usually detected and quantified using luminescent labels attached to target DNA.

If test samples contain mRNA this is converted to cDNA, which becomes the target DNA, and dyes are attached before the hybridisation process.

The greater the level of hybridisation, the greater the presence of the gene and the more the gene is expressed.

How can proteins in the blood be tracked?

Blood proteins can be tracked by attaching radioactive or other markers to them. It can be a useful technique in diagnosis and treatment.

Transferrins are glycoproteins found in the blood, which bind to iron and control the level of iron in the plasma. Transferrin receptor (TfR) is a receptor in cell membranes and is involved in the uptake of iron from transferrin and with the regulation of cell growth. Tumour cells can be found by linking luminescent tracking probes to transferrin molecules, which then attach to the TfRs. In this way, luminescence can be used both to measure levels of TfRs and to identify tumour cells in the body.

What is biopharming and how is it used?

DEFINITION

BIOPHARMING is the use of genetic engineering to add genes to animals or plants so that they produce useful pharmaceuticals.

Biopharming can be used to produce therapeutic proteins such as ATryn®, proteins for use in vaccines and also antibodies. These are complex proteins which cannot be produced in bacterial cells because bacteria do not carry out modifications to proteins after translation.

At present transgenic goats produced by nuclear transfer have been used to good effect because:

- Harvesting from milk is the most popular way of accessing recombinant proteins from transgenic organisms.
- Milk is produced in large quantities and proteins can easily be purified from it.
- Goats are well suited to biopharming as they produce more milk than sheep.
- Females goats mature quicker than sheep and have a gestation period of just 6 months.

Antithrombin deficiency causes blood clots during surgery and ATryn® is antithrombin, produced commercially for people with the deficiency. Genes for the protein, together with promoters and genes to ensure the protein is produced in milk, are introduced into goat oocytes to produce cloned, transgenic offspring.

Biopharming in plants is possible for vaccines, which have been produced in tobacco leaves; and for enzymes, for example glucocerebrosidase, which is produced in bioreactors containing duckweed (*Lemna minor*) and is used to treat Glaucher's disease.

TEST YOURSELF B.7

 Biopharming can be described as which of the following:
- **A** growing animals for farming
- **B** genetically modifying animals to produce novel products
- **C** producing transgenic animals for farming
- **D** creating clones of useful animals

How are viral vectors used in gene therapy?

Viruses are very efficient at entering the cells of organisms, and can be used as vectors for the delivery of therapeutic genes into cells. Some viruses can incorporate the genes they carry into the cells they enter.

Retroviruses, single stranded RNA viruses are often used.

- They enter via specific receptors.
- Their RNA is converted to DNA.
- The DNA is integrated in the host cell genome.
- It remains there for the life of the cell.
- Integrated DNA can be passed on when the cell divides.

Before a virus can be used, it must be modified so that it will enter but not replicate inside a target cell, as this would destroy the cell. Viral genes involved in replication are removed or inactivated. Non-viral genetic material is inserted and these viruses are then known as vectors.

There has been some success in treating SCID and cystic fibrosis using gene therapy.

TEST YOURSELF B.8

 Which of the following statements about transgenic organisms is true:

A they contain genes from another species   **C** they are from different geographical areas

B they are used to produce human antibodies   **D** statements **A** and **B** only are true

B5 Bioinformatics (HL)

Key information you should revise:

- Databases provide easy access to information and the amount available is increasing exponentially.
- BLAST search can identify similar sequences in different organisms.
- Model organisms with similar sequences are used to study gene function.
- Sequence alignment software compares sequences from different organisms.
- BLASTn allows nucleotide sequence alignment and BLASTp allows protein alignment.
- Databases allow newly identified sequences to be compared with known function sequences in other organisms.
- **EST (expressed sequence tags)** are used to identify potential genes.

How are databases used in genetic research?

Biological databases are enormous electronic records of information from experiments, scientific papers and computer analyses of data. Databases contain collections of structured, searchable and up-to-date data maintained electronically.

Information is stored from research in:

- genomics – records of nucleotide sequence
- proteomics – records of protein sequence data
- metabolomics – pathway data on enzyme controlled reactions
- microarray – results on genes and mRNA expressed in different cells
- phylogenetic – studies of evolution.

The amount of information stored in this way is thought to be increasing exponentially.

Nature of Science. Co-operation between groups of scientists using internet databases allows free access to information.

How are BLAST searches used and what can they show us?

BLAST is an algorithm used to compare sequence information, such as the amino acid sequences in different proteins or the nucleotide sequences in DNA from different organisms. The BLAST programme was first published in 1990 and now researchers can use a BLAST search to compare a sequence of DNA or amino acids with a database containing known sequences. The search will reveal all the known sequences that have more than a certain proportion of resemblances to the sequence being investigated.

What is the difference between a BLASTn and a BLASTp search?

The BLASTn programme allows nucleotide sequence alignments to be made. BLASTn can be used for several purposes, such as the identification of species, establishment of evolutionary relationships, and DNA mapping and comparison.

- BLASTn can help to determine the origin of a certain sequence of DNA. It can search for related species with similar sequences.

- Using the results from BLASTn, a phylogenetic tree can be built up. Although phylogenies based on BLASTn alone are not 100% reliable and are always used in conjunction with other phylogenetic analyses.

- In DNA mapping, BLASTn can compare the chromosomal position of a gene sequence of a known species with the positions of other sequences in the database, or locate genes that are common in related species to map differences and similarities between one organism and another.

The BLASTp programme allows amino acid sequence alignments to be made and matches to be found between newly discovered sequences and known sequences. Questions it can help to answer include:

- Do analogous proteins from different species share similar amino acid sequences, and if so are the species likely to be related in evolutionary terms?

- Where in a protein is a particular sequence of amino acids located?

How are databases used to investigate newly identified sequences?

Databases can be used to compare newly discovered sequences with sequences whose function is already known.

TEST YOURSELF B.9

 State the type of data that can be accessed in a BLASTn search.

How are model organisms such as knock out mice used in research?

DEFINITION

A **MODEL ORGANISM** is a species that has been studied by many scientists because it is assumed that discoveries made in the species will have relevance to other organisms. Examples include the mouse, the fruit fly, the yeast *Saccharomyces cerevisiae* and the plant *Arabidopsis thaliana*.

Model organisms such as knock out mice are used to study gene function, especially genes that have been sequenced but whose functions are not known.

A knock out mouse is genetically modified so that certain genes are inactivated. Thousands of different strains exist. Each is named after the 'knocked out' gene. Knocking out genes changes the phenotype of the mouse so that it looks or behaves in a way that researchers can see or it has different biochemical characteristics that can be monitored.

1 Outline what is meant by a model organism. **[1]**

2 State two named examples of model organisms. **[2]**

3 Why are model organisms important in research? **[1]**

What are expressed sequence tags (ESTs)?

ESTs are tags that can be used to identify potential genes in a sequence of DNA.

An EST is the nucleotide sequence of a tiny portion of a known gene, which computers can use to scan databases to help make a match with unknown genes and to map their positions within a genome. This information can help in genome mapping.

ESTs are short sequences (usually between 300 and 500 nucleotides long) that occur at one or both ends of a gene. ESTs effectively 'represent' the genes expressed in certain cells. Researchers use them to locate a gene in a portion of chromosomal DNA from a different organism by matching up the base pairs. ESTs provide a route for finding new genes and for obtaining data on gene expression and regulation.

A database called dbEST records data about ESTs. All ESTs that are submitted to the genetic database GenBank are checked and annotated and then lodged in dbEST.

List three types of information that might be collected in a genetic database.

> **hint**
>
> Notice that the command word in Test yourself question **B.11** is 'list' so do not waste time adding unnecessary detail. This will not gain extra marks.

ECOLOGY AND CONSERVATION

This chapter covers the following topics:

☐ Species and communities

☐ Communities and ecosystems

☐ Impacts of humans on ecosystems

☐ Conservation of biodiversity

☐ Population ecology (HL)

☐ The nitrogen and phosphorus cycles (HL)

C1 Species and communities

Key information you should revise:

- The distribution of species is affected by limiting factors.
- Each species plays its own role in a community because of the combination of its spatial habitat and interactions with other species.
- Interactions are classified by their effect in a community.
- Two species cannot survive indefinitely in the same habitat if they have identical niches.
- Community structure is affected by keystone species.

What are limiting factors and how do they influence species distribution?

If there is insufficient light or if the temperature is too low plants will die, so these conditions are known as limiting factors for the distribution of plant species.

Plant distribution is limited by the following: temperature, light intensity, pH of soil, water availability, salinity and availability of minerals. Animal distribution is limited by the following: temperature water, food availability, number of breeding sites and availability of territory.

How can the distribution of a species be investigated and related to abiotic factors?

DEFINITION

ABIOTIC FACTORS are non-living components of an ecosystem such as soil type or light intensity.

Sampling methods such as the use of quadrats and transects are used. Samples must be randomised, using random number tables.

A quadrat is a square made of metal or wood that is placed on the ground so that the organisms present inside the square can be counted. The sizes of the quadrats vary according to the sampling area.

A transect involves sampling a line or belt through an area and can show the distribution of a species in relation to a particular abiotic factor. It can also show successions or changes in communities of organisms across a habitat. Transects provide a method of systematic rather than random sampling.

☆ Model answer C.1

Think of a plant or animal species that is found in the area where you live. Note how each of the factors listed previously affects its distribution.

Nettles are wild plants that cannot grow in cold conditions and are not found in areas where the temperature is regularly below 10°C. They need light for photosynthesis and grow in open ground or under hedges. They are tolerant of a range of pH levels but will not be found in very acid soils. They require water but do not grow in waterlogged soils or desert conditions. They are limited by salinity and are not found in coastal areas where the soil is salty. They grow well where there are high levels of nitrogen and are often found along the edges of cultivated fields where fertilisers have run off the land.

What gives each species its unique position within a community?

DEFINITION

A **COMMUNITY** may be described by the geographical area it occupies, a lake community for example, or by the dominant plant species present, coniferous forest, for instance.

The organisms present in a community depend on the other organisms living there. These other species provide food or are predators. Abiotic aspects such as soil, rock formation and weather are also important. In all communities each species plays a unique role. This role is determined by its place in the habitat and the interactions that it has with other species.

DEFINITION

HABITAT is an area offering living space to a number of different types of organism and includes all the physical and abiotic factors in the environment.

Every organism occupies its own space in an ecosystem, which is known as its spatial habitat. The surroundings are changed by the presence of the organism. For example, a woodpecker lives inside hollow trees, adapting them to provide nesting places and shelter.

DEFINITION

A **NICHE** is the particular environment and 'lifestyle' that is adopted by a species. It includes the place where the organism lives and breeds (its spatial habitat), as well as its food and feeding method and its interactions with other species.

As an organism feeds within its niche, it affects the other organisms that are present. For example, an owl feeding on mice in woodland helps to keep the population of mice at a stable level. A habitat comprises a number of niches, each one is unique to its particular species because it offers the exact conditions that the species needs.

What is meant by competitive exclusion?

Competition occurs when two organisms need the same limited resource and they may find themselves in competition for the same niche. The principle of **competitive exclusion** states that no two species can occupy the same niche. The species cannot exist together because one will come to dominate and exclude the other.

Ecology and conservation

A famous study on competition was carried out in 1934. A Russian scientist, Gause, experimented with two species of *Paramecium*, *P. aurelia* and *P. caudatum*. If the two species were allowed to grow in separate cultures where they were fed on bacteria, both species grew well. When the two species were cultured together with an identical food source, *P. aurelia* survived while *P. caudatum* died out. Both species had similar needs in the culture but *P. aurelia* had an advantage that enabled it to outgrow *P. caudatum*.

TEST YOURSELF C.1

 The kite diagram (Figure **C.1**) shows the distribution of five species of mollusc on a rocky shore.

1 Which is the most abundant species at the high tide mark (30 m). **[1]**

2 Suggest two abiotic factors that could affect the distribution of the five species shown in the diagram. **[2]**

3 Suggest two reasons for the different distributions of *Littorina neritoides* and *L.littorea*. **[2]**

4 Outline reasons for the distribution of *Nucella lapillus* in relation to (i) *Patella vulgata* and (ii) *Littorina* species. **[3]**

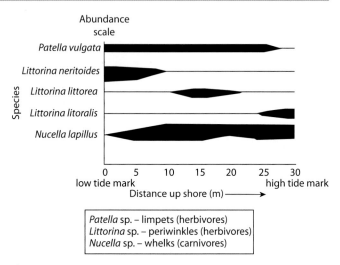

Figure C.1

What are some of the interactions between species that have an effect on the community?

Organisms interact with other organisms living in the same community. The interactions include competition, herbivory, predation, parasitism and **mutualism**. These interactions are defined in Table **C.1**.

Table C.1

Interaction	Effects
competition	• two species require the same resource • one may exclude the other (see below)
herbivory	• herbivores feed on plants • different organisms eat leaves, stems or roots • herbviores may cause damage to plants
predation	• predators catch and kill prey and reduce their numbers
parasitism	• one species feeds in or on another living organism which suffers as a result

The effect of interactions between two species is summarised in Table **C.2**.

Table C.2

		Effects on organism 1	
		Benefit	Harm
Effects on organism 2	Benefit	mutualism	predation/parasitism
	Harm	predation/parasitism	competition

Name the three types of species interaction.

What is a keystone species and how does it affect community structure?

DEFINITION

A **KEYSTONE SPECIES** is one that has a disproportionate effect on the structure of a community.

Keystone species include specific predators or grazers. For example, limpets are a keystone species on a rocky shore because they control the level of algae as they graze.

Lobsters are a predatory keystone species. We can see how important they are from observations of over-fishing. When fishermen removed too many lobsters from the Atlantic Ocean, there were not enough left to control the sea urchin population. Numbers of sea urchins increased and destroyed large areas of kelp, a species of seaweed. As the kelp disappeared, the complex community of molluscs and other small organisms that lived in it was also destroyed. The diversity of species and the complexity of the food webs were much reduced.

TEST YOURSELF C.3

State one example of a mutualistic and one of a parasitic relationship.

C2 Communities and ecosystems

Key information you should revise:

- Species occupy different trophic levels in multiple food chains.
- A food web show possible food chains in a community.
- The percentage of ingested energy converted to biomass depends on respiration rate.
- We can predict the appearance of stable ecosystems based on climate.
- In closed ecosystems energy is exchanged with the surroundings but matter is not.
- If an ecosystem is disturbed its structure and rate of change are affected.

What is a trophic level and how do species occupy more than one trophic level?

Before you revise this section, refresh your memory by looking back at Chapter **4**, Section **4.2**.

What are pyramids of energy?

DEFINITION

PYRAMIDS OF ENERGY are diagrams that model the flow of energy through an ecosystem.

When herbivores feed, the energy transferred from plant to herbivore is also not 100% efficient. Not all of the plant material is eaten, not all the material is absorbed in the gut, and some energy is lost in movement and respiration. The same is true for carnivores eating prey animals. Only about 10% of the energy in producers is passed to herbivores and a similar low percentage of energy is passed from herbivores to carnivores.

Ecology and conservation

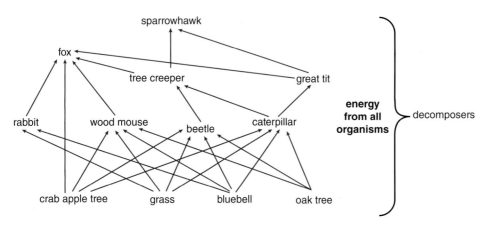

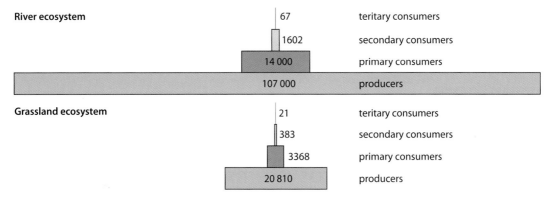

Ecologists show the availability of energy in an ecosystem in energy pyramids. It is also possible to construct pyramids of numbers and biomass.

Figure C.2 In a food web such as this, species may feed at different trophic levels, depending on what they eat.

Figure C.3 Pyramids of energy for a river ecosystem and a grassland ecosystem. Each bar represents a trophic level and the width of the bar indicates how much energy it contains. Energy is measured in $kJ\,m^{-2}\,y^{-1}$. Only a small percentage of the energy in each level is transferred to the next level.

📝 Annotated exemplar answer C.1

Explain why the biomass of species at higher trophic levels tends to be small. **[5]**

This is an essay-style question with five available marks, so make sure you answer fully in the space available to you. You will need to include information from Chapter 4 in your answer.

At each trophic level energy is used. ——— To gain the mark here you must say what energy is used for – respiration, reproduction, growth, movement and some is lost as heat.

So only a small proportion of the energy taken in can be used to build biomass. ——— This is good, the correct term 'biomass' has been included.

As organisms on the next trophic level feed, they take in only about 10% of the energy ——— To improve your mark, add, 'for life processes.'
and biomass in the level below.

They too use energy.

So at each trophic level the energy available to produce new biomass is less than the level below.

TEST YOURSELF C.4

 Outline the difficulties of placing organisms in the correct trophic level, use named examples in your answer. **[3]**

What is a food conversion ratio?

In commercial food production, farmers measure the food conversion ratio (FCR) of their animals. The FCR is a measure of an animal's efficiency in converting food mass into increased body mass (biomass). It is calculated by dividing the mass of food eaten by the gain in body mass over a period of time.

A lower food conversion ratio can show that the process of farming is more energy efficient.

Table C.3

Animal	Approximate FCR
farmed salmon	1.2
poultry	2
pigs	3.5
sheep	8
cattle	8

What are primary and secondary succession?

DEFINITION

SUCCESSION is the process of change to communities in a particular area over a period of time, so that the appearance of the whole area evolves and changes.

Succession involves interactions between the biotic and abiotic components of the area. If an area of land is left bare as a result of a volcanic eruption, fire or land clearance, early 'pioneer' communities modify the physical environment, which, in turn, modifies the biotic community. This enables more species to move in and modify the physical environment still more, and so on until a stable situation is reached.

A typical succession in the northern hemisphere might be:

Species: bare rock → lichens → mosses → grass and small shrubs → fast-growing trees → slow-growing trees

Approximate years: 2–3   3–10   10   15–20   25–50   100–200

DEFINITIONS

PRIMARY SUCCESSION begins when an area of bare ground or rock, with no existing soil, is colonised for the first time.

SECONDARY SUCCESSION occurs where there has been land clearance in an established ecosystem and soil is already present.

How can we predict the type of ecosystem that will develop in an area?

The type of stable ecosystem, known as a **climax community,** that emerges following a succession depends on the local climate.

A climograph can be used to predict the type of stable ecosystem that will emerge from information about the mean annual temperature and mean annual precipitation in a region.

A hot desert ecosystem has rainfall less than 50 mm per year while a tropical rainforest has between 3000 mm and 4500 mm per year. The mean annual temperatures of both these ecosystems are between 20 °C and 30 °C. Tundra is an ecosystem with low rainfall and low temperatures.

Ecology and conservation

What is a closed ecosystem?

Many ecologists now study ecosystems using the systems approach. The systems approach studies an ecosystem as a whole, rather than examining individual parts such as a food chain within it. Systems are divided into three types: open, closed and isolated. Living systems may be either open or closed.

An *open system* exchanges both matter and energy with its surroundings across the boundaries of the system. Most living systems and all ecosystems are open systems, which exchange energy and matter with their environment. Inputs can include light, carbon dioxide minerals. Outputs can be water and heat from respiration.

In a *closed system* energy, but not matter, is exchanged across the boundaries of the system. These systems are very rare in nature. Most examples are set up for experiments and are artificial. Examples include bottle gardens and projects such as the Biodome experiment in Arizona.

How is an ecosystem affected by disturbance?

Disturbance, caused by natural events such as flood, drought or human interference, influences both the structure and the rate of change in an ecosystem. Some examples include:

- Extreme climatic events can destroy all or part of a food web.
- The nutrient cycles within the system (Section **C.6**) can be disrupted by harvesting crops in agriculture, which removes nutrients from the system.
- Human populations encroach into the territories of carnivores.
- Pesticides remove selected and non-selected organisms from food chains and cause disruption to the system.

☆ Model answer C.2

Gersmehl diagrams can be used to compare ecosystems

Gersmehl diagrams show how nutrients are transferred and stored in three parts of a system: litter (L), biomass of organisms (B) and soil (S). The size of circles and arrows is proportional to the amount of nutrients stored or transferred. Other arrows show inputs such as rainfall and nutrients made available by weathering, and outputs such as run off and leaching.

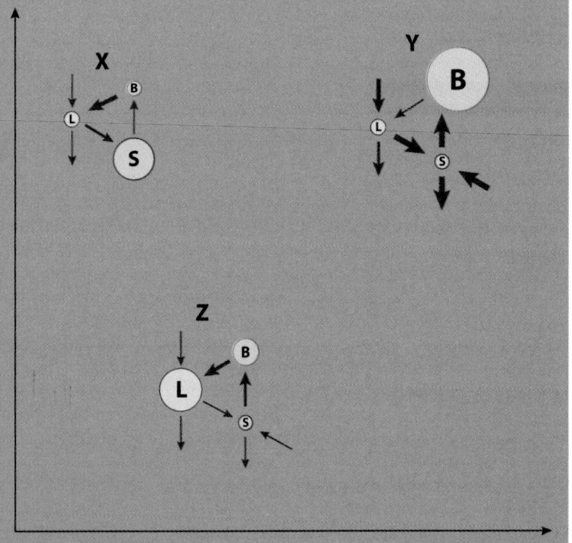

a Identify which of the three diagrams in Figure C.4 represents a desert ecosystem.

b Explain your reasons for this choice.

c Which of the three ecosystems represents a tropical rain forest?

d Why is it difficult for this ecosystem to recover from deforestation?

e In diagram Z identify the arrow that represents mineral absorption by plants.

Figure C.4

> **a** Area X is likely to be a desert.
>
> **b** This is because it has very low levels of biomass and litter but higher amounts of soil and rock (sand).
>
> **c** Area Y because of its high biomass.
>
> **d** There is not a high level of nutrients in either the soil or the litter of area Y. If trees are removed it will be difficult for new trees to become established because of the low levels of resources available to them.
>
> **e** The arrow that passes from the soil to biomass shows uptake of minerals by plants.

C3 Impacts of humans on ecosystems

Key information you should revise:

- Introduced, alien species can be come invasive if they escape into the local ecosystems.

- Endemic species can be reduced when alien species invade because of competitive exclusion and the absence of predators.

- Pollutants become concentrated at higher trophic levels by biomagnification.

- Microplastic and macroplastic debris has accumulated in the marine environment.

What is an alien species and how can they become invasive?

DEFINITION

ALIEN SPECIES are species that have been introduced into an area where they did not previously occur.

There are many examples of organisms that have been introduced from one ecosystem to another, in most cases introduction of alien species is harmful to the locally occurring species. Introduction can occur:

- accidentally – e.g. zebra mussels carried in the ballast of a ship from Russian lakes to the Great Lakes in the USA

- deliberately – e.g. orchids, bamboo and rhododendron brought from oriental regions to European gardens for their flowers and exotic foliage

- for biological control of a pest – e.g. the cane toad taken from Puerto Rica to Australia to control sugar cane beetles.

Alien species are described as invasive when their numbers increase significantly. Limiting factor, such as predators and diseases that should control them are not present in their new habitat, so they grow unchecked.

How do alien species compete with endemic species?

Introduced species are only a problem if their numbers increase significantly and the species spreads.

Alien species will increase in numbers in a new environment if:

- there are no natural predators or diseases present

- there are no local competitors

- the alien species outcompetes local species.

Alien species can dominate a new environment and threaten biodiversity. If a local organism occupies the same or a similar niche, competitive exclusion will mean that either:

- the two species occupy smaller niches
- the alien species will dominate and exclude the local organism.

Two examples of competitive exclusion are:

- Grey squirrels, which were introduced into the UK and occupy similar niches to the native red squirrel. In areas where grey squirrels are present, red squirrels are excluded.
- In Australia's Queensland, New South Wales and Northern Territory the introduced cane toad excluded local amphibians, which breed more slowly and later in the season.

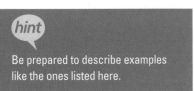

How are alien species controlled?

Biological control and eradication programmes, using pesticides, trapping and culling, can limit or remove the problems caused by alien species.

Biological control

The prickly pear cactus (*Opuntia* sp.) was deliberately introduced to Australia as a source of cattle feed. It rapidly became invasive and grew out of control because the climate was ideal and there were no native animals that ate it. Scientists found a natural consumer for the prickly pear, the caterpillar of the cactus moth (*Cactoblastis cactorum*) in its homelands of the USA and Mexico. This caterpillar was deliberately introduced into Australia and now keeps the plant under control.

Eradication programmes

A 6-year restoration programme was used on Montague Island in New South Wales, Australia, to remove kikuyu grass (*Pennisetum clandestinum*) and other non-endemic plants that had been introduced to help stabilise the sandy soil and provide food for grazing animals. The kikuyu grass had spread and displaced seabird nesting areas and killed many native little penguins *(Eudyptula minor)*, which became trapped or strangled in the grass. It also threatened other birds. Management techniques included, clearing the grass by controlled burning and spraying with herbicide, followed by re-vegetation of the island with endemic plant species.

TEST YOURSELF C.5

 Suggest three key requirements for a successful eradication programme.

What is biomagnification and how do pollutants become concentrated at the end of a food chain?

DEFINITION

BIOMAGNIFICATION is the process that leads to accumulation of chemical substances in food chains; the chemicals become more concentrated at higher trophic levels.

Some chemical pesticides are taken into living organisms but accumulate in their body tissues because the organism cannot break them down and excrete them. Insecticides

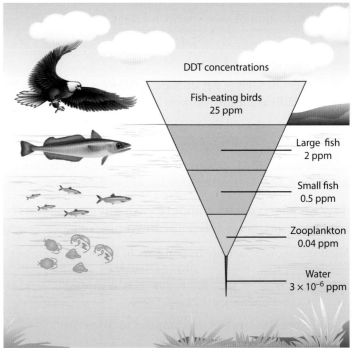

Figure C.5 An example of how DDT concentrations increase up the trophic levels of an estuarine food chain.

such as DDT and dieldrin are well-studied examples of the way toxic chemicals can accumulate in the environment by **biomagnification**.

DDT is now a banned insecticide in most parts of the world.

DDT is an organochlorine (OC) insecticide that was widely used to kill mosquitoes that carry the malarial parasite. It is stored in the fatty tissues of animals that have ingested it. It is not readily biodegradable and can remain in the environment for up to 15 years.

TEST YOURSELF C.6

 Define the term 'biomagnification'.

What damage is caused by plastic debris in the oceans?

Two types of plastic account for the majority of debris in the marine environment:

- macroplastic – large visible debris more than 1 mm across
- microplastic – produced by physical breakdown of macroplastic; fragments that are less than 1 mm.

The debris is carried by ocean currents and becomes concentrated in certain areas known as gyres found in the Pacific, Atlantic and Indian Oceans.

Plastic is ingested by marine organisms, which mistake them for food or take tiny fragments in as they filter feed. Plastic can:

- block or damage their intestines
- accumulate in their cells
- entangle organisms that drown or suffocate
- prevent feeding and cause starvation
- release persistent chemicals into the ocean as they are degraded.

The Laysan albatross is an example of a species that has suffered harm from plastic debris. Parent birds feed plastic fragments to their chicks, mistaking them for food. Adults can regurgitate some plastic but chicks cannot and are killed by plastic that may cut their stomach or remain undigested, preventing them from feeding.

TEST YOURSELF C.7

 Sea turtles feed on jellyfish in the oceans. Since the 1950s the number of turtles found with plastic debris in their stomachs has increased by 40%. Suggest two reasons for this increase. **[2]**

C4 Conservation of biodiversity

Key information you should revise:

- An indicator species is an organism used to assess a specific factor in the environment.
- Indicator species can be used to calculate the value of a biotic index.
- *In situ* conservation requires active management of nature reserves.
- *Ex situ* conservation preserves species outside their natural habitats.
- Biogeographic factors affect species diversity.
- Richness and evenness are factors in assessing biodiversity.

Ecology and conservation

What is an indicator species?

An **INDICATOR SPECIES** is one that is used to monitor or assess a specific environmental condition.

Examples of indicator species include lichens, which are very intolerant of pollution, and stonefly nymphs, which are intolerant of low oxygen concentrations in water. The presence of large lichens indicates that air is clean and free of pollutants, such as sulphur dioxide. If stonefly nymphs are found in streams it indicates that the water is clean and well oxygenated.

How is a biotic index calculated?

A **biotic index** is calculated from the relative numbers of indicator species present in a habitat. An index is calculated from a survey of organisms.

To calculate a biotic index for a stream, all parts of the stream are sampled and each family present is recorded. Scores are added together to give a BMWP (Biological Monitoring Working Party) score that provides a measure of water quality.

BMWP scores are one of several different biotic indices that are used. All use the same principles but the details of the methods may be different.

Each family is given a score from 1 to 10 depending on their pollution tolerance, 10 being the most intolerant.

Table C.4

Example organisms	Score
caddis flies	10
freshwater crayfish, stoneflies	9
dragonflies, damselflies	8
mayfly, tube-making caddis flies	7
small air-breathing snails, amphipod crustaceans	6
pond skaters, water striders, creeping water bugs	5
small mayflies, freshwater leeches, alderflies	4
valve snails, bladder snails	3
non-biting midges	2
segmented worms	1

Table C.5

BMWP	
Score	Water quality
>150	very good biological quality
101–150	good biological quality
51–100	fair biological quality
16–50	poor biological quality
0–15	very poor biological quality

Table C.6

ASPT	
Score	Water quality
>4.4	very good
4.81–4.4	good
4.21–4.8	fair
3.61–4.2	poor
<3.61	very poor

In this system, the efficiency of sampling and sample size are taken into account using the Average Score Per Taxon (ASPT). ASPT is the BMWP score divided by the number of families (taxa) in the sample. This gives an idea of the diversity of the community. The overall water quality is assessed by looking at both BWMP and ASPT scores.

 Define the term indicator species and give one example.

What is meant by the term *in situ* conservation?

IN SITU **CONSERVATION** protects species within their normal habitat by maintaining the environment, often within a nature reserve or national park.

In situ conservation work can involve:

- removal of invasive species that compete with the species being conserved
- protecting the species from predators and poaching
- feeding the protected species
- protecting the habitat and limiting access of visitors.

Provided there are sufficient numbers in the population, *in situ* conservation should provide sufficient genetic diversity for a population to be sustained.

TEST YOURSELF C.9

 Which *in situ* methods would be used to conserve rhinos in a game park?

What is meant by *ex situ* conservation?

DEFINITION

EX SITU CONSERVATION involves preserving a species whose numbers are very low in a captive-breeding programme in a zoo or botanic garden to prevent it dying out.

In situations where **in situ conservation** is difficult or inadequate, **ex situ conservation** must be used as a back up. This is not ideal, because an organism behaves differently outside its natural habitat. But it does give the opportunity to protect young offspring and use modern technology, such as IVF in and embryo transfer for captive-breeding of rare species.

TEST YOURSELF C.10

 Outline the advantages of *in situ* conservation. **[4]**

Which components do we use to estimate biodiversity?

Biodiversity is estimated from two components:

- richness – the number of different species present
- evenness – how similar in numbers populations of each species are.

🔲 Worked example C.1

The data in Table C.7 shows the number of butterfly species present in two areas of meadowland.

a Which of the two meadows showed the greater richness?

b Which had the greater evenness?

For richness you must look for the area that has the greater number of different species – in this case Meadow 1.

For evenness look at how many of each species are present. Even though Meadow 2 has fewer species, it is not dominated by any one species; the numbers of each species present is about the same. Meadow 2 has greater evenness.

Table C.7

Species	Meadow 1	Meadow 2
A	25	0
B	1	0
C	6	6
D	2	5
E	9	7
F	4	0

How is the Simpson diversity index calculated and used?

The Simpson diversity index takes into account both richness and evenness. It is calculated using the formula:

$$D = \frac{N(N-1)}{\sum n(n-1)}$$

where D is the diversity index, N is the total number of organisms in the habitat, n is the number of individuals of each species. The lowest value possible for D is 1, if an area contains only one species.

> **hint**
>
> This formula is the reciprocal index of diversity and will be the one used in your exam. Other formulae are used and will produce different results.

⚙ Worked example C.2

If data is collected for two areas of woodland and the results in Table C.8 are collected, which area has greater diversity?

Table C.8

Species	Site A	Site B
woodrush	2	0
holly	8	6
brambles	1	24
wood anemone	1	0
sedge	3	3
total (N)	15	33

For site A:

$$D = \frac{15(14)}{2(1) + 8(7) + 1(0) + 1(0) + 3(2)}$$

$$D = \frac{210}{64} = 3.3$$

For site B:

$$D = \frac{33(32)}{6(5) + 24(23) + 3(2)} \qquad D = \frac{1056}{588} = 1.8$$

Site A has a higher value for the index than site B, so we conclude that site A has a higher biodiversity. It contains more species (richness) and is not dominated by one species, so is also more even.

How do biogeographic features influence species diversity?

DEFINITION

The study of spatial distribution of organisms, species and ecosystems is known as **BIOGEOGRAPHY**.

As more protected areas are set aside to provide regions where organisms are safeguarded, many biogeographic factors must be taken into account to ensure they are successful in conserving diversity.

The chosen areas must have biogeographic features such as:

- the correct climate and terrain to support the species
- the size of the area must be large enough; small reserves can only support small populations and inbreeding may occur
- one large area is better than many small ones but wildlife corridors can help link small areas together
- the total length of its boundary are important – edges have different features from the centre of reserves (the 'edge effect').

C5 Population ecology (HL)

Key information you should revise in this subtopic is:

- Population size is estimated using sampling techniques.
- In an unlimited environment population growth may be exponential.
- Population growth slows as the carrying capacity of the environment is reached.
- Phases in a sigmoid population growth curve can be explained by rates of natality, mortality, immigration and emigration.
- Limiting factors can be top-down or bottom-up.

How are sampling techniques used to estimate population size?

A population is a group of individuals of the same species that live in the same area. Population numbers change over time and are affected by a number of factors in the environment. It is usually impossible to count individual members of a species, so to assess the size of a population sampling techniques such as the capture–mark–release–recapture (or Lincoln index) method is used:

1 A sample of the population is collected by netting or trapping. The sample must be as large as possible and trapping must not harm the animals.

2 The number of organisms in the sample is counted and recorded.

3 Each captured animal is inconspicuously marked – for example, with non-toxic paint for invertebrates or by trimming a concealed area of fur for small mammals.

4 The animals are returned to the wild and left for long enough to mix with the rest of the population.

5 A second sample of the population is collected after this time.

6 The number of marked and unmarked individuals in the second sample is counted.

7 The population size (N) is calculated using the Lincoln index formula: $N = \dfrac{n_1 \times n_2}{n_3}$

N is the total population; n_1 is the number of organisms caught originally: n_2 is the number caught in the second sample: n_3 is the number of marked individuals in the second sample.

TEST YOURSELF C.11

1 State three factors that must be taken into account when using the Lincoln index.

2 Give three examples of organisms that can be sampled in this way.

How do graphs show population growth patterns?

Plotting the number of individuals in a population over a period of time can show how the population is changing. In perfect conditions where resources are unlimited, a population graph would show an exponential rise in population numbers. In most cases, there are limiting factors, which restrict the number of individuals the environment can support.

Ecology and conservation

What is shown by the phases of a sigmoid curve?

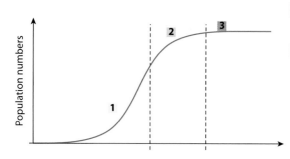

3 Plateau phase
In this phase the number of births plus immigration is equal to the number of deaths plus emigration.

2 Transitional phase
One or more factors in the environment are limiting the rate of reproduction. These might be competition for resources such as food, space or mates, increased predation and disease, or an abiotic factor such as oxygen might be in short supply.

1 Exponential phase
Population increases with no restraint on growth. Nutrients are abundant and there is little accumulation of waste.

Figure C.6 The sigmoid population growth curve for a model species such as duckweed (*Lemna* sp.), growing in a stable environment.

At the plateau phase the population is unable to increase any further and the population numbers will stabilise at a level known as the carrying capacity of the environment.

The human population growth graph has not followed the sigmoid pattern shown. Since the evolution of humans, no plateau has been reached, and instead the global population continues to rise exponentially.

Why do population sizes change?

There are a number of important reasons why a population may change in size:

- natality – the birth rate may change
- mortality – the number of deaths may change
- emigration – members of the population may move away to new habitats
- immigration – new members of the species may arrive from elsewhere.

A population will be stable if: births + emigration = deaths + immigration.

What are top-down and bottom-up limiting factors?

Top-down limiting factors are those that involve an organism higher up the food chain, limiting the numbers of a species at a lower trophic level, usually through predation or herbivory. For example, lobsters control the population of sea urchins in the Atlantic Ocean.

Bottom-up control by limiting factors occurs when the nutrient supply and productivity of primary producers (plants and phytoplankton) control the structure of the ecosystem. In marine coastal ecosystems, plankton populations depend on and are controlled by the availability of nutrients.

Bottom-up and top-down control tends to keep a stable population at the carrying capacity of the ecosystem. The bottom-up resources set the limit for the maximum sustainable population, while top-down control removes individuals from a large population, with the result that resources are not over-exploited.

TEST YOURSELF C.12

 State one example of top-down and one example of bottom-up limiting factors.

C6 The nitrogen and phosphorus cycles (HL)

Key information you should revise in this subtopic is:

- Nitrogen-fixing bacteria convert nitrogen from the atmosphere into ammonia.
- *Rhizobium* sp. form mutualistic relationships with the roots of certain plants.
- Denitrifying bacteria reduce nitrate in the soil when oxygen is not present.
- Phosphorus can be added to the phosphorus cycle in the form of fertilisers or removed from it as crops are harvested.
- The turnover rate of the phosphorus cycle is much slower than that of the nitrogen cycle.
- Phosphate may become a limiting factor in agriculture in the future.
- Leaching of minerals from agricultural land can lead to eutrophication and increased biochemical oxygen demand.

What are the important features and bacteria of the nitrogen cycle?

Key bacteria to remember are:

- *Azobacter and Rhizobium* – nitrogen-fixing bacteria
- *Nitrosomas and Nitrobacter* – nitrifying bacteria
- *Pseudomonas* – denitrifying bacteria.

hint

Practise drawing the key features of the nitrogen cycle. Start with air, soil and plants and make as many connections as you can.

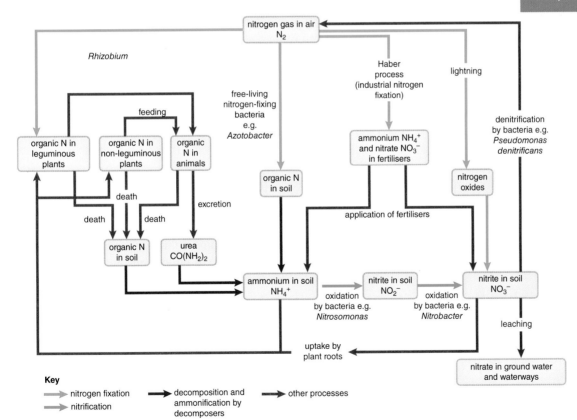

Figure C.7 The nitrogen cycle.

What is nitrogen fixation?

NITROGEN FIXATION is the conversion of nitrogen gas in the air into ammonia and nitrates which can be used by plants.

Azotobacter and *Rhizobium* are able to 'fix' nitrogen from the air and convert it into ammonia. Ammonia formed by both organisms reacts with organic acids to form amino acids.

Rhizobium form a mutualistic relationship with the roots of leguinous plants such as peas, beans and clover and form nodules on the roots. The bacteria receive sugars from the plant, and the plant in turn receives nitrates from the bacteria.

Nitrogen can also be fixed by lightning, which combines nitrogen gas in the air with oxygen, forming nitrates that enter the soil and in industry. The Haber process is used to manufacture fertilisers.

What is nitrification?

NITRIFICATION is the conversion of ammonium compounds and nitrites into nitrates.

Nitrification is important because plants cannot use ammonia and nitrite. Nitrates are soluble and plants can absorb them through their roots and assimilate them into biomass. Nitrification is an oxidation reaction and is favoured by neutral pH and well-aerated soil.

What is denitrification?

DENITRIFICATION converts nitrates into nitrogen gas.

Denitrifying bacteria, for example *Pseudomonas denitrificans,* are found in anaerobic conditions in compacted or waterlogged soils. Waterlogging reduces the cycling of nitrogen and causes a lack of nitrifying and nitrogen-fixing bacteria. Denitrification reduces the fertility of soil so that it may not be useful for cultivation.

TEST YOURSELF C.13

 Outline the impact of humans on the global nitrogen cycle. **[4]**

How do plants survive in nitrogen poor soils?

A few unusual plants supplement their nitrogen levels by capturing and feeding on insects. Insectivorous plants, such as the Venus fly trap and sundew digest their prey and extract nitrogen to build their own proteins.

TEST YOURSELF C.14

 List two abiotic conditions that favour nitrification.

What are the features of the phosphorous cycle?

Phosphorus is needed for DNA, RNA and ATP formation as well as to build bones and cell membranes. Phosphorus is often the limiting element for animal and plant production. The rate of turnover is much slower in the phosphorus cycle than the nitrogen cycle because it involves weathering and erosion, which are slow, long-term processes.

What effect does agriculture have on soil phosphorus?

Phosphorus is added to the soil in fertilisers and removed when crops are harvested. Phosphate is mined on a large scale to make fertilisers. In the 1900s about 5 million tonnes of phosphorus were mined, but by the early 2000s the level had risen to 150 million tonnes. The amount of phosphorus available may limit agriculture of the future.

Today plant and animal health problems caused by lack of phosphate have been eliminated in developed countries but without fertiliser, agricultural yields would fall dramatically and could lead to starvation.

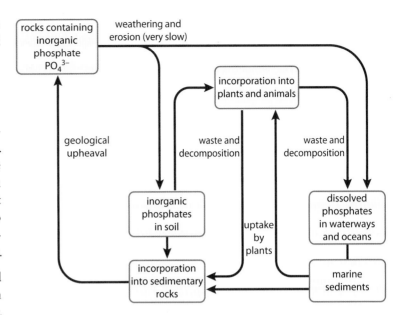

Figure C.8 The phosphorus cycle.

What measures could help in the supply of phosphorus in future?

Some measures suggested include:

- crop rotation
- recovery of phosphorus from sewage (human urine contains phosphorus)
- use of bacteria that selectively absorb phosphorus in sewage treatment
- development of genetically modified animals such as the Enviropig®, which excretes less phosphate in its manure, leading to less run off from livestock farms.

How does leaching from the soil cause eutrophication?

Leaching is caused when rain falls on farmland and water-soluble nutrients are carried into waterways and streams. Nutrient enrichment in this way causes **eutrophication**:

- Nutrients encourage the growth of algae on the water surface.
- Algal blooms block light to water plants below them.
- If the algae and plants die, bacteria feed on them and use up oxygen causing a higher biological oxygen demand (BOD).
- The reduced levels of oxygen lead to the death of sensitive organisms, such as invertebrates and fish.

Eutrophication can also be caused by the release of untreated sewage.

TEST YOURSELF C.15

 1 State two indicator species that might be lost if a stream suffered eutrophication. **[2]**
2 Farmyard manure consists of a mixture of animal dung and straw.
   a Suggest three reasons why farmyard manure is a good fertiliser. **[3]**
   b Describe how ammonium compounds liberated into soil from manure become nitrates. **[3]**
   c Why is manure less effective in waterlogged soils? **[2]**

HUMAN PHYSIOLOGY

This chapter covers the following topics:

- ☐ Human nutrition
- ☐ Digestion
- ☐ Functions of the liver

- ☐ The heart
- ☐ Hormones and metabolism (HL)
- ☐ Transport of respiratory gases (HL)

D1 Human nutrition

Key information you should revise:

- Which nutrients are essential for health and what problems are caused by a shortage of them.
- The differences between vitamins and minerals and what they are used for in the body.
- What happens when a person is malnourished or suffers from starvation.
- How appetite is controlled.
- What problems are caused by being overweight.

What are 'essential' nutrients?

DEFINITIONS

A **NUTRIENT** is a chemical substance taken in by a living organism and used for growth or metabolism.

ESSENTIAL NUTRIENTS are defined as those substances that cannot be made in the body and must be obtained from our food.

Essential nutrients you should remember are:

- essential amino acids
- essential fatty acids
- vitamins
- minerals
- water

Note that not all amino acids and fatty acids are 'essential' the body can produce some. Also notice that carbohydrates are not included on this list. There are no specific carbohydrates that are essential.

What's the difference between vitamins and minerals?

Vitamins and minerals are often listed together in diet information but they are quite different. The differences are shown in Table **D.1**. Remember that both are essential nutrients.

Table D.1

Vitamins	Minerals
made in plants	derived from rocks or dissolved in water
compounds	elements in ionic form (e.g. phosphate (PO_4^-)
organic e.g. vitamin C ($C_6H_8O_6$)	inorganic e.g. Iron (Fe^{2+}), calcium Ca^{2+}

State two differences between vitamins and minerals.

What happens if we do not have enough of the essential nutrients?

The effect of a deficiency in nutrients depends on which nutrient is missing. A deficiency can lead to malnutrition; this is not the same as starvation.

A person who doesn't have enough of the essential amino acids may suffer from protein deficiency malnutrition because they cannot make all the proteins they need. Kwashiorkor is a protein deficiency disease seen in young children. The child's abdomen becomes swollen because they cannot produce plasma proteins properly. Tissue fluid is not absorbed and leads to swelling called edema.

A shortage of certain vitamins has different consequences. Lack of vitamin C can lead to scurvy. Vitamin C helps protect the body from infection and is needed for the synthesis of the protein collagen.

Vitamin D (calciferol) is needed to ensure calcium is absorbed from the gut. Without it bones can be malformed. Vitamin D can be produced in the skin when it is exposed to sunlight and it is stored in the liver.

Nature of Science. Although humans cannot synthesise vitamin C, some animals can. In early experiments rats and mice were deprived of vitamin C but did not suffer from scurvy. These animals are able to synthesise their own vitamin C.

hint

Be prepared to answer questions about the balance of risks between sitting in the sun and producing vitamin D in the skin and excessive exposure to UV light.

 Why is a diet, which consists mainly of one type of food, such as potatoes or rice, unlikely to be healthy even if it does provide enough energy?

What is the difference between starvation and malnutrition?

Starvation occurs when a person does not have enough to eat. It can lead to body tissues being broken down as energy reserves are used up.

Malnutrition occurs when a person does not eat a balanced diet. Their diet may lack a nutrient or contain an excess of a particular nutrient. A person can eat a lot of food but still be malnourished.

 Why must all humans take in proteins in some form?

How do we know when we have eaten enough? How is appetite controlled?

Our appetite control centre is in the **hypothalamus** at the base of the brain. Appetite is suppressed in four ways:

- Receptors in the stomach wall signal the hypothalamus when the stomach is full.
- As food enters the small intestine a peptide hormone PYY 3–36 is released.

- The hormone leptin is released by adipose (fat) cells.
- Insulin is released as food is absorbed.

But we can override these controls if we are tempted by the smell or sight of delicious foods and eat too much.

Why is it bad to be overweight?

If we eat more carbohydrate foods than we need for everyday activity, the excess is stored as glycogen in the liver and muscles or as fat. Fat contains twice as much energy as carbohydrate, so too much fatty food is also likely to lead to obesity.

hint

Remember that correlation and cause are different. Being overweight contributes to these health problems but other factors also influence them.

Being overweight is correlated with several serious health issues:

- type II diabetes – the inability to control blood sugar levels.
- hypertension – high blood pressure, which can increase the risk of stroke or heart attack
- coronary heart disease (CHD) – blockages of the arteries, formation of clots in arteries of the heart and heart attacks.

TEST YOURSELF D.4

1 Define the term essential amino acid. **[1]**
2 Discuss the relationship between nutrition and hypertension (high blood pressure). **[3]**

hint

Test yourself **D.4** is typical of the type of question that you will see in Paper **3**. Note the number of marks for each section. Write answers that only include the key facts.

Which foods cause particular problems?

There is a correlation between eating a diet that is high in saturated fats and an increased risk of CHD and other circulatory diseases. These fats can be deposited in the arteries with cholesterol and may lead to **atherosclerosis** (blockages in the arteries).

Another indicator of CHD is the level of cholesterol in a person's blood. Cholesterol is a steroid that is made in the liver but taken in with foods of animal origin. Cholesterol is transported into the body in the form of two types of lipoprotein.

- LDL – low-density lipoprotein is often called 'bad' cholesterol because it does not travel easily in the blood and can clog arteries.
- HDL – high-density lipoprotein is known as 'good' cholesterol because it does not block arteries and can even remove LDLs from them.

D2 Digestion

Key information you should revise:

- How the type and volume of digestive juices that are secreted is controlled by nerves and hormones.
- What type of glands secrete these juices.
- Why the acidic conditions in the stomach are useful but can be harmful if acidity is excessive.
- How cells in the epithelium of the small intestine are adapted to absorb digested food.
- What is meant by transit time and how it is correlated with fibre content in the diet.
- What happens to undigested food.

What is a digestive juice and how is it different from an enzyme?

Digestive juices are secretions, which enter the intestine to aid digestion. Many of them do contain enzymes and other substances, which help with digestion. Digestive enzymes are biological catalysts that speed up the breakdown of food molecules into simple absorbable substances.

The secretions are produced by **exocrine glands** in the mouth, stomach and pancreas. Examples are shown in Table **D.2**. The enzymes are shown in blue.

Table D.2

Digestive juice	Site of production	Contents
saliva	salivary glands in the mouth	• water • mucus • salivary amylase
gastric juice	gastric glands in the stomach wall	• water • mucus • pepsin secreted as pepsinogen • hydrochloric acid
pancreatic juice	exocrine cells in the pancreas	• water • pancreatic amylase • trypsin secreted as trypsinogen • pancreatic lipase • carboxypeptidase chymotrypsin • hydrogencarbonate (HCO_3^-) ions

Notice that the protein digesting enzymes pepsin and trypsin are secreted in an inactive form so that they do not harm cells in the intestine.

What are the differences between an exocrine and an endocrine gland?

An exocrine gland produces digestive juices and secretes them via a duct into the digestive (or another) system. Sweat glands are also exocrine glands that secrete onto the surface of the skin.

An endocrine gland is part of the endocrine system and produces hormones that are secreted directly into the blood stream without passing along a duct.

hint

You may be asked to discuss the effect of pH and temperature on enzyme activity. You can find this information in Chapter **2**.

Why is the stomach acidic?

The stomach is acidic because cells in the walls of the stomach release hydrochloric acid to maintain the contents at pH 2, the optimum pH for the action of protease enzymes. The acidic conditions denature proteins so that peptide bonds are exposed to the enzymes. The acid also kills bacteria that may be in the food we eat.

TEST YOURSELF D.5

Why is it important for the pH of the stomach to be acidic?

What is acid indigestion and what causes it?

Excess acid in the stomach can cause indigestion or 'heartburn'. In most cases a simple indigestion remedy will neutralise the acid and relieve the problem. But if a person suffers with indigestion over a long period of time, the acid must be controlled so that it doesn't damage the stomach lining. This is done with drugs called PPIs (proton pump inhibitors), which also treat acid reflux and stomach ulcers. PPIs block hydrogen potassium pumps and ATPase enzymes in the acid secreting cells to switch off acid release.

How is the secretion of digestive juices controlled so we have the right amount at the right time in the right place?

Both nerves and hormones control these processes. Here is a checklist of what happens as you eat.

- From experience you know that sight and smell of food stimulates the production of saliva. Nerve impulses that cause this response also stimulate the release of gastric juice in the stomach.
- Touch and stretch receptors stimulate the release of gastric juice as food enters the stomach.
- Chemoreceptors also send impulses to the brain to maintain gastric juice secretion.
- Nerve impulses stimulate endocrine glands in the stomach wall to produce the hormone gastrin that stimulates the release of protease and hydrochloric acid.
- If fats have been eaten, the hormone enterogasterone slows the exit of these foods from the stomach.
- In the small intestine, two further hormones (secretin and CCK-PZ) control the secretions from the pancreas and gall bladder as food arrives.

TEST YOURSELF D.6

 State the role of the hormone gastrin.

What can go wrong in the intestine?

Stomach ulcers

Cause: Until the mid 1980s most doctors believed that stomach ulcers were caused by stress and poor eating habits, but then two Australian scientists, Marshall and Warren, discovered a bacterium that they suggested was the real cause. *Helicobacter pylori* is an unusual bacterium that is able to survive in the acid conditions of the stomach.

 Nature of Science. Following a series of experiments, which even involved infecting themselves with the bacteria, the Australians convinced the medical profession that treatment with antibiotics that killed *H.pylori* would cure ulcers.

hint

Two serious infections that you must be able to discuss are stomach ulcers and cholera; both are caused by bacteria.

Symptoms: Stomach pain, excess acidity, acid reflux.

Treatment: Antibiotics that kill *H pylori*.

The work of Marshall and Warren led to a *paradigm shift* in the understanding and treatment of stomach ulcers. This concept is part of your *Theory of Knowledge* studies.

Cholera

Cause: The toxin of the cholera bacterium *Vibrio cholerae* binds to the surface of intestinal cells and modifies a chloride **channel protein**. Chloride ions are pumped out and are followed by water, sodium ions, potassium ions and hydrogen carbonate ions. Cells replace the lost substances by taking them from the blood.

Symptoms: Severe dehydration and diarrhoea.

Treatment: Antibiotics and rehydration therapy.

Transmission: The feces of infected people contain the bacteria and if these contaminate water supplies, the bacteria are passed on. This may happen during times of war or a natural disaster, such as an earthquake.

How is the small intestine adapted for the absorption of food?

Before you revise this section, refresh your memory about the structure of the intestine by looking at Section **6.1**, in particular Figure **6.2** and **6.3**.

Adaptations:

- The intestine is long and has a large surface area for absorbing food.
- Villi on the inner surface increase the surface area.
- Microvilli increase it further.
- The epithelium lining is thin so digested food can pass through easily.
- A capillary network inside the villi carries away absorbed molecules.
- A lacteal carries away absorbed fatty acids.
- Longitudinal and circular muscles move food along the intestine by peristalsis.

You should be able to make a simple drawing of a section through the small intestine and of a villus.

It's very important that you can locate and identify all the features in a diagram of a section through the small intestine.

TEST YOURSELF D.7

 Name three adaptations of the small intestine for the absorption of digested food.

☆ Model answer D.1

Explain how the structure of a villus is related to its function [4]

A villus is a small fold in the lining of the small intestine; it is adapted to function as an absorptive surface for digested food molecules. It has a large surface area; enhanced by the presence of microvilli; each villus contains a network of capillaries to carry away digested food and maintain a diffusion gradient; and a lacteal that carries away triglycerides.

How does digested food pass into the villi and then the blood stream?

Digested food passes through the membranes of microvilli and into the villi to reach a blood vessel or lacteal. Digested molecules are small and movement may occur by means of: simple diffusion, active transport, facilitated diffusion and pinocytosis (endocytosis).

Most molecules pass straight through the cells of the villi into the capillaries.

How are cells of the villi adapted to absorb food?

- Each cell is linked to neighbouring cells by tight junctions so that absorbed materials pass directly through the cell to the capillary.
- Cells have many mitochondria to provide ATP for active transport.
- Pinocytotic vesicles are present as some substances are absorbed by endocytosis.

What happens to material that isn't digested?

Undigested material, which is mostly cellulose, lignin and plant fibre, passes into the large intestine. Water and bile salts are reabsorbed. What remains, together with dead intestinal cells, passes out of the body as feces.

DEFINITION

TRANSIT TIME is the time food takes to pass through the whole intestine from ingestion (being eaten) to egestion (being expelled as feces). It varies depending on a person's diet content and fibre intake.

D

Human physiology

What is 'fibre' and why is it important?

Fibre is material in cereals, fruits and vegetables that we do not have the enzymes to digest. There are two types of fibre and both are important to human health. They add bulk to feces, which pass through the colon more easily, preventing constipation. 'Soluble fibre' absorbs water. It helps to slow down the rate of digestion and helps the contraction of muscles of the small intestine. 'Insoluble' fibre does not absorb water and tends to speed up transit time. There is a positive correlation between the amount of insoluble fibre in your diet and the transit time through the large intestine.

☆ Model answer D.2

Which of the graphs shows the correct relationship between the amount of fibre in a person's diet and the time that food spends in the intestine? Explain why. Also, explain why the remaining two graphs do not show this relationship.

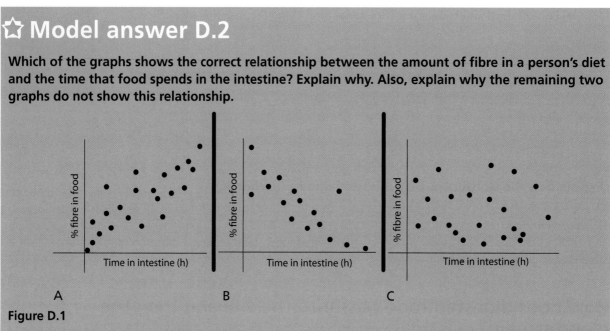

Figure D.1

Graph A shows a positive correlation, as fibre increases so does the time in the intestine. Graph B shows a negative correlation between the variables and graph C shows no correlation between the variables.

D3 Functions of the liver

Key information you should revise:

- How the liver is supplied with blood from the small intestine and also the hepatic artery.
- How the liver regulates the levels of toxins, nutrients, and cholesterol of the blood that leaves it.
- The liver's role as a storage organ for iron, glycogen and vitamins A and D.
- The role of the liver in the breakdown of red blood cells and storage of iron.
- How the liver produces both bile and plasma protein.

Which blood vessels supply the liver?

DEFINITION

HEPATIC means concerned with the liver.

216

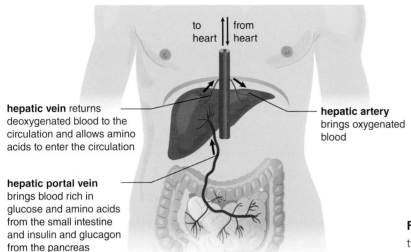

hepatic vein returns deoxygenated blood to the circulation and allows amino acids to enter the circulation

hepatic artery brings oxygenated blood

hepatic portal vein brings blood rich in glucose and amino acids from the small intestine and insulin and glucagon from the pancreas

to heart ↑↓ from heart

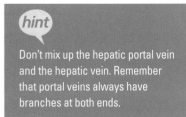

hint

Don't mix up the hepatic portal vein and the hepatic vein. Remember that portal veins always have branches at both ends.

Figure D.2 The liver receives blood from two large vessels but blood leaving it is carried in just one, the hepatic vein.

📑 Annotated exemplar answer D.1

Outline the circulation of blood through the liver. **[4]**

There are four marks to be awarded here so make sure you make four key points in your answer. It is always useful to include a diagram in a question like this.

Blood is brought to the liver in the hepatic artery and from the hepatic portal vein.

Good to identify the blood vessels but you should state where each one comes from. Say that the hepatic artery comes from the aorta and hepatic portal vein from the intestine.

These vessels divide into smaller vessels between rows of hepatocytes.

The questions asks for 'circulation', so sinusoids must be mentioned, you'd lose a mark if you forget this.

Blood then flows into the central vein and on to the hepatic vein, which takes blood back to the vena cava.

This is good; the return route must be included.

(2/4)

Where are hepatocytes and Kupffer cells in the liver?

The structure of the liver can look complicated but it's the same all through.

- It's made of many cylinders (lobules) packed together.
- Each lobule has rows of hepatocytes radiating out from the centre.
- Between each lobule are branches of the hepatic artery and hepatic portal vein, branches from these, called sinusoids pass between the hepatocytes.
- In the centre of each lobule is a central vein, which leads to the hepatic vein. This takes blood away from the liver (see Figure **D.2**).
- Kupffer cells line the walls of the sinusoids and engulf damaged red blood cells.

hint

Try imagining hepatocytes as rows of recycling and storage factories that process different substances. As blood in the sinusoids flows past the factories they remove certain substances, so that blood flowing into the central vein contains regulated amounts. At the back of the factories some reprocessed material flows out into bile.

Organisation of tissues

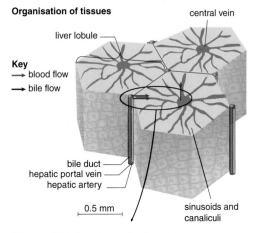

Structure

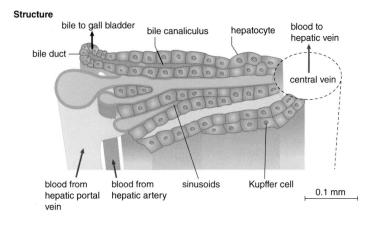

Figure D.3 Structure of a liver lobule.

1 List three functions of hepatocytes.
2 What is the role of Kupffer cells?

How does the liver control the levels of substances in the blood?

The liver:

- has a role in detoxification and removes alcohol, food additives and pesticides
- breaks down old red blood cells and recycles their components
- synthesises cholesterol and controls its level in the blood
- controls blood sugar level and storing glycogen, lipids, iron and vitamins A and D (it has a role in homeostasis).

Detoxification

Hepatocytes absorb toxins and convert them to non-toxic or less toxic products. Examples are:

- lactate from anaerobic respiration is broken down to carbon dioxide and water
- hydrogen peroxide is a by-product of metabolism and detoxified by the enzyme catalase
- ethanol (alcohol) is converted to acetaldehyde and then metabolised
- toxic nitrogenous waste is converted to urea, which is excreted by the kidneys.

Red blood cells

The Kupffer cells absorb cell fragments and hemoglobin from worn out red blood cells by phagocytosis. The hemoglobin is recycled in a sequence of steps shown in Figure **D.4**. Notice that almost all the components are recycled.

Cholesterol

Cholesterol, needed for cell membrane formation, is produced by hepatocytes. Any excess in the blood is excreted in bile. Blood cholesterol levels may be linked to a person's diet. High levels can lead to blockages in the arteries and CHD (see Section **D.4**).

Control of nutrient levels

Molecules absorbed from the small intestine travel to the liver. A high carbohydrate meal raises blood glucose levels, so the liver absorbs the glucose from the incoming blood and stores it as glycogen. Blood that leaves the liver contains a regulated amount of glucose. The liver releases some of its stored glycogen as glucose to rebalance the level if blood glucose levels fall.

If the incoming blood contains vitamins A and D, which are fat-soluble, the liver can store these. It also stores iron and copper.

Excess amino acids from absorbed food or other sources are 'deaminated' and converted to urea. Urea travels from the liver to the kidneys for excretion in urine.

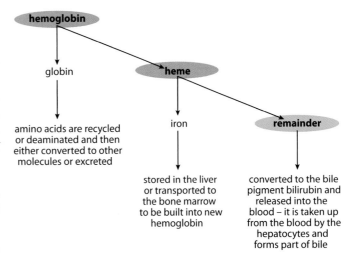

Figure D.4 The breakdown of hemoglobin. Hemoglobin is split into heme groups and globin. Globin is hydrolysed to amino acids, which can be re-used. Iron is removed from the heme group and either stored or taken to the bone marrow where it is used to produce hemoglobin for new red blood cells. The remaining part of the molecule becomes part of bile.

DEFINITION

DEAMINATION is the removal of an amine group (NH_2) from an amino acid if a person has excess protein. The amino group is converted to ammonia (which is toxic) and then to urea in the liver.

TEST YOURSELF D.9

 1 In what form is excess glucose stored in the liver?
2 Which hormone controls this process?

 See Chapter **6** to revise the roles of insulin and glucagon in controlling blood glucose.

What substances does the liver produce?

Bile and plasma proteins are two important products of the liver, and so is cholesterol.

Plasma proteins help regulate the osmotic balance of body fluids and the movement of water between plasma and tissue fluid. They are synthesised by the endoplasmic reticulum and assembled in the Golgi apparatus of hepatocytes. Globulins and albumen and the blood-clotting protein, **fibrinogen** are all plasma proteins.

Bile is produced by the Kupffer cells in the liver, passed into the bile canal (see Figure **D.4**) and stored in the gall bladder. Bile contains bile pigment, bilirubin from the breakdown of red blood cells. This pigment is responsible for the brown colour of feces. Bile salts are produced from excess cholesterol and emulsify fat in the small intestine (see Chapter **6**).

What causes jaundice?

Jaundice is a disease caused by the build up of bilirubin in the blood and tissues. It can be caused by any disruption to the flow of bilirubin, such as infections that damage red blood cells, liver damage or blockages of the bile duct.

D4 The heart

Before you begin revising this section, check Chapter **6** to make sure you are confident about the structure of the heart.

Key information you should revise:

- The structure of heart muscle and how electrical impulses pass through it.
- How impulses pass from the **sinoatrial node** to control heart rate.
- How contraction of the ventricular wall is coordinated.
- How heart sounds are made by closing of valves.
- Interpretation of graphs showing pressure and volume changes in the heart.
- Causes and consequences of hypertension and thrombosis.

How is cardiac muscle different from other muscles?

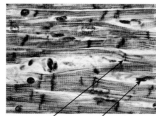

intercalated   nucleus   50 μm
disk

Figure D.5 Muscle fibres of the heart.

Heart muscle has a unique structure that is unlike striated muscle found in the limbs or involuntary muscle found in the gut.

- Cardiac muscle has striped, or striated fibres joined by cross-connections to form a network.
- Cardiac muscle cells contain actin and myosin fibres, which produce the striped appearance.
- Cardiac muscle cells are **myogenic** and can contract over and over again without becoming tired.
- Cardiac muscle is stimulated by the autonomic nervous system, which can speed, up or slow down its contractions.

DEFINITION

MYOGENIC MUSCLE has the ability to contract without receiving impulses from nerves. The contraction originates from the muscle itself.

Table D.3

Cardiac muscle	Striated muscle	Involuntary muscle
• striations present • fibres branch • fibres divided longitudinally by intercalated discs • cells contain a central nucleus • contraction is myogenic and not controlled consciously	• striations present • consists of bundles of unbranched fibres • nuclei are along the length of each fibre • contraction controlled consciously by nerve impulses. • found in muscles of the limbs	• cells not arranged in fibres • each cell has a nucleus • actin and myosin fibres not highly organised • found in intestine, blood vessels. • contraction is not controlled consciously

TEST YOURSELF D.10

 State one consequence of the arrangement of cells in cardiac muscle.

How does cardiac muscle structure help electrical impulses pass through the heart?
Linkages between cells in the heart make it easy for action potentials to spread rapidly and this allows the heart muscle fibres to act together and contract simultaneously.

What stimulates the heart to change its rate of contraction?

The heart beats in a repeated sequence of events known as the cardiac cycle.

The pacemaker (sinoatrial node or SAN) found in the right atrium controls heart rate. The cells initiate action potentials without nervous stimulation, but when the rate needs to change, impulses from the brain are important (See Section **6.2**).

The sequence of events is as follows:

- Impulses from the medulla oblongata in the brain stem pass to the SAN and initiate an action potential. The action potential spreads through the atria, which contract.
- The impulse can't pass directly to the ventricles but it does stimulate a group of cells called the AVN (atrioventricular node) which is close to the ventricles.
- The AVN sends impulses to the base of the ventricles down two bands of non-stimulatory fibres, running down the centre of the heart.
- At the base of the ventricles Purkinje fibres branch out between the muscle fibres and stimulate the ventricles to contact from the base (or apex) of the heart, upwards to complete the cardiac cycle.

hint

If you are asked to describe the stimulation of the heart during the cardiac cycle, draw a simple diagram to show the location of the SAN and AVN to help your explanation.

Heart rate changes with our level of activity or stress. During exercise the heart rate increases as more impulses are sent from the medulla.

When we are afraid or excited the pacemaker is also stimulated by the hormone epinephrine (adrenaline).

TEST YOURSELF D.11

State two ways in which the body can stimulate the SAN to increase heart rate.

What causes the sound of a heart beat?

Valves between the atria and ventricles make heart sounds. Once blood has passed through them, the valves snap shut with the characteristic sound that you can hear with a stethoscope. This is followed by a second sound as the semilunar valves in the arteries leaving the heart also close. Together the sets of valves make the familiar 'lub-dub' sound of a heartbeat.

hint

Don't make the mistake of saying that muscle contraction causes heart sounds. Muscles contract silently as they pump blood.

Recall from Chapter **6** (Figure **6.8**) that atria contract together, so the two atrioventricular valves closing at the same time make the first heart sound.

TEST YOURSELF D.12

Name the valves that separate the atria and ventricles.

📝 Annotated exemplar answer D.2

a On the diagram below, indicate the positions of the SAN and the AVN. **[2]**

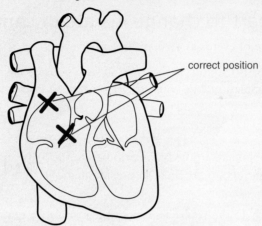

correct position

Figure D.6

b Cardiac muscle is described as myogenic define this term. **[2]**

c Outline the role of the SAN in the control of heart rate. **[3]**

a. A cross or other indication in the top left hand corner of the diagram labelled SAN and a cross at the top of the atrioventricular valve labeled SVN.

Don't forget to label the positions you mark on the diagram; you will lose all the marks if you do not.

b. Myogenic means that the cardiac muscle cells can contract on their own.

Use scientific terms. To get the mark here add 'independently without external stimulation'.

c. The SAN receives impulses from the nervous system (the medulla oblongata) and responds by increasing or decreasing impulses to heart muscle.

It's good to identify the part of the nervous system 'the medulla oblongata'.

The SAN may also be stimulated by the hormone epinephrine, which speeds up the heart rate.

This is an important point to include.

Increased stimulation of the SAN means that more impulses are passed to cardiac muscle which contracts more frequently.

This is a clearly worded answer and would gain full marks..

(6/7)

What is shown on a pressure, volume and ECG trace?

hint

Diagrams like Figure 6.9 can look confusing, but if you study each line in turn they are much easier to interpret.

Look at Figure **6.9** (ECG trace) again. Notice that the top three lines refer to the pressure in the heart and use the scale on the left. Pressure rises as the chambers are stimulated to contract during **systole** and falls as they empty and relax during **diastole**.

The blue line shows the volume of the ventricles, which falls as blood is expelled and rises again as blood enters during diastole.

The lowest line is an ECG trace, which shows the rhythm and electrical activity of the heart.

DEFINITIONS

SYSTOLE is contraction of the heart muscle.

DIASTOLE is relaxation of the heart muscle.

HEART RATE is the number of times the heart beats per minute.

HYPERTENSION means high blood pressure.

THROMBOSIS is the formation of a blood clot in a blood vessel.

hint

You should be able to answer questions about the pressure in chambers of the heart from a graph.

What are the causes and consequences of hypertension and thrombosis?

Hypertension is caused when arteries are narrowed or blocked and blood flow is restricted. The heart has to pump harder to produce the greater pressure needed to enable blood to pass through.

One common cause of blockages is atherosclerosis, a build up of material called plaque inside an artery. Plaque begins as damage to the artery lining and is thickened by fatty deposits. A diet high in saturated fatty acids and high levels of blood cholesterol is linked to the occurrence of atherosclerosis.

Consequences of hypertension include:

- damage to artery linings
- bulging or aneurysm in an artery
- kidney failure if glomerular capillaries are damaged.

If the rate of blood flow is too slow, clots may form on the artery wall and restrict it even more. If a clot breaks free, it can block a smaller artery elsewhere. If a clot blocks a coronary artery it may cause a coronary **thrombosis** or heart attack. Cells beyond the blockage are deprived of oxygen and may die. If a clot blocks an artery supplying the brain, it may cause a stroke.

hint

These diseases are mentioned in several parts of the IB syllabus. You may find an exam question on them in any of the three papers.

hint

Be prepared to discuss the factors linked to diseases of the heart and circulation. Remember the difference between cause and effect, because there are many factors including diet, exercise, lifestyle, age and genetics and it is impossible to say with certainty that any one factor is a direct cause of heart disease.

TEST YOURSELF D.13

 Define the terms systole and diastole.

D5 Hormones and metabolism (HL)

Before you begin this section, prepare yourself by reading through your notes on hormones and homeostasis from Sections **6.6** and **11.3**.

Key information you should revise:

- Endocrine glands secrete directly into the blood stream.
- Different types of hormone work in different ways to influence a cell.
- Steroid hormones bind to receptor proteins in the cytoplasm of the target cell to form a receptor–hormone complex that promotes transcription of specific genes.
- Peptide hormones bind to receptors in the plasma membrane of the target cell and activate a second messenger inside the cell.
- The hypothalamus controls hormone secretion by the lobes of the pituitary gland.

- Pituitary hormones control growth, developmental changes, reproduction and homeostasis.
- Some athletes use hormones illegally.
- Hormones control milk production after a baby is born.

What is the difference between and endocrine gland and other glands in the body?

Endocrine glands only produce hormones. They are arranged around blood vessels and their secretions pass directly into the blood. Other glands such as sweat glands or salivary glands have a tube or duct, which takes their secretions to a specific place.

How many types of hormone are there?

Hormones are divided into three categories based on their chemical structure.

Table D.4

Chemical make up of hormone	Examples
proteins	insulin, FSH, LH
steroids derived from cholesterol	testosterone, progesterone
tyrosine derivatives	thyroxin

What are the differences between the way that protein and steroid hormones work?

Hormones only affect their specific target cells and regulate their activities. Protein and steroid hormones work in different ways:

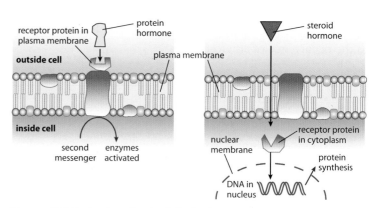

Figure D.7 Endocrine glands of the body.

Table D.5

Protein hormones	Steroid hormones
bind to a receptor on plasma membrane of the target cell. Do not enter the cell	pass through the plasma membrane and enter the cell
binding triggers the release of a second messenger from the inside of the membrane.	hormone binds to a receptor in the cytoplasm to form a hormone–receptor complex
messenger controls the activities of the cell, e.g. by activating or inhibiting an enzyme	hormone–receptor complex enters the nucleus and regulates transcription

TEST YOURSELF D.14

 Name two examples of steroid hormones.

Why are the hypothalamus and pituitary glands so important?

The hypothalamus and **pituitary gland** are located at the base of the brain.

The hypothalamus provides a link between the nervous and hormonal systems. It monitors hormone levels and indirectly controls body temperature, hunger and sleep.

The pituitary gland has two parts, an anterior lobe and a posterior lobe. They differ in their connections to the brain and the hormones they secrete.

Table D.6

Anterior lobe	Posterior lobe
controlled by releasing hormones produced by neurosecretory cells in hypothalamus and transferred via blood capillaries	controlled directly by different neurosecretory cells which link the hypothalamus and posterior lobe
hormones from the anterior lobe include FSH and LH, HGH (human growth hormone), TSH (thyroid stimulating hormone)	hormones produced include oxytocin and ADH

Secretions from neurosecretory cells are often called 'hormones' but a more correct termed is neurohormones because they are not produced by endocrine glands. They are usually peptides that travel as droplets along the **axons** of the neurosecretory cell.

 TEST YOURSELF D.15

Which type of hormone binds to receptors on the outside of the target cell?

Why do some athletes use HGH and other hormones?

Some athletes, particularly in power sports such as bodybuilding, swimming and weight lifting, have used human growth hormone (HGH) to promote muscle growth in an attempt to improve performance. The Olympic Committee banned the hormone in 1989, but there is evidence that it is still used. Some steroid hormones, such as testosterone or synthetic versions of HGH, have also been used.

How do hormones control the production of milk?

During pregnancy, progesterone and estrogen from the placenta promote the growth of breast tissue but suppress milk production, see also Chapter **11**.

At the end of pregnancy progesterone levels fall and *oxytocin* is released from the posterior pituitary gland. Oxytocin stimulates contractions of the uterus and also controls milk release from the mammary glands.

After a baby has been born another hormone, *prolactin* is released from the anterior pituitary gland to stimulate milk production. As a baby suckles more prolactin is secreted and oxytocin is also released. Oxytocin causes contraction of **smooth muscle** that squeezes milk into the duct system of the breasts.

Hormones control milk production in all mammals to balance supply and demand. Oxytocin and prolactin are released in proportion to the amount of milk that the young mammal takes. When a baby is weaned and no longer takes milk, hormone levels decrease.

 TEST YOURSELF D.16

Which part of the pituitary gland releases:

a prolactin   **b** ADH

☆ Model answer D.3

Epinephrine (adrenalin) increases the rate of conversion of glycogen to glucose. The method by which the hormone works is shown in Figure D.8.

a **(i) State whether epinephrine is a protein-based or steroid hormone. [1]**

    (ii) Give a reason for your answer. [1]

    (iii) Outline how the release of the hormone during exercise is of benefit to the body. [2]

b (i) The pituitary gland is often called the 'master gland' of the hormone system. Suggest reasons for this name. [1]

(ii) Describe how the hypothalamus communicates with the pituitary gland. [2]

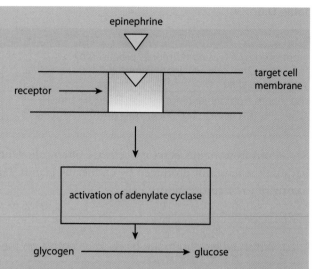

a (i) A protein-based hormone

(ii) Because the hormone does not enter the cell but interacts with a protein receptor on the membrane.

(iii) During exercise muscles require more energy in the form of glucose; glycogen is a stored in muscles and the liver and can be converted to glucose when it is needed; the release of epinephrine increases the rate of conversion.

b (i) Pituitary hormones control the secretions of other endocrine glands e.g. FSH stimulates the ovaries and testes.

(ii) Nerve centres in the hypothalamus secrete releasing hormones to the anterior pituitary via a portal vessel so that it releases its secretions, e.g. prolactin; nerve connections from the hypothalamus transmit impulses to the posterior lobe to stimulate release of hormones such as ADH.

Figure D.8 The modes of action of protein and steroid hormones.

D6 Transport of respiratory gases (HL)

Review the information in Section **6.4** so that you can explain the structure of the respiratory system.

Key information you should revise:

- The affinity of hemoglobin for oxygen changes at different partial pressures.
- How to interpret a dissociation curve.
- Carbon dioxide is carried in different ways in the blood.
- The Bohr shift explains increased release of oxygen by hemoglobin in active tissues.
- Chemoreceptors are sensitive to pH changes in the blood.
- Ventilation rate increases during exercise as carbon dioxide levels in the blood rise.
- The respiratory centre in the **medulla oblongata** controls ventilation rate.
- Oxygen can be transferred across the placenta because fetal hemoglobin differs from adult hemoglobin.

What is partial pressure?

DEFINITION

The **PARTIAL PRESSURE** of a gas in a mixture of gases is the pressure that a gas exerts in the mixture. It is proportional (but not equal) to its percentage in the mixture.

Pressures of gases are measured in kPa (kiloPascals). For dry air at sea level, atmospheric pressure is 101.3 kPa.

Oxygen makes up 21% of the air. Its partial pressure is calculated as follows:

$$\frac{21}{100} \times 101.3 \, \text{kPa} = 21.3 \, \text{kPa}$$

Nitrogen makes up 79% of the air. Try calculating its partial pressure in the same way.

TEST YOURSELF D.17

 Define partial pressure.

How does the affinity of hemoglobin for oxygen change as the partial pressure of oxygen changes?

When hemoglobin comes into contact with air, which has a partial pressure of oxygen of 21.3 kPa, it binds with the oxygen molecules and becomes almost 100% saturated with oxygen. Where the oxygen levels and partial pressure are lower, fewer hemoglobin molecules carry their full complement of oxygen and hemoglobin may be only 50% saturated.

Each hemoglobin molecule can bind four oxygen molecules via the iron (heme) group it contains.

The pattern of affinity of hemoglobin for oxygen in different partial pressures is shown as an oxygen dissociation curve like the one in Figure **D.9**.

These curves are constructed by exposing hemoglobin to different partial pressures of oxygen in experiments but the results are important in explaining how oxygen is carried by hemoglobin in our bodies.

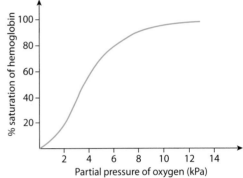

Figure D.9 Oxygen dissociation curve.

How are dissociation curves interpreted?

In the lungs there is a lot of oxygen as fresh air is inhaled. Here the partial pressure is high and hemoglobin becomes fully saturated. Look at the right hand side of Figure **D.10** to see this.

In areas where oxygen levels are lower, for example in respiring tissues, the amount of oxygen bound to hemoglobin is lower. Oxygen and hemoglobin molecules dissociate and oxygen is released. In active tissues the partial pressure may be about 4–5 kPa, so that 50% of the oxygen brought to them is released. Look at the middle part of the graph in Figure **D.10**, where the curve is steepest to see this.

In this way hemoglobin acts as a transport system for oxygen, binding to it where there is a high level and releasing it where the partial pressure is lower and cells need it. The steep S shape of the dissociation curve shows how the affinity of hemoglobin for oxygen changes at the different partial pressures.

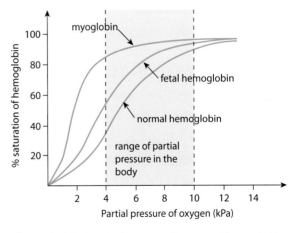

Figure D.10 Dissociation curves for normal hemoglobin, fetal hemoglobin and myoglobin. The curves are constructed using the normal range (at sea level) of partial pressures of oxygen in the body. The partial pressure of oxygen in alveolar air is about 14 kPa due to the presence of water vapour, which forms about 6% of alveolar air.

What about different pigments and different shapes of dissociation curve?

The dissociation curve in Figure **D.10** shows both hemoglobin and myoglobin, which is a pigment found in muscle cells.

The curve for myoglobin is to the left of the one for hemoglobin. If you look at the graph you will see that for almost all partial pressures of oxygen, myoglobin remains saturated. Myoglobin can bind to oxygen, which is released by hemoglobin, in muscles and remain fully saturated (i.e. hold on to the oxygen) until the partial pressure of oxygen is very low in the 0–2 kPa range. Myoglobin acts as a reserve supply of oxygen that is released when we are very active.

hint

Place a ruler on the graph at the 50% saturation level and check the partial pressure of oxygen for each type of hemoglobin.

The dissociation curve shows curves for both adult and fetal hemoglobin. Fetal hemoglobin also has a higher affinity for oxygen than adult hemoglobin. Its structure is slightly different and it can pick up oxygen released in the placenta by maternal hemoglobin.

Look at the graph, at a partial pressure of 4 kPa, the mother's hemoglobin is only 50% saturated, but fetal hemoglobin becomes approximately 70% saturated. Fetal hemoglobin carries oxygen to the baby's body and releases it into the respiring fetal tissues.

TEST YOURSELF D.18

 What is shown by a dissociation curve?

How is carbon dioxide carried back to the lungs?

Carbon dioxide from respiration returns to the lungs in the blood. It is transported in one of three ways.

   1 About 70% of carbon dioxide enters red blood cells and is converted to HCO_3^- (hydrogen carbonate) ions.

   2 About 7% remains in the blood and is transported dissolved in plasma.

   3 The remainder is bound to hemoglobin.

TEST YOURSELF D.19

 How does myoglobin differ from hemoglobin in its affinity for oxygen?

What is the chloride shift?

Carbon dioxide reacts with water to form carbonic acid, which dissociates to form hydrogen carbonate ions and hydrogen ions:

$$CO_2 + H_2O \rightarrow H_2CO_3 \rightleftharpoons H^+ + HCO_3^-$$

Hydrogen ions bind to plasma proteins and have a buffering effect, so that there is not a big fall in pH in the blood. This reaction in the plasma is slow.

Most carbon dioxide (about 70%) diffuses into the red blood cells where the same reaction is catalysed by the enzyme carbonic anhydrase.

Hydrogen carbonate ions move out of the red blood cells by facilitated diffusion and are exchanged for chloride ions. Thus the balance of charges on each side of the membrane is maintained. This process is called the chloride shift.

What is the Bohr shift?

From the dissociation curve you can see that the affinity of hemoglobin for oxygen is reduced in high carbon dioxide concentrations. As the partial pressure of carbon dioxide rises, the ability of hemoglobin to combine with oxygen falls and the curve moves to the right. This is known as the **Bohr shift**. It is caused when hydrogen ions produced from carbonic acid combine with hemoglobin.

Some carbon dioxide binds to hemoglobin to form carb-aminohemoglobin and forces hemoglobin to release its oxygen. This happens in active respiring tissues where the partial pressure of carbon dioxide is high.

In the lungs the carbaminohemoglobin releases carbon dioxide, which is exhaled and hemoglobin is available again to collect oxygen.

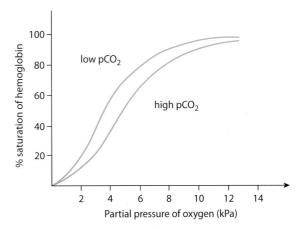

Figure D.11 The Bohr shift.

How and why does our ventilation rate increase when we exercise?

Ventilation rate is controlled by the breathing centre of the medulla oblongata, which receives impulses from chemoreceptors in the inner wall of the aorta and carotid arteries. These receptors respond to a fall in blood pH caused by an increase in blood carbon dioxide levels.

The breathing centre matches ventilation rate and tidal volume (the depth of breathing) to activity levels. Working muscles need oxygen and as exercise increases, so does the rate of oxygen consumption and carbon dioxide production.

If blood returning to the lungs has a high level of carbon dioxide an increase in ventilation rate draws in more fresh air to maintain the concentration gradient between the alveolar air and the blood. More oxygen can be absorbed and carbon dioxide removed.

What happens to the body when we move to high altitudes?

At high altitude, the percentage of oxygen in the air is the same as it is as sea level, but because air pressure is lower, the partial pressure of oxygen is reduced. At low partial pressures, hemoglobin does not become fully saturated with oxygen so that when a person moves from low to high altitude they may experience headaches and breathlessness and other symptoms of 'altitude sickness'.

Over a period of time the body will adjust by increasing:

- the number of red blood cells
- the level of myoglobin
- the density of blood capillaries in lungs and muscles.

Some athletes train at high altitude because, back at sea level, these factors improve their performance.

People who live at high altitude permanently have a larger lung capacity and tidal volume than those at sea level.

Revise the structure of alveoli, including the importance of pneumocytes from Section **6.4**. You must be able to label a diagram of an alveolus if you are given one.

Human physiology

What is emphysema and how can it be treated?

Emphysema is a chronic obstructive pulmonary disease (COPD), which slowly destroys the structure of alveoli in the lungs so that eventually they burst. The main symptom of emphysema is shortness of breath, which usually begins gradually. In more advanced stages of emphysema the lungs become so damaged that sufferers struggle to breathe even while resting.

The most common cause of emphysema is smoking, but long-term exposure to air pollution, industrial pollutants and coal or silica dust can also be causes. Treatments such as bronchial dilators to relax muscles in the bronchi can reduce some of the symptoms of emphysema, but the damage it causes is permanent. In severe cases patients must inhale oxygen from a cylinder.

☆ Model answer D.4

The graph shows the results of an experiment to investigate the effect of the partial pressure of carbon dioxide on the oxygen dissociation curve of human blood.

a **Explain the results shown by the three lines. [3]**

b **State the name given to the position of line 1 in relation to line 2. [1]**

c **Give an example of a location in the body and type of activity which would produce line 1. [2]**

d **Suggest two reasons why an athlete may decide to complete a period of training at high altitude. [2]**

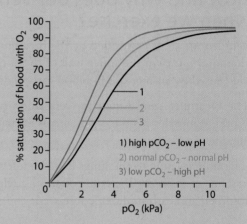

Figure D.12

a Line 2 represents the 'normal' situation in the body. Line 1 shows how the percentage saturation of the blood is different if there is a higher level of carbon dioxide present in the blood. It shows that hemoglobin in the blood dissociates more readily from oxygen (has a lower affinity for oxygen) if the partial pressure of carbon dioxide is high. Line 3 shows the opposite effect; if levels of carbon dioxide in the blood are low, hemoglobin has a higher affinity for oxygen, which remains bound to it more strongly.

b It is known as the Bohr shift.

c The Bohr shift occurs in an active muscle, where a lot of carbon dioxide is being released from respiring cells during vigorous exercise.

d After a period of some weeks at high altitude the human body adapts to lower partial pressures of oxygen by producing additional red blood cells and growing additional capillaries in lung and muscle tissue. These two adaptations enable a person to supply more oxygen to their muscles during exercise at sea level and can give an advantage in athletic performances.

GLOSSARY

abiotic aspect of the environment that is not living

absorption the taking up of a substance by a tissue

absorption spectrum wavelengths of light that a pigment is able to absorb

action potential a rapid wave of depolarisation at a cell surface causing an impulse in a neuron

activation energy the energy a substrate molecule must achieve before it can change chemically

active site the region on the surface of an enzyme to which the substrate molecule binds

active transport transport of a substance across a membrane against the concentration gradient

allele an alternative form of a gene found at a specific locus on a chromosome

analogous structures structures with similar functions but with different evolutionary origins

antibiotic organic compound produced by microorganisms to kill or inhibit other microorganisms

antibody one of millions of blood proteins produced by plasma cells in response to specific antigens

antigen a substance that stimulates the production of antibodies

atherosclerosis hardening and loss of elasticity in the arteries

ATP (adenosine triphosphate) a universal energy storage nucleotide formed in photosynthesis and respiration from ADP and P_i

autosome any chromosome other than a sex chromosome

axon a cytoplasmic process that transmits action potentials from the cell body of a neuron

biomagnification the process by which chemical substances accumulate at each trophic level in a food chain

bioremediation use of microorganisms to treat areas contaminated by pesticides

biotic index a measure of the biodiversity, of a given ecosystem or habitat obtained by surveying the organisms present

Bohr shift the reduction in hemoglobin's affinity for oxygen caused by an increase in the partial pressure of carbon dioxide

Bowman's capsule the cup-shaped part at the beginning of a nephron

Calvin cycle cycle of light-independent reactions in the stroma of the chloroplast

carbon fixation the conversion of carbon atoms into a combined organic form

cell theory the theory that organisms consist of cells and that all cells come from pre-existing cells

central nervous system (CNS) the brain and spinal cord of a vertebrate

centromere the region where sister chromatids are joined

cerebral cortex a highly folded layer of nerve cell bodies that forms the surface of the cerebrum

cerebral hemispheres (cerebrum) the main part of the human brain, the coordinating system of the nervous system

chemiosmosis the passive flow of protons down a concentration gradient

chiasma (chiasmata) point of crossing over between homologous chromosomes

cholesterol a lipid formed in the liver and carried in the blood as lipoprotein

chromatid one of the two copies of a chromosome after it has replicated and before the centromeres separate at anaphase

chromosome in eukaryotes, long thread of DNA and protein that carries the genetic information in bacteria, the DNA molecule that contains the genetic information

clade all the organisms both living and fossil descended from a particular common ancestor

cladistics classifying organisms using lines of descent

climax community the stable stage at the end of a succession of communities in an ecosystem

clone genetically identical cells or organisms produced from a common ancestor by asexual reproduction

codon a triplet of three nucleotides in mRNA that specify the position of an amino acid in a polypeptide

cohesion forces of attraction between water molecules, which enable them to stick together in a lattice

competitive exclusion two species that compete for the same resources cannot coexist indefinitely

competitive inhibitor substance similar to the substrate of an enzyme, which binds to the active site

complementary base pairing pairing of bases A–T and G–C in double stranded DNA, and of A–U and C–G between DNA and RNA

concentration gradient a difference in concentration of a substance between one area and another

condensation reaction a reaction in which two molecules bonded covalently and a molecule of water is released

continuous variation variation in a species which is controlled by several genes

corpus luteum mass of cells which develops from an ovarian follicle after the release of the oocyte

cortical reaction release of cortical granules at fertilisation to prevent polyspermy

cristae folds of the inner membrane of mitochondria

crossing over exchange of genetic material between homologous chromosomes during meiosis

cytokinesis division of cytoplasm after the nucleus has divided

Glossary

denaturation a change in the structure of a protein that results in a loss of its function

diffusion passive, random movement of molecules from an area of high concentration to an area of lower concentration

discrete variation variation in characteristics so that types can be grouped into specific categories

DNA gyrase an enzyme that relieves the tension on a DNA molecule during replication

DNA helicase an enzyme that unwinds and separates the two strands of a DNA molecule

DNA ligase enzyme that links Okazaki fragments during DNA replication

DNA microarray a glass or silicon chip with DNA probes attached to its surface

DNA polymerases a group of enzymes that catalyse the formation of DNA strands from a DNA template

electron transport chain (ETC) a series of carriers that transfer electrons along a redox pathway, enabling the synthesis of ATP during respiration

electrophoresis separating components in a mixture of chemicals by means of an electric field e.g. DNA

embryonic stem cells cells derived from an embryo that retain the potential to differentiate into any other cell

emergent property a property of a complex system that arises from interactions of its component parts

end-product inhibition control of a metabolic pathway in which a product within or at the end of the pathway inhibits an enzyme found earlier in the pathway

endocrine gland a ductless gland that secretes hormones into the bloodstream

endosymbiosis a theory which proposes that mitochondria and chloroplasts evolved from bacteria that became part of a larger cell

epinephrine (adrenalin) the 'flight or fight' hormone produced by the medulla of the adrenal gland

eukaryotic an organism whose cells contain a membrane-bound nucleus

eutrophication an increase in the concentration of nutrients such as nitrate in an aquatic environment so that primary production increases

evolution the cumulative change in the heritable characteristics of a population

exocrine gland a gland whose secretion is released via a duct

exocytosis the active movement of substances out of a cell in vesicles

exon portion of RNA transcript that codes for part of a polypeptide in eukaryotes (compare with intron)

facilitated diffusion diffusion across a membrane through specific protein channels in the membrane

fibrinogen the soluble plasma protein, converted to fibrin during the blood-clotting process

fluid mosaic model the structure of a membrane that includes a phospholipid bilayer in which proteins are embedded

gene a heritable factor that controls a specific characteristic

gene pool all the genes and their alleles present in a breeding population

genetic modification (GM) alteration of genes, often using genes from a different species, in order to modify an organism's characteristics

genome the complete genetic information of an organism or an individual cell

genotype the exact genetic constitution of an individual feature of an organism; the alleles of an organism

glucagon hormone released by the pancreas, which stimulates the breakdown of glycogen in the liver to increase blood glucose

glycogen polymer of glucose used as a storage carbohydrate in liver and muscle tissue

glycolysis the first stage of respiration during which glucose is converted to pyruvate

helper T cells cells that activate B cells and other T cells in the immune response; target of the HIV virus

hemodialysis a method of treating kidney failure by filtering blood through a machine which removes urea and other unwanted substances

heterozygous having two different copies of an allele of a gene

histamine a molecule released during allergic reactions

histone one of a group of basic proteins that form nucleosomes and act as scaffolding for DNA

homeostasis maintenance of a constant internal environment

homologous chromosomes chromosomes in a diploid cell that contain the same sequences of genes but which are derived from different parents

homologous structures similar structures due to common ancestry

homozygous having two identical copies of an allele

hybridoma a cell formed by the fusion of a plasma cell and a cancer cell

hydrolysis reaction reaction in which hydrogen and hydroxyl ions (water) are added to a large molecule to cause it to split into smaller molecules

hydrophilic water loving

hydrophobic water hating

hypertonic a more concentrated solution (one with a less negative water potential) than the cell solution

hypothalamus control centre of the autonomic nervous system and site of release of releasing factors for the pituitary hormones

immune response the production of antibodies in response to the presence of antigen

intron a non-coding sequence of nucleotides in primary RNA, in eukaryotes (compare with exon)

karyogram a diagram or photographic image showing the number, shape and types of chromosomes in a cell

karyotype the number, shape and types of chromosomes in a cell

keystone species a species that is important in maintaining community structure in an ecosystem because it reduces competition in other trophic levels

Krebs cycle a cycle of biochemical changes that occur in the mitochondrial matrix during aerobic respiration

lagging strand the daughter strand that is synthesised discontinuously in DNA replication

light-dependent reactions stages in photosynthesis that occur on the grana of the chloroplasts in which light is used to split water, and produce ATP and NADPH + H$^+$

light-independent reactions stages in photosynthesis that take place in the stroma and use the products of the light-dependent reactions to produce carbohydrate

limiting factor a resource that influences the rate of processes (such as photosynthesis or population growth) if it is in short supply

locus the specific location on a chromosome of a gene

luteinising hormone (LH) a hormone produced by the anterior pituitary gland that stimulates the production of sex hormones by ovaries and testes

medulla oblongata the part of the brain stem that controls breathing and other reflex actions

meiosis a nuclear division that produces cells containing half the number of chromosomes of the parent cell

memory cells cloned lymphocytes which remain in the blood stream after an infection to give protection against the same infection (antigen) later

mRNA (messenger RNA) a single-stranded transcript of one strand of DNA

metabolic pathway a series of chemical reactions that are catalysed by enzymes

metabolism integrated network of all the biochemical reactions of life

metaphase stage in nuclear division; chromosomes become arranged on the equator of the spindle

microvilli folded projections of epithelial cells, such as those lining the small intestine, that increase cell surface area

mitotic index a measure of cell proliferation; the ratio between the number of cells in mitosis and the total number of cells in the sample

mitosis cell division that produces two daughter cells with the same chromosome compliment as the parent cell

monomer a small molecule which can link with other identical molecules to form a polymer

monosaccharide a simple sugar (monomer) that cannot be hydrolysed

motor neuron nerve cell that carries impulses away from the brain

mutagen an agent that causes mutation

mutation a permanent change in the base sequence of DNA

mutualism a type of symbiotic relationship in which both organisms benefit

myogenic a contraction of heart muscle that originates in heart muscle cells

negative feedback a regulating mechanism in which a change in a sensed variable results in a correction that opposes the change

neurotransmitter a substances produced and released by a neurone, which passes across a synapse and affects a post-synaptic membrane

non-competitive inhibitor an inhibitor of an enzyme that binds at a site away from the active site

non-disjunction failure of sister chromatids to separate in mitosis or meiosis II, or of homologous chromosomes to separate in meiosis I

nucleosome a part of a eukaryotic chromosome made up of DNA associated with histone molecules

nucleotide the basic chemical unit of a nucleic acid; an organic base combined with pentose sugar (either ribose or deoxyribose) and phosphate

Okazaki fragments newly formed DNA fragments that form part of the lagging strand during replication

oncogene a cancer-initiating gene

oogenesis female gamete production

pentadactyl having limbs that end in five digits

peptide bond a covalently bonded linkage between two amino acids

phagocyte a type of white blood cell which removes harmful particles by engulfing them

phagocytosis modifying the shape of a phagocytic cell so that it can engulf bacteria or other particles

phenotype the characteristic or appearance or an organism which may be physical or biochemical

phloem tissue that carries food in the stem of a plant

phospholipid important constituent molecules of membranes

phosphorylation the addition of a phosphate group to a molecule

photolysis the splitting of water molecules in the light-dependent stage of photosynthesis

photophosphorylation the formation of ATP using light energy in the grana of chloroplasts

phototropism the tropic response of plants to light

phytochrome a pigment found in plants that regulates several processes including the flowering pattern in response to day length

pinocytosis a form of endocytosis, taking extra cellular fluids into a cell by means of vesicles

pituitary gland 'master gland' whose hormones control the activities of other glands

placenta a structure of maternal and fetal tissues in the uterus

plaque the build up of fatty deposits in artery walls

plasma cells antibody-secreting cells that develop from a B cell

plasmid a small circle of DNA found in bacteria

platelets cell fragments found in the blood that are concerned with blood clotting

Glossary

pneumocyte cells found in alveoli. Type 1 are responsible for gas exchange, type 2 produce surfactant

polar body a non-functioning nucleus produced during meiosis; three are produced during human oogenesis

polygenic phenotypic characteristics that are determined by the collective effects of several different genes

polymer a substance built up from a series of monomers

polymerase chain reaction (PCR) process by which small quantities of DNA are multiplied

polypeptide a chain of amino acids linked by peptide bonds

polysaccharide carbohydrates formed by condensation reactions between large numbers of monosaccharides

population a group of organisms of the same species that live in the same area at the same time

positive feedback a control mechanism in which a deviation from the normal level stimulates an increase in the deviation

proteome the complete set of proteins expressed by a genome

R group a side chain attached to an amino acid

recessive allele an allele that has an effect on the phenotype only when present in the homozygous state

recombinant DNA DNA that has been artificially changed, involving the joining of genes from different species

reflex action a rapid automatic response

refractory period the time after an action potential during which another action potential cannot occur

regulator gene a gene determining the production of a protein that regulates the activity of structural genes

replication fork the point at which DNA is replicating

resting potential the potential difference across the membrane of a neurone when it is not being stimulated

restriction enzyme (endonuclease) one of several enzymes that cut nucleic acids at specific sequences

RNA a nucleic acid that contains the pentose sugar ribose and bases adenine, guanine, cytosine and uracil

RNA polymerase an enzyme that catalyses the formation of RNA from a DNA template

RNA primase an enzyme that catalyses the synthesis of RNA primers as the starting point for DNA synthesis

RNA splicing modification of RNA to remove introns and rejoin the remaining exons

sarcomere contractile unit of skeletal muscle between two Z lines

saturated a hydrocarbon in which all carbon atoms are linked by single bonds to other carbon or hydrogen atoms

sense strand the coding strand of DNA, which is not transcribed

sex chromosomes chromosomes that determine the sex of an individual

sinoatrial node (SA node) the pacemaker cells in the wall of the right atrium, which initiate the heart beat

sister chromatids two joined copies of a chromosome after it has replicated and before the centromeres separate

skeletal (striated) muscle voluntary muscle which has multinucleated cells with actin and myosin microfilaments

smooth muscle sheets of mononucleate cells that are stimulated by the autonomic nervous system

somatic cell body cell, not a gamete producing cell

speciation the evolution of new species

species a group of individuals of common ancestry that are normally capable of interbreeding to produce fertile offspring

supercoiling additional coiling of the DNA helix

systole contraction of the chambers of the heart during the cardiac cycle

telomere region of nucleotide sequences at the end of a chromatid

thrombosis the blockage of a blood vessel by a blood clot

transcription copying a sequence of DNA bases to mRNA

tRNA (transfer RNA) short lengths of RNA that carry specific amino acids to ribosomes during protein synthesis

translation decoding of mRNA to produce an amino acid sequence

transpiration loss of water vapour from the leaves and stem of plants

trisomy containing three rather than two members of a chromosome pair

trophic level a group of organisms all have the same number of energy transfers from the source of energy

tropism a growth response of plants; the direction of growth is determined by the direction of the stimulus

tumour a disorganised mass of cells

type II diabetes diabetes which results from the body developing an insensitivity to insulin

ultrafiltration process that occurs through tiny pores in the capillaries of the glomerulus

unsaturated fats that contain at least one double bond between carbon atoms in their molecules

urea a molecule formed from excess amino acids in the liver

vaccination injection of an antigen to induce antibody production

variation differences in the phenotype of organisms of the same species

vascular bundles a length of vascular tissue in plants consisting of xylem and phloem

vector a plasmid or virus that carries a piece of DNA into a bacterium during recombinant DNA technology

villi (villus) a fold in the lining of the small intestine where absorption occurs

ANSWERS TO TEST YOURSELF QUESTIONS

1 Cell biology

1.1 All cells arise from other cells; living organisms are made of cells; cells are the smallest units of life.

1.2 The ratio decreases.

1.3 As a cell or other small object, such as a sphere or cube, increases in size, its surface area and volume do not change in the same proportions / the ratio between surface area and volume is not a linear correlation / the ratio of the surface area to volume decreases, as the cell grows larger; this means there is less surface area for the diffusion of substances in and out of the cell; large cells would be unable to obtain what they need to live through their surfaces, so cells divide and remain small.

1.4 **1** They retain the capacity to differentiate into any other cell type.

    2 D

1.5 D

1.6 Protein synthesis

1.7 **a** A is a mitochondrion; B is rough endoplasmic reticulum

    b A is the site of respiration; B is the site of protein synthesis

    c Use the formula 1:1500 (1500x)

$$\text{Magnification} = \frac{\text{measured length of cell}}{\text{actual length of cell}}$$

    d The scale line represents $0.5\,\mu m$ so the mitochondrion is approximately $4 \times$ this length, $2\,\mu m$.

1.8 'Water hating'

1.9 Cholesterol changes the fluid properties of the membrane.

1.10 Diffusion is the movement of particles from an area of high concentration to an area of lower concentration, whereas osmosis is the movement of water molecules from an area of high concentration to an area of lower concentration. No energy is needed for either process.

1.11 C

1.12 Pasteur's experiment showed that cells did not spontaneously appear. They grew from other cells.

1.13 Prophase, metaphase, anaphase, telophase

1.14 The number of cells in a sample and the number undergoing mitosis.

2 Molecular biology

2.1 **1** alpha-D-glucose (note the position of the OH group on the right hand side of the molecule)

    2 A polypeptide

    3 Peptide bonds

2.2 Water has a high heat capacity and a lot of energy is lost when it changes from liquid to vapour when sweat evaporates.

2.3 **1** B

    2 Hydrophobic means water hating.

    3 Lipids have no polar groups and are large molecules; thus they do not dissolve in water.

2.4 It is formed of long straight molecules linked together by H bonds.

2.5 Condensation

2.6 Condensation reaction and a peptide bond

2.7 20   **2.8** B

2.9 Leucine   **2.10** B

2.11 The rate of reaction increases until all the active sites are filled and then it levels off.

2.12 **1** 350 because each T pairs with A.

    2 GC pairs – because they have three hydrogen bonds holding them together but AT pairs have only two.

2.13 C

2.14 **1** methionine (start) aspartic acid, serine, cysteine

    2 AGA or AGG and UAU or UAC

    3 TCT or TCC and ATA or ATG

2.15 **1** RNA nucleotide

    2 tRNA contains the bases A, C, G and U whereas DNA contains A, C, G and T; tRNA is a single stranded nucleic acid whereas DNA is double stranded.

    3 **a** ACG   **b** serine

Answers to Test yourself questions

2.16 B

2.17 ATP and lactate (lactic acid)

2.18 **1** A – pyruvate (or pyruvic acid); B – lactate (or lactic acid); C – ethanol; D carbon dioxide

2 Q - anaerobic respiration: R - aerobic respiration

3 In mitochondria

2.19 Red and blue wavelengths

2.20 Light dependent reactions: require light energy; light energy is absorbed by chlorophyll; light energy is used to split water molecules in a process called photolysis to produce ATP. Light-independent reactions: do not require light energy; do not split water molecules but do fix carbon dioxide by combining it with hydrogen and ATP; produce glucose and other organic compounds.

2.21 **1** **a** light intensity **b** temperature

2 The graph shows that increasing carbon dioxide concentration increases the rate of photosynthesis, so farmers might choose to increase CO_2 levels inside their glasshouses if they are sealed from the atmosphere. Increasing light intensity also increases the rate of photosynthesis so lighting the glasshouse could also increase photosynthesis. Increasing photosynthesis would lead to an increase in growth of the tomato plants.

3 A limiting factor is a resource that influences the rate of photosynthesis if it is in short supply. If light intensity increases, plants will increase their rate of photosynthesis until another factor, such as carbon dioxide concentration or temperature limit the reaction.

3 Genetics

3.1 B

3.2 If DNA sequences are known, the proteins produced by a gene can be identified and new therapeutic drugs can be developed if a gene is faulty; evolutionary relationships can be established/ variations in proteins between organisms identified.

3.3 **1** The diploid number.   **2** 15

3.4 Genome size of an organism is measured as the number of base pairs in a complete genome.

3.5 **1** The chromosomes are linear not circular; bacteria have a single chromosome and the karyogram shows many chromosomes.

2 There are 44 autosomes (or 22 pairs).

3.6 **1** D   **2** A

3.7 **1** Prophase

2 Anaphase 1

3 Anaphase 2

3.8 **a** There is a 50% chance that their daughters would be colour blind because there is a 50% chance that they would inherit the recessive alleles from both their parents.

b There is a 50% chance that their sons would be colour blind because there is a 50% chance that they would inherit the recessive allele from their mother (and their Y chromosome from their father).

3.9 A

3.10 PCR produces many copies of small samples of DNA – often DNA samples are very small and couldn't be used on their own.

3.11 **1** Restriction enzymes which cut DNA in specific places and ligases that join up 'sticky ends' to insert the new DNA. (Restriction enzymes are also used in the PCR.)

2 C

3.12 D

3.13 The genetic code is universal – the code found in one species will produce the same protein in any other species.

4 Ecology

4.1 B

4.2 Several are possible, but should have wheat seeds in level 1; sparrow and mouse in level 2 and fox, cat and hawk in level 3; hawk and fox could be in level 4.

4.3 The length of a food chain is determined by the loss of energy at each transfer when animals feed. Many animals use energy to maintain body temperature. In aquatic systems most organisms are not homeotherms (warm-blooded), so the energy they need to maintain temperature is less and more energy is available to be passed up the food chain to the next consumer. Water also supports the bodies of aquatic organisms, so less energy is needed to build bones and muscles.

4.4 D

4.5 Any six of the following points in a suitable order would gain marks here.

- Energy flows from one trophic level to another as animals feed.

- The first trophic level is green plants, which start a food chain such as:

- Grass → mouse → owl
- Energy passes to the mouse as it feeds on grass seeds.
- The mouse is at trophic level 2.
- The energy in the seeds is used by the mouse to make new tissues and grow, or for respiration or it is lost in feces.
- Only energy, which is stored in the mouse, can pass to trophic level 3, the owl.
- The owl will use the energy it obtains to live, respire and grow.
- Only stored energy can be passed to the next trophic level.
- At each energy transfer there is less energy available to the next trophic level because energy lost as heat from respiration or in feces cannot be passed on.
- When animals die the energy in their bodies passes to decomposers.

4.6 Photosynthesis and dissolving in oceans

4.7 Fossil plants; compressed bodies of ancient sea organisms; mollusc shells and coral skeletons

4.8 **1** Humans use all three substances as sources of fuel. As they are gathered and burned, carbon is oxidised to carbon dioxide gas and the amount of carbon locked up in the three reserves is reduced.

2 Vegetation in very wet areas such as wetlands and bogs dies; the vegetation starts to rot on the surface due to the action of aerobic bacteria; the process is interrupted as more vegetation piles up on top; only anaerobic bacteria can survive under these layers and decomposition slows or stops so that eventually peat forms. (3 marks for any three points)

3 Peat is not a renewable source of energy because it takes up to 5000 years to form and is used up much more quickly than this.

4.9 A

5 Evolution and biodiversity

5.1 Organisms do not change if there is no environmental pressure to do so. Modern organisms will resemble their fossil ancestors if their environments have remained stable.

5.2 It describes how humans have selected and changed the characteristics of domestic animals and plants to suit our needs, so that they are now very different from their original ancestors.

5.3 Bones of the foot, bones of the flipper, bones supporting the wing membrane.

5.4 Meiosis, sexual reproduction, mutations.

5.5 **1** The main difference is in the shape of the beak.

2 This suggests the birds feed on different types of food

3 The birds began to feed on different food as their numbers grew and there was more competition. The birds with the best beak shape for the new food survived and passed on their beak shape to their offspring. Gradually different populations of finches came to feed on insects, seeds and so on.

4 If the birds cannot interbreed they must now be different species.

5.6 Breeds of dog are not different species because they can interbreed and produce fertile offspring, even though they may not do so.

5.7 It is an artificial classification because it does not relate to the evolution of the food plants from a common ancestor, but only relates to the way humans use the plants.

5.8 You would need to analyse the DNA or proteins from the two groups to test the hypothesis.

5.9 **1** Because Latin is an unchanging language; that is accepted by scientists all over the world.

2 Analogous structures; because they are structurally dissimilar but they carry out the same function.

3 Bryophyta

5.10 **1** Analogous structures have similar functions but not similar structure.

2 a Cladogram 3

b Cladogram 3 shows that B and C share a common ancestor; in all the other cladograms C and D share a common ancestor.

6 Human physiology

6.1 C   **6.2** The pancreas

6.3 Amino acids   **6.4** D

6.5 **1** Pressure is highest at about 0.3 seconds because at this point the muscles of the ventricles have contracted to force blood into the aorta.

2 At approximately 0.2 seconds, when the atria have contracted and the atrium is filling with blood. The valve closes as pressure builds up in the ventricles and prevents blood flowing back into the atria.

Answers to Test yourself questions

3 At 0.4 seconds, the semi-lunar valves shut to prevent blood flowing back from the arteries and the atrio-ventricular valves open to let blood flow from the atria to refill the ventricles.

6.6 If they were active, blood would clot as it flowed in blood vessels.

6.7 B

6.8 Antibodies are produced in the human body but antibiotics are produced by organisms such as fungi; antibodies are specific to one type of pathogen but antibiotics affect bacterial metabolism so can kill different types of bacteria; antibodies can kill viruses but antibiotics cannot.

6.9 Longitudinal and circular muscles in the intestine; external and internal intercostal muscle in the ribs.

6.10

Feature of alveoli	Why it is important for gas exchange
many small, spherical alveoli	*provide a large surface area for gas exchange*
thin walls made of flat cells	*short diffusion distance*
rich blood supply from capillaries	*maintains concentration gradient and carries absorbed gases away rapidly*

6.11 Tiredness can be a sign of slow metabolism and a person with emphysema will have difficulty obtaining sufficient oxygen for respiration. Also emphysema makes ventilation difficult and more effort is needed to inhale and exhale, leading to tiredness.

6.12 During the refractory period, the resting potential is re-established; by the action of the sodium–potassium pump; at this time an action potential cannot start; so an action potential can't be started in the part of the axon from which an action potential has come.

6.13 **1** C **2** D **3** B

6.14 **1** There is no direct correlation between the diameter of the axons and their speed of transmitting impulses. The data from the myelinated axons of the toad and cat with the same diameter show that cat axons transmit data more quickly than toads. But if the squid and the toad are compared, the big diameter of the squid axon enables it to transmit impulses at the same speed as the toad.

2 There is no direct evidence that myelination can increase the speed of transmission. The unmyelinated cat axon transmits impulses much more slowly than the myelinated cat axon but this may be due to the diameters of the two axons rather than their myelin covering.

6.15 **1** The pancreas is the gland which is the effector for blood glucose levels.

2 Insulin is released by the pancreas when blood glucose levels rise. Glucagon is released when blood glucose levels fall.

6.16 **1** The (red) line represents insulin because the level of the hormone rises *after* the level of glucose. Glucose stimulates the pancreas to release insulin.

2 Glucose is stored as glycogen in muscles and the liver. It may be stored as fat if there is a very high level of glucose present.

3 If the person did not eat lunch the level of glucose in the blood would fall below the $90\,mg\,100\,cm^{-3}$ line. Insulin levels would fall as insulin would not be released.

6.17 **1** 04:00

2 The person is likely to be getting up at 08:00 cortisol will increase heart rate and metabolic rate as the day begins.

3 Adrenaline because the heart rate tends to be lower at night and thyroxin because metabolism is lower at night.

6.18 LH (luteinising hormone)

6.19 B   **6.20** **1** A   **2** B

7 Nucleic acids (HL)

7.1 D   **7.2** D

7.3 The anti-sense strand is transcribed but the mRNA strand has the same base sequence as the sense strand (but with U instead of T).

7.4 mRNA construction proceeds in a 5' to 3' direction as the 5' end of a nucleotide is added to the 3' end of the growing molecule. This is the same for all nucleotide linkages.

7.5 C   **7.6** B

7.7 AUGCUAGAC

7.8 **a** 75 + 6; each amino acid is coded for by a triplet of bases, plus a start and stop codon.

b At least 81 – there may be more bases in DNA because exons will have been removed.

7.9. **1** The active site is the place on an enzymes surface where a substrate must bind. It must be a specific three-dimensional shape to accommodate the substrate, so the three-dimensional structure is essential.

2 a True

b True, mRNA and tRNA

c False, amino acids attach to tRNA not mRNA

d True many ribosomes can attach to one strand of mRNA

e False ribosomes attach to mRNA not DNA

f False, mRNA moves to the cytoplasm for translation

8 Metabolism, cell respiration and photosynthesis (HL)

8.1 a The line should follow the horizontal parts of the graph but be drawn underneath the area where energy level rises.

b The enzyme lowers the activation energy; which is the energy needed to bring the substrate(s) to their transition state; so that products are formed more quickly.

8.2 C

8.3 Competitive

(i) structurally similar to the substrate

(ii) occupies and blocks the active site

(iii) at low concentrations of inhibitor, increasing the substrate concentration reduces inhibition

Non-competitive

(i) structurally unlike the substrate

(ii) site binds at a site away from the active site but reduces access to it

(iii) at low concentrations of substrate, increasing the concentration of substrate has no effect on inhibitor binding so inhibition stays high

8.4 The inter-membrane space contains a high concentration of H^+ ions, so the pH here will be higher than that in the matrix.

8.5 A   **8.6** A

8.7

Stage	Site	Oxygen needed	Processes
glycolysis	cytoplasm	no	Glucose is converted to pyruvate. Hydrogen is removed and passed to electron carriers.
link reaction	mitochondrial matrix	yes	Pyruvate enters the mitochondrion is decarboxylated, dehydrogenated and combined with CoA to produce acetyl coenzyme A. Hydrogen is removed and passed to electron carriers.
Krebs cycle	mitochondrial matrix	no	A cyclical reaction, hydrogen is passed to electron carriers, carbon dioxide is removed and a starting reactant is regenerated.
electron transport chain	inner membranes (cristae)	yes	Hydrogen from the previous reactions is split to release electrons. These pass through carriers and generate ATP. Hydrogen is combine with oxygen to release water.

8.8 Thylakoid membrane and stroma

8.9 1 1 = outer membrane; 2 = granum; 3 = stroma; 4 = lipid droplet; 5 = starch grain

2 a Light-dependent reactions occur in structure 2;

b light-independent reactions (or Calvin cycle) occur in structure 3.

8.10 To raise electrons to a higher energy level.

8.11 NADPH + H+ and ATP

8.12

	True/False
electrons are excited by photons	✓/x
electrons pass to carriers	✓/x
oxidative photo-phosphorylation is involved	✓/x
ATP is produced from ADP and phosphate	✓/x
ATP is produced in light and dark	x/✓

Answers to Test yourself questions

9 Plant biology (HL)

9.1 **1** Stomata were open and the sub-stomatal space contained water vapour which was lost from the leaves.

2 The rate of water loss decreased because the plant was losing water from its cells which is a slower process; turgor reduces as water is lost via the stomata and is not replaced. Stomata were closing and rate of loss decreased.

3 The geranium was plant 2 because a thick cuticle and hairy covering reduced overall water loss.

9.2 Any three of: xylem is not living, phloem is alive; xylem tissue forms a continuous tube; phloem cells are separated by perforated ends; xylem carries water up the stem; phloem carries substances (sugars) both up and down the stem.

9.3 Green photosynthesising leaves

9.4 The hydrostatic pressure in the phloem is greatest close to the source. This pressure drives the flow in the phloem, which is also greatest close to the source.

9.5 **1** Cells from the stem tip (meristem) are able to produce undifferentiated cells, leaves and plantlets; different genes can be switched on by different concentrations of plant hormones so the cells must contain a complete genome.

2 To grow whole plants the grower must start with plantlets, the ratio of auxin to cytokinin that does this is 10:50 or 1:5.

3 Plants will be identical, so if cells for culture are taken from a good quality plant, all the new plants will be the same quality; there will be fewer losses due to failed germination and young plants can be kept in controlled conditions in the lab until they are ready for planting out.

9.6 **1** Plant B **2** P_{fr}

3 Slowly converted to P_r

9.7 D

10 Genetics and evolution (HL)

10.1 D

10.2 **1** C

2 Genes consist of alleles at corresponding places (loci) on homologous chromosomes; all alleles on a chromosome must be carried together as they are inherited; but if a chiasma forms some of these alleles will be exchanged with those on a sister chromatid; thus the lleles in a linkage group are changed.

3 Meiosis reduces the diploid number of chromosomes to the haploid; fertilisation joins two haploid nuclei to re-establish the diploid number.

10.3 B

10.4 **1** The inherited characteristics do not behave in a Mendelian way.

2

Phenotype	Observed (O)	Expected (E)	(O – E)	(O – E)²
grey/normal wing	180	145	35	1225
black/vestigial wing	52	16	36	1296
grey/vestigial wing	14	48	−34	1156
black/ normal wing	11	48	−37	1369

3 $\chi^2 = 1225/145 + 1296/16 + 1156/48 + 1369/48 = 142.1$

4 3

5 Reject the null hypothesis because the value is greater than the critical value

6 The characteristics are linked. The alleles are on the same chromosomes. Black with vestigial wing and grey to normal wings.

10.5 **1** Cross-pollination can only occur within the existing gene pool of a species; thus it cannot bring new genes into the gene pool because a species is by definition reproductively isolated.

2 An individual will be affected by the environment and this can modify its phenotype; some alleles have multiple effects in a phenotype.

10.6 **1** A = stabilising; B = directional; C = disruptive

2

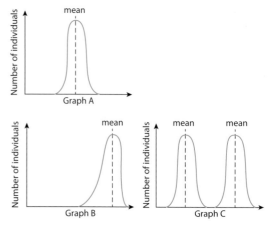

3 The mean is indicated on the graphs shown in 2.

11 Animal physiology (HL)

11.1 Phagocytes are able to move out of the capillaries more easily; and engulf pathogens and damaged cells which have entered the body, but may not be in the circulation.

11.2 The receptor sites on both B and T cells are very specific to just one antigen molecule.

11.3 Donated organs have proteins on their cell surfaces which are recognised as 'non-self' by the recipient; B and T cells would destroy the transplanted organ; immunosuppressant drugs reduce the rejection of the transplanted organ but also reduce the patient's ability to destroy other antigens and fight infections.

11.4 C

11.5 1 P = myosin, Q = actin, R = Z line

2 The muscle is relaxed and not contracting.

3 D

4 Antagonistic muscle would have to contract to pull this muscle back to position A.

5 Calcium ions bind to troponin; which causes tropomyosin to move and expose the binding sites on the actin molecule; myosin heads then bend and move the actin filament a short distance towards the centre of the sarcomere.

11.6 Blood in renal artery contains: more oxygen than the blood in the renal vein; more urea than the blood in the renal vein; more glucose than the blood in the renal vein. Blood in the renal artery has a variable content of salts and water but in the renal vein there is a regulated amount.

11.7 D   **11.8** A

11.9 It maintains the corpus luteum, so that secretion of estrogen and progesterone continues; and maintains the uterus lining (endometrium).

11.10 LH is high; FSH is high; estrogen is high; progesterone is low.

A Neurobiology and behaviour

A.1 In the first month after conception

A.2 Neurons will move to different areas of the brain as it develops before taking up their final positions.

A.3 1 Shrews and bats

2 The relationship shows a positive correlation but is not directly proportional as the bodyweight is shown on a logarithmic scale.

3 A human might have a ratio of brain: body weight mass of 10 but for a whale this ratio is 1 and for a mouse it would be 1000. It is difficult to draw conclusions from this data. We cannot say that humans have the largest relative brain mass.

A.4 Memory and learning; cerebral hemispheres

A.5 Ability to speak and write

A.6 There is one type of rod, but three types of cone; rods are found throughout the retina, but cones are only found in the centre of the retina directly behind the pupil; rods are linked to ganglion cells with several cells per ganglion, whereas cones are linked individually.

A.7 A stimulus is a change in the internal or external environment that is detected by a receptor and prompts a response; response is a change in the behaviour, in reaction to a stimulus; reflex is a rapid and unconscious response.

A.8 Male birds sing to attract females for reproduction and to establish territorial boundaries; birds are born with an (innate) template song of their own species; they must listen to the song of adult birds so that they can (learn) adapt their song to be similar to that of successful adults; both innate and learned behaviour are important.

A.9 1 Causes hyperpolarisation of post-synaptic membrane; so they are more difficult to stimulate.

2 Reduces inhibitions, can affect co-ordination and speech.

A.10 1 Dopamine is a neurotransmitter released in the 'reward' pathways. It modulates mood and pleasure.

2 MDMA raises levels of dopamine and serotonin. Dopamine produces feelings of well-being but repeated stimulation can cause them to be desensitised so that more and more of the drug is needed to maintain feelings of well-being; serotonin regulates mood and sleep so if its levels fall rapidly a person may feel anxious and depressed.

A.11 1 If prey is abundant feeding on small numbers of large prey requires less energy expenditure

2 At low prey densities fish eat whatever prey is available rather than not feeding.

A.12 1 If different individuals have slight variations in their phenotypes, they may respond differently. A favourable behavioural response can be advantageous, and lead to survival and reproduction of those animals that carry the favourable allele. Over time the allele and the

Answers to Test yourself questions

behaviour will become prevalent. One example is the migration pattern of the black cap (*Sylvia atricapilla*). The birds' original migration pattern from their German breeding ground was to the south of Spain; but some individuals began to travel west to the UK. These individuals had the advantage of mild winters and a shorter journey, which led to greater reproductive success as they returned to their breeding grounds earlier than other birds.

2 Unrelated females share blood with other females as well as their sisters and mothers; blood given to another animal reduces the amount the donor has for itself; there is no reproductive benefit to the donor as the animals may not share the same genes.

B Biotechnology and bioinformatics

B.1

Condition	Leads to	Controlled by
rising temperature	enzyme inefficiency	cooling jackets
low oxygen levels	aerobes cannot respire	stirrers and air input
carbon dioxide production	changes in pH	monitoring and release of gases

B.2 1 Batch production

2 temperature; concentration of oxygen; quantity of nutrients added at the start of the reaction

3 A secondary metabolite is not essential for the normal functioning of the *Penicillium* cells.

4 80 hours or 10 hours either side

B.3 Marker genes, regulator genes

B.4 They do not produce amylose; amylose reduces the usefulness of starch in industrial processes, such as paper and adhesive production, so the starch produced is easier to process or more useful.

B.5 Microorganisms reproduce quickly; they are able to metabolise substrates such as heavy metals and hydrocarbons (oil or petrol).

B.6 The method microorganisms use to communicate, it involves releasing chemical signals into the nearby environment.

B.7 B   **B.8** D

B.9 The sequence of nucleotides in a gene or open reading frame.

B.10 1 Model organisms are common species that have been studied in laboratories for a long time.

2 Mouse, *Drosophila* (fruit fly) *Arabidopsis*, yeast, *E. coli* (any two).

3 They can provide data that is relevant to other species.

B.11 Nucleotide sequences, protein sequences, microarray data, metabolic pathway data (any three).

C Ecology and conservation

C.1 1 *Nucella lapillus* is most abundant at the high tide mark (this is shown by the width of the 'kites' in the diagram).

2 The species are likely to be affected by temperature and the time that they are exposed (not covered by sea water) at different times of the day.

3 The two species may feed on different vegetation which grows at different distances from the low tide mark; the two species may have different tolerances to exposure at low tide so *Littorina neritoides* is less tolerant and lives closer to the low tide mark.

4 (i) The whelk (*Nucella lapillus*) is a predator but it shares a similar distribution to the limpets (*Patella vulgata*) and is found at all distances up the shore, this suggests that the limpets are not eaten by whelks in large numbers, this might be due to protection of the limpets shells or availability of easier prey for the whelks.

(ii) Whelks are likely to feed on *L. littoralis* at the low tide mark, *L. littorea* in the mid shore and *L. neritoides* at the high tide mark.

C.2 Predation, herbivory, mutualism

C.3 Mutualism – plants and their pollinators; parasitism – mosquitoes or tapeworm and humans (or other suitable example)

C.4 Few consumers feed at just one trophic level. For example a chimpanzee will feed on fruit and leaves but may also kill and eat monkeys. When it eats fruit it must be placed at TL2 but when eating meat it is feeding at TL3. Predatory birds, such as bald eagles may eat mice or ducks, placing them at TL3 or snakes which are carnivores (TL3) and then the eagles would be placed at TL4.

C.5 Removing the invader faster than it can reproduce; support of the local people; maintenance of the control to ensure the species does not re-emerge; knowledge of the organism (e.g. time of reproduction).

C.6 The accumulation of a non-biodegradable toxic chemical in the higher levels of a food chain.

C.7 Turtles feed by catching floating jellyfish so may easily mistake clear plastic bags for food; the amount of plastic used by people since the 1950s has increased significantly in all parts of the world.

C.8 An indicator species is one which is used to assess a specific environmental condition. An example is that the presence of nettles indicates a high level of nitrate in the soil/leafy lichens indicate clean air or other suitable example.

C.9 All of them could be used but protection, controlling poaching and limiting visitors are the most likely.

C.10 *In situ* conservation means that species are conserved in their natural habitat. This is achieved by removing competitors, reducing predation and in some cases feeding the endangered species. The advantages of this method are: species are already used to/adapted to living in the location (or there will be no need to reintroduce the species back into the habitat after the conservation programme); their behaviour is unlikely to be affected; so breeding behaviour will occur as normal; the species can continue to interact with other species in the area.

C.11 1 Marking must not harm the animals or make them conspicuous; there should be no immigration or emigration in the population; measurements must be taken with in one life cycle of the organism.

    2 Woodlice, snails, small mammals that do not have large territories.

C.12 Top-down – a predator such as the lobster in the Atlantic Ocean or a lion in the savannah. Bottom – up Eutrophication in ponds caused by use of fertilisers can lead to bottom-up control as algae build up, they block light reaching other species and limit the growth of pond plants and animals which depend on them.

C.13 Humans affect the nitrogen cycle by: adding fertilisers to soil, which increases nitrogen in one part of the cycle; harvesting crops, which removes nitrogen compounds that would otherwise be recycled; monoculture, which interrupts the natural cycling of nitrogen; irrigation, which can lead to waterlogging and denitrification; draining wetland which reduces denitrification. (any 4)

C.14 Neutral pH and well-aerated soil

C.15 1 Mayfly nymphs, dragonfly nymphs, air breathing snails or other suitable example.

    2 a It is a good source of ammonium compounds; nitrates; mineral salts; it adds to the humus/ organic matter of the soil; it improves the aeration and drainage of the soil (any 3)

    b Ammonium compounds oxidised to nitrites and then to nitrates; *Nitrosomonas*; (ammonium compounds to nitrites); *Nitrobacter*; (nitrites to nitrates)

    c Waterlogged soils contain little or no oxygen; *Nitrosomonas* and *Nitrobacter*/nitrifying bacteria only live in aerobic conditions

D Human physiology

D.1 Vitamins are organic, minerals are inorganic; vitamins are compounds, minerals are ions; vitamins are made in plants, minerals are derived from rocks.

D.2 A healthy diet must contain a balance of nutrients including protein, fats, vitamins and minerals. It is unlikely that one food would contain all these nutrients.

D.3 Proteins are needed to build new cells and animals cannot synthesise all the amino acids to do this. There are 20 essential amino acids, which must be eaten in the form of protein.

D.4 1 An essential amino acid is one which cannot be made in the body and can only be obtained from foods we eat.

    2 Poor nutrition can lead to weight gain if too many carbohydrate and fatty foods are eaten. Weight gain leads to higher output of blood from the heart, which can raise blood pressure. Layers of fat in the abdomen can produce resistance to blood flow and raise blood pressure. Also clogged arteries may be narrower, which increases blood pressure.

D.5 Acidic conditions provide the optimum conditions for protease enzymes in the stomach and also kill bacteria.

D.6 Gastrin stimulates the release of acid and pepsinogen from the cells of the stomach lining.

D.7 Folded to produce a large surface area, many villi increase surface area still further; rich blood supply to carry food away; thin diffusion distance from intestine to blood.

D.8 1 Absorption of excess glucose; absorption of vitamins A and D; production of immunoglobulins; synthesis of cholesterol (any 3)

    2 Kupffer cells engulf damaged red blood cells and break them into their components for recycling.

Answers to Test yourself questions

D.9   **1** Glycogen   **2** Insulin

D.10 Action potentials can move quickly through the cells which contract in a coordinated manner.

D.11 Nervous or hormonal stimulation

D.12 Atrio-ventricular valves

D.13 Systole is contraction of the heart muscle; diastole is relaxation of heart muscle.

D.14 Estrogen and progesterone

D.15 Protein hormones

D.16 **a** Anterior   **b** Posterior

D.17 The pressure exerted by a gas in a mixture.

D.18 A graph showing the affinity of hemoglobin (or other respiratory pigment) at different partial pressures of oxygen

D.19 Myoglobin has a higher affinity from oxygen than hemoglobin. It can combine with oxygen at lower partial pressures than hemoglobin.

INDEX

Index

Index